IMAGES
of America

UPPER SANDUSKY

On the Cover: The *Union Republican* newspaper was located at 113 West Wyandot Avenue in Upper Sandusky. In 1914, the *Wyandot Union* and *Union Republican* merged and became the *Wyandot Union Republican*. In 1938, it was renamed the *Daily Chief Union* and is still printing today. (Courtesy of the Wyandot County Historical Society.)

IMAGES
of America

UPPER SANDUSKY

Tom Hill and Ashlie Payton
on behalf of the
Wyandot County Historical Society

ARCADIA
PUBLISHING

ISBN 978-0-7385-7736-4

Published by Arcadia Publishing
Charleston, South Carolina

Printed in the United States of America

Library of Congress Control Number: 2009930493

For all general information contact Arcadia Publishing at:
Telephone 843-853-2070
Fax 843-853-0044
E-mail sales@arcadiapublishing.com
For customer service and orders:
Toll-Free 1-888-313-2665

Visit us on the Internet at www.arcadiapublishing.com

To Bailey, Brooke, Marnie, and family, and the late Ron Klink.

—Tom Hill

For Marjorie Rickenbacher, Ryan, my family, and David Fadley.

—Ashlie Payton

Contents

Foreword		6
Acknowledgments		7
Introduction		8
1.	Trial and Tribulation	9
2.	The Life of a Warrior	27
3.	Expansion and Enterprise	41
4.	Education and Faith	73
5.	A Portrait in Time	89
6.	Home Life and Happy Times	109

Foreword

In Upper Sandusky, we are lucky to have a rich heritage combined with a deep sense of community. We work hard to keep the traditions and memories of the past alive. From school field trips to the Old Mission Church to reenactments at the county museum, we make it a priority to keep even the youngest citizens involved with and interested in their community. Roots run deep in our town. The neighbor one sees sipping coffee at the local cafe is likely to have ancestors buried at one of our historic cemeteries. The fisherman pulling in a bass from the Sandusky River may have a surname found in the county census records from the 19th century.

Located between Marion and Findlay on U.S. Route 23, Upper Sandusky is a pleasant one-hour drive from either Toledo or Columbus. This convenient location, combined with the quiet atmosphere and abundance of local shopping and recreation, makes the town perfect for the family looking to escape from urban traffic or suburban homogeneity.

Although Upper Sandusky is a bustling and modern small town, there remain pockets of wilderness that invite the visitor to think back to the time when Ohio was the frontier, and tribes such as the Wyandots, Delaware, and Senecas lived in the area. Someone who takes a moment to peep through the woods that line the walking path at Stepping Stones Park may see deer, raccoons, rabbits, and muskrats—all animals that helped sustain pioneers through long Midwestern winters.

Visitors will want to see the Wyandot County Museum. Located in a pre–Civil War mansion, the museum has been operated by the Wyandot County Historical Society since 1962. In addition to displays about the history of Upper Sandusky and the surrounding area, the museum hosts period teas and dances, reenactments, guest speakers, and visiting exhibits.

It is my sincere hope that this book does more than offer the reader a glimpse of the historical importance of Upper Sandusky to Ohio and the United States. I hope it gives the residents of our town a renewed respect for our shared heritage.

Whether one's family has lived in Wyandot County for generations or one has only recently heard of the area, I hope to see everyone in Upper Sandusky, where our pride in the past inspires us to make a better future.

—Scott Washburn
Mayor, Upper Sandusky
May 2009

Acknowledgments

First of all, I would be remiss if I did not acknowledge a very special person for the help she gave me and Ashlie in getting this book ready for Arcadia to publish. If there could have been another author for this work it would have been Janet Engle who shared her expertise, time, and skills. Undertaking to put Upper Sandusky into a photographic history was a monumental achievement to say the least and without her help this project would not have been done.

The Wyandot County Historical Society must also be thanked for sharing most of the wonderful photographs used to get this book into publication. This photographic journey would have been nonexistent without their help. Photographs in this book are from the historical society unless otherwise marked. Ray Gottfried's 1976 book on Wyandot County was another invaluable source of information in our endeavor.

We also thank our mayor, Scott Washburn, who shared his thoughts and help despite his busy schedule.

When I first thought of doing this book, I had very little skills to take on this task and without the help of the people mentioned it would not have come to be. Thanks to John and Mary Jane Constien for their help with furnishing photographs. Mary Jane's book on Upper Sandusky businesses was a great help on locations and dates. Last but not least, I need to thank my granddaughters, Bailey and Brooke, for sharing their time with papa to work on this book, and my wife, Marnie, for her help.

INTRODUCTION

From the time it started as a Wyandot Indian village in 1773 to the present, Upper Sandusky has been an important crossroads in the history of Ohio. In 1782, Col. William H. Crawford fought a Revolutionary War battle against Indian and British troops, because the area was a hotbed of activity hostile to the fledging American nation. In 1812, Gen. William Henry Harrison had his headquarters at Fort Ferree in Upper Sandusky and courted the Wyandots to align with American forces against the British. In 1843, Upper Sandusky became the county seat of newly formed Wyandot County. In 1913, the great flood not only devastated the state of Ohio but also played havoc with the residents of our city. This journey in photographs was made to show the history of Upper Sandusky and its importance not only to the local population but also to the state of Ohio. In 1962, Doris Day played Cathy Timberlake and mentions she is from Upper Sandusky in the movie *That Touch of Mink*. In 1994, the movie *The Shawshank Redemption* used the Wyandot County courthouse for the trial scene of Tim Robbins and the Stephan Lumber Company building for the prison woodshop scenes. For 167 years, Upper Sandusky has grown and flourished into the community it is today and will be for years to come.

One

TRIAL AND TRIBULATION

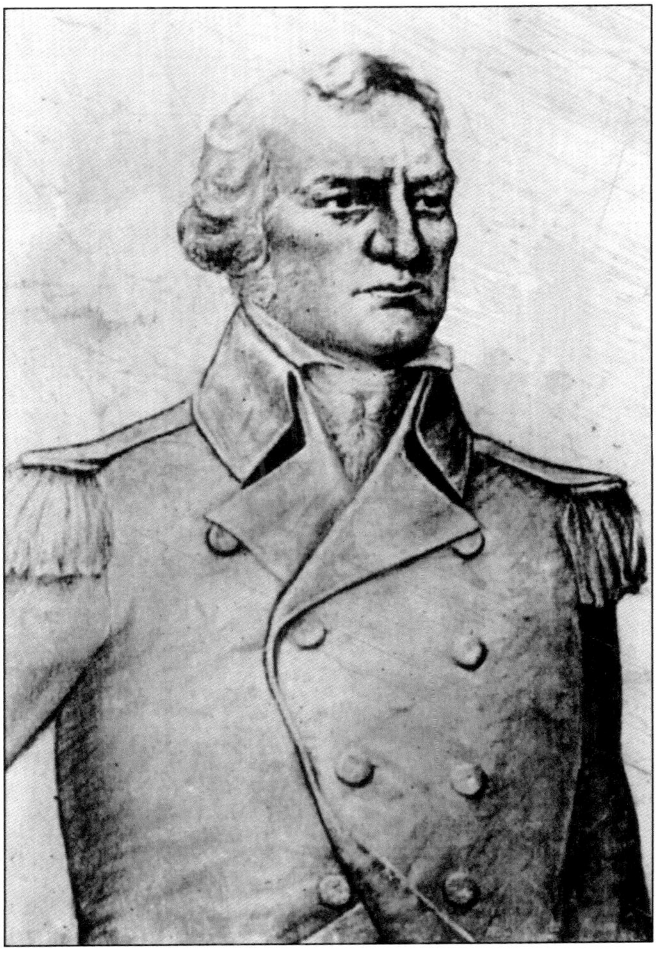

This early drawing of Col. William H. Crawford shows him when he was an officer during the Revolutionary War. General Irving of Fort Pitt asked Colonel Crawford and Col. David Williamson to lead an expedition to Upper Sandusky for the purpose of destroying the Native American villages there. By the vote of the men, Crawford was elected to command the expedition, and Williamson was to be second in command.

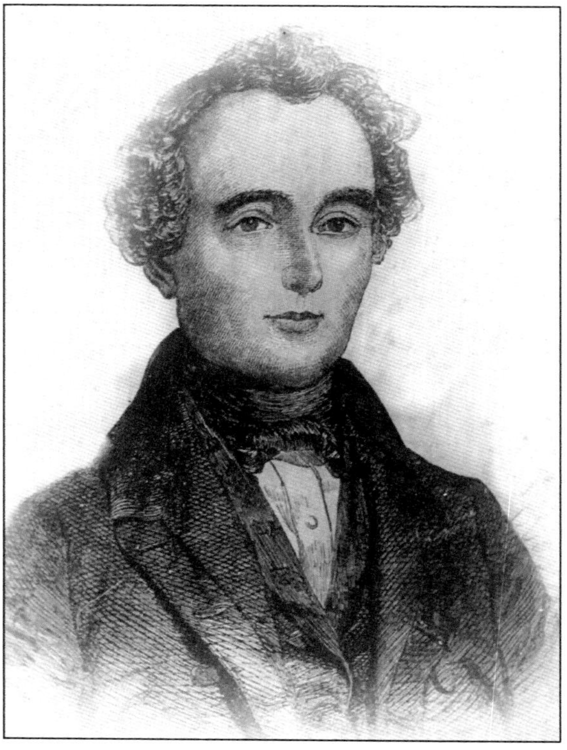

This rendition of Colonel Crawford shows him around the time he lead the Sandusky Plains Campaign to Upper Sandusky in 1782. The campaign's goal was to destroy the surrounding Indian villages. (Photograph from the collection of Tom and Marnie Hill.)

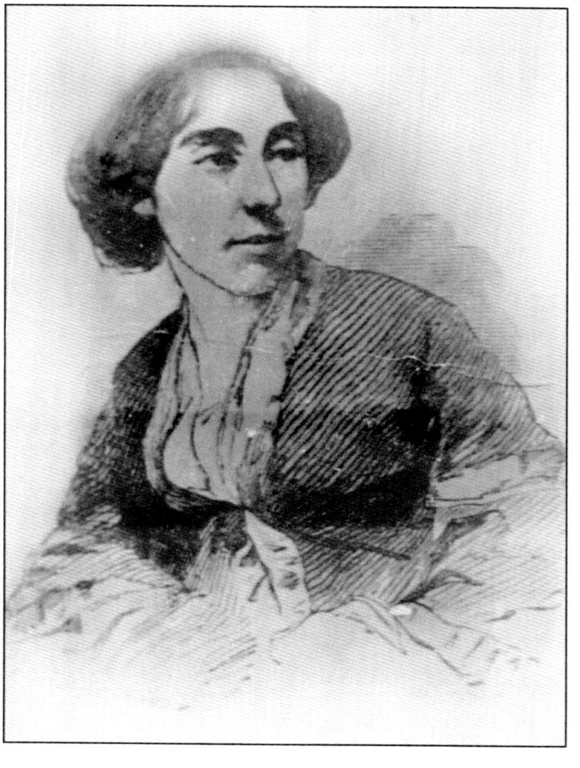

Hannah Vance Crawford was the wife of Colonel Crawford. She came to Upper Sandusky much later and was shown the site of Crawford's execution by one of the participants.

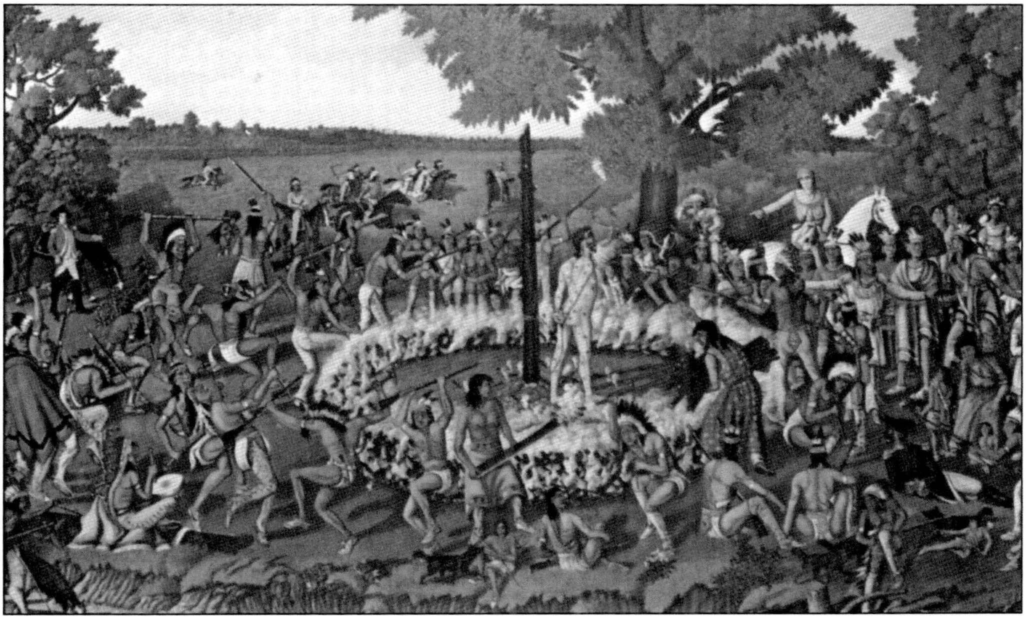

Continental surgeon Dr. John Knight witnessed the death of Colonel Crawford. Crawford received at least 70 shots of black powder to his body. His ears were cut off and red-hot sticks were applied to ignite the powder embedded in his skin. After two hours of torture, Crawford was scalped. An old Indian squaw went to his prostrate body and threw hot coals on the scalp wound. Crawford then rose and seemed to be impervious of pain until his death.

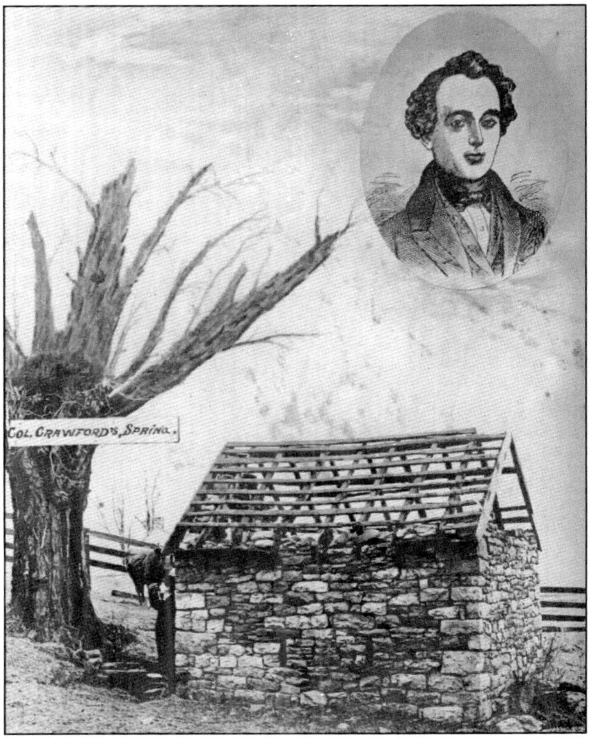

This photograph of a building on Colonel Crawford's land in Connellsville, Pennsylvania, is labelled "Col. Crawford's Spring." George Washington, a good friend of Crawford's, spent time here with Crawford and his family on visits to the area. Washington owned thousands of acres in the Ohio area because of surveying projects that William and Valentine Crawford did for him.

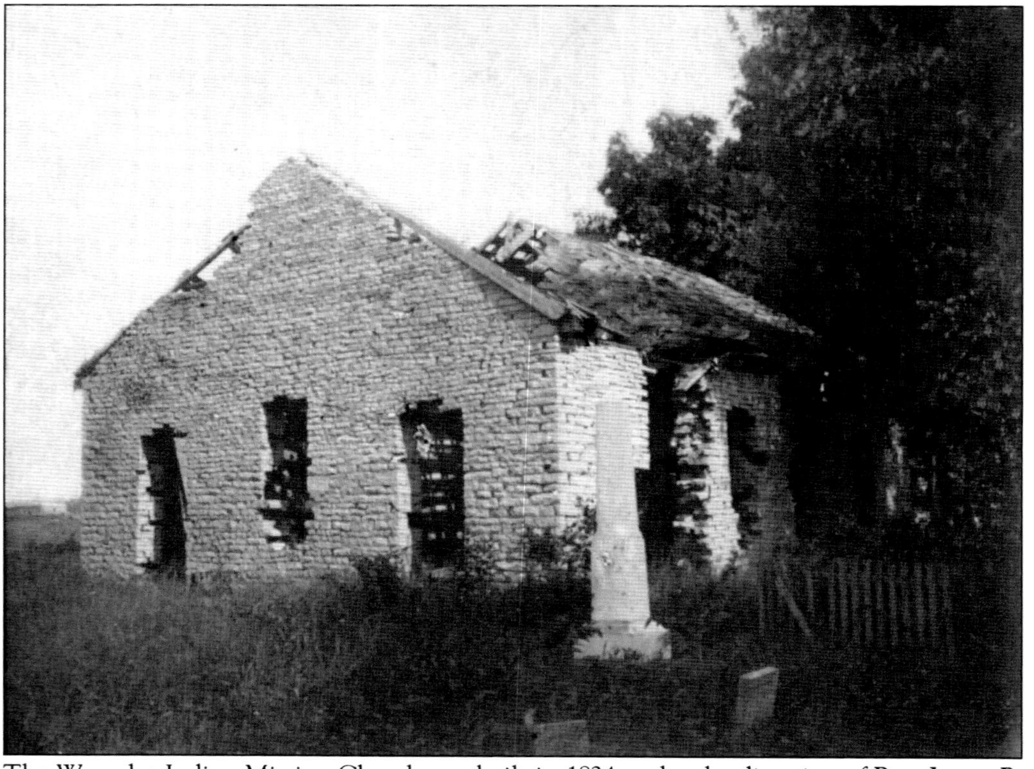

The Wyandot Indian Mission Church was built in 1824 under the direction of Rev. James B. Finley with $1,333 given to the Wyandot tribe by the federal government. The limestone used to build the mission came from the Sandusky River.

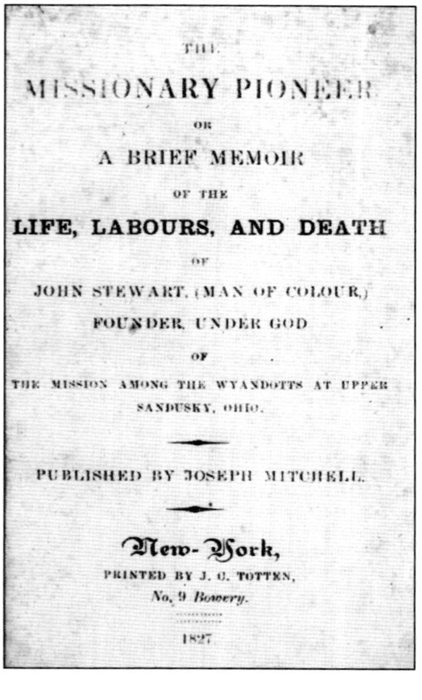

THE

MISSIONARY PIONEER

OR

A BRIEF MEMOIR

OF THE

LIFE, LABOURS, AND DEATH

OF

JOHN STEWART, (MAN OF COLOUR,)

FOUNDER, UNDER GOD

OF

THE MISSION AMONG THE WYANDOTTS AT UPPER SANDUSKY, OHIO.

PUBLISHED BY JOSEPH MITCHELL.

New-York,

PRINTED BY J. C. TOTTEN,

No. 9 Bowery.

1827

The Missionary Pioneer was published in 1827 by Joseph Mitchell. The book told about John Stewart's life among the Wyandot Tribe in Upper Sandusky.

John Stewart (rendition at right) received his calling to preach the word of God while recovering from alcoholism in 1816. He traveled the Ohio wilderness and settled with the Wyandots in Upper Sandusky. Missionaries had tried to convert the tribe to Christianity before and were unsuccessful. Stewart asked Indian agent William Walker for help. Walker introduced Stewart to Jonathan Pointer, an African American who had been kidnapped by Wyandots and who served as an interpreter for Stewart's sermons.

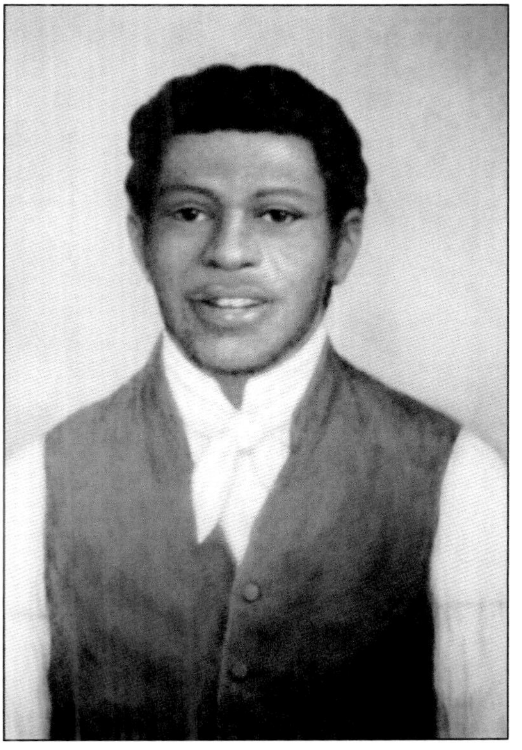

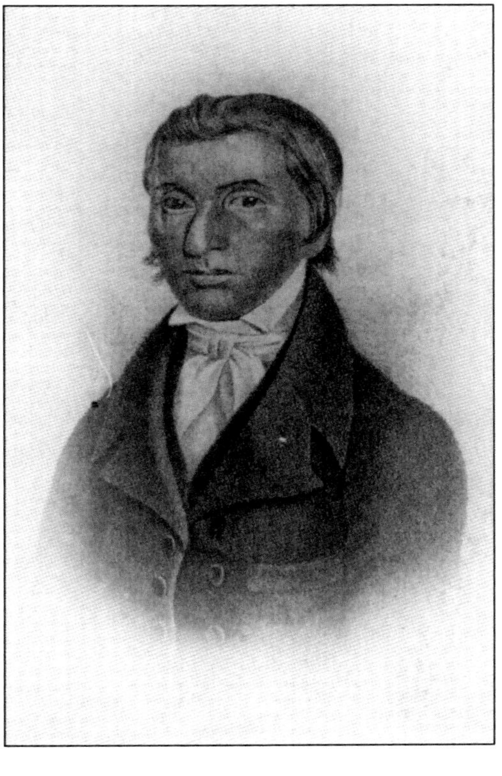

Wyandot chief Between the Logs was to become one of John Stewart's first converts to Christianity. In 1817, the Wyandots were disappointed with the Treaty of the Maumee Rapids. Between the Logs went to Washington with a delegation and spoke to President Monroe, the U.S. secretary of war, and Congress, to no avail. In 1818, Between the Logs was head of a delegation at Saint Mary's and asked for a revision of the 1817 treaty. As a result of his leadership, the reservation was expanded by about 87 square miles.

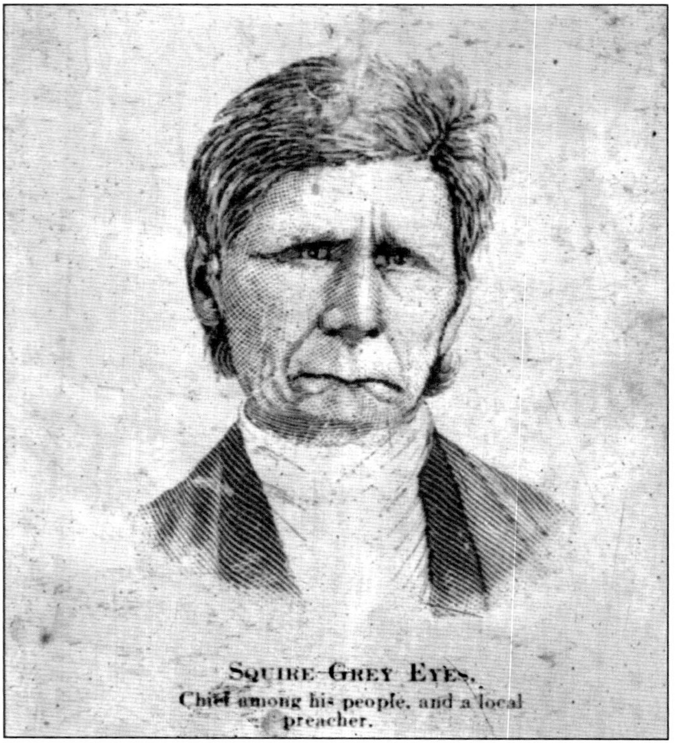

The Wyandots gathered at the Old Mission Church before leaving Upper Sandusky for the Indian reservation in Kansas on July 9, 1843. Six-hundred-and-sixty-four members of the Wyandot nation gathered for the farewell speech given by Squire Grey Eyes.

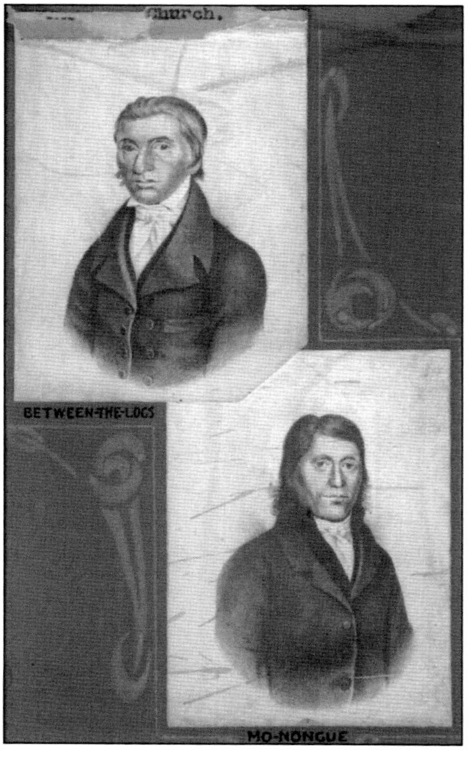

This photograph is of chiefs Between the Logs and Mononocue. Both Wyandot chiefs were converted to Christianity and by 1821 were helping to convert more of their tribe to the Christian faith.

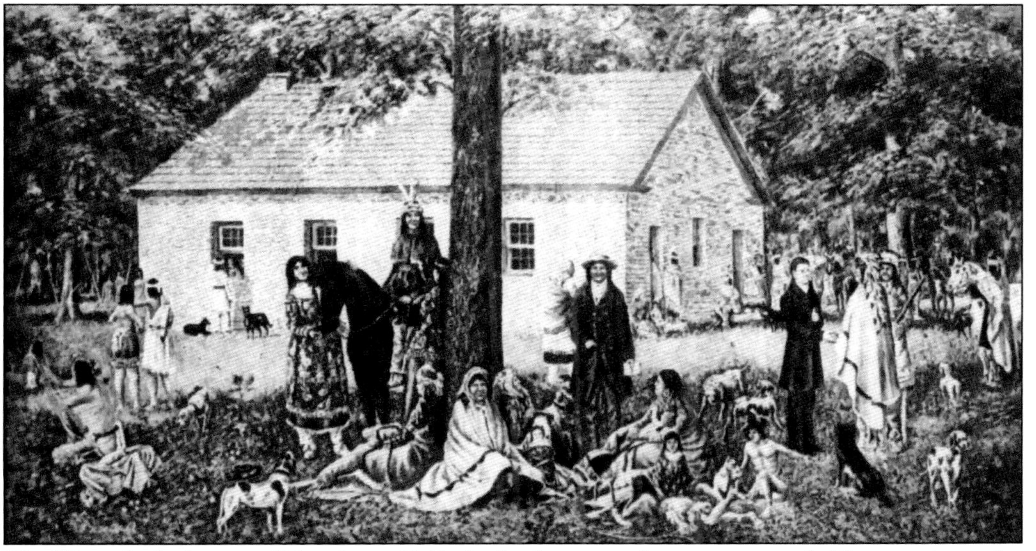

The Wyandot Indians and Rev. James B. Finley had many gatherings to preach Christianity at the Wyandot Mission Church in Upper Sandusky. (From the collection of Tom and Marnie Hill.)

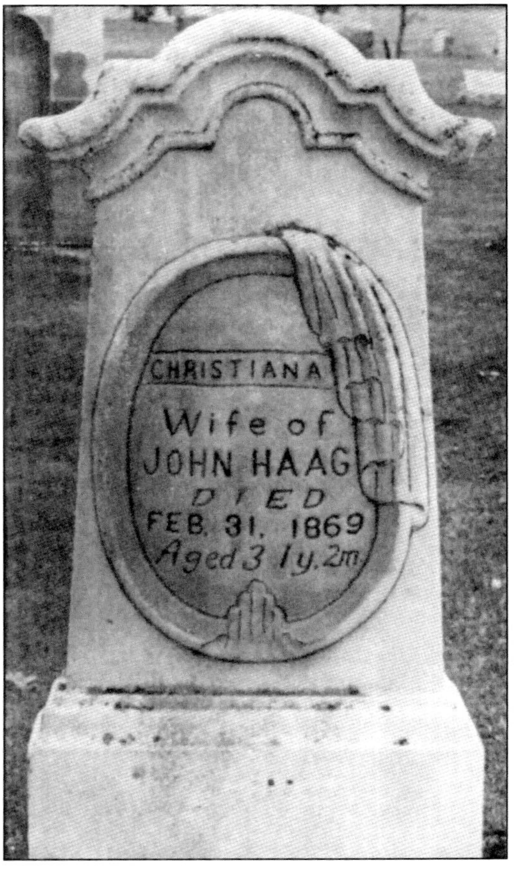

The grave marker of Christiana Haag at the Mission cemetery was mistakenly dated February 31, 1869 by a stonecutter. The correct date is believed to be December 31, 1869. (Photograph from the collection of Tom and Marnie Hill.)

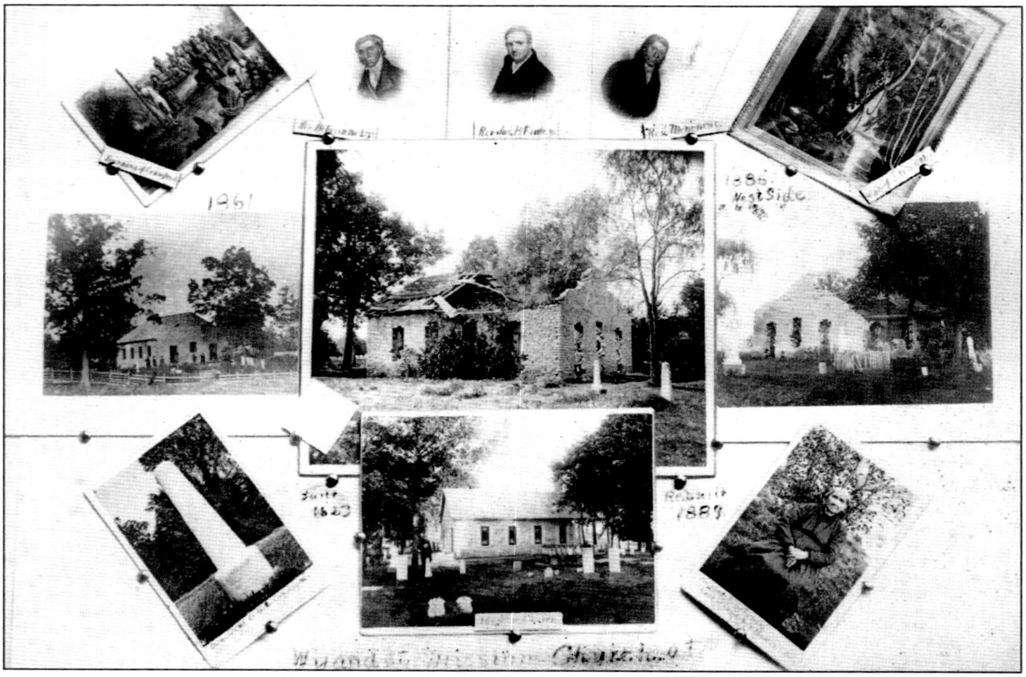

This collage shows Col. William Crawford's burning, Wyandot Rev. Between the Logs, Rev. James B. Finley—Methodist Missionary, Wyandot Reverend Mononocue, Crawford's monument, and Margaret (Mother Solomon) Grey Eyes. (Photograph from the collection of Tom and Marnie Hill.)

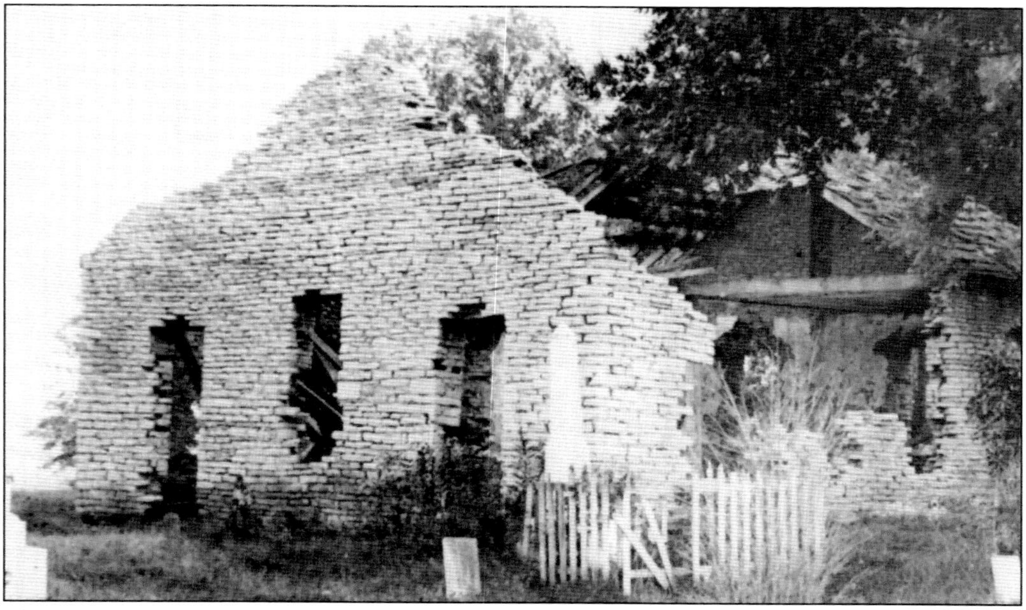

The Wyandot Indian Mission Church was built in 1824 by John Owens, under contract to Reverend Finley. After the Wyandot tribe left the area, the mission was neglected. The church was restored in 1889. It was designated a National Shrine of the Methodist Church in 1960. (Photograph from the collection of Tom and Marnie Hill.)

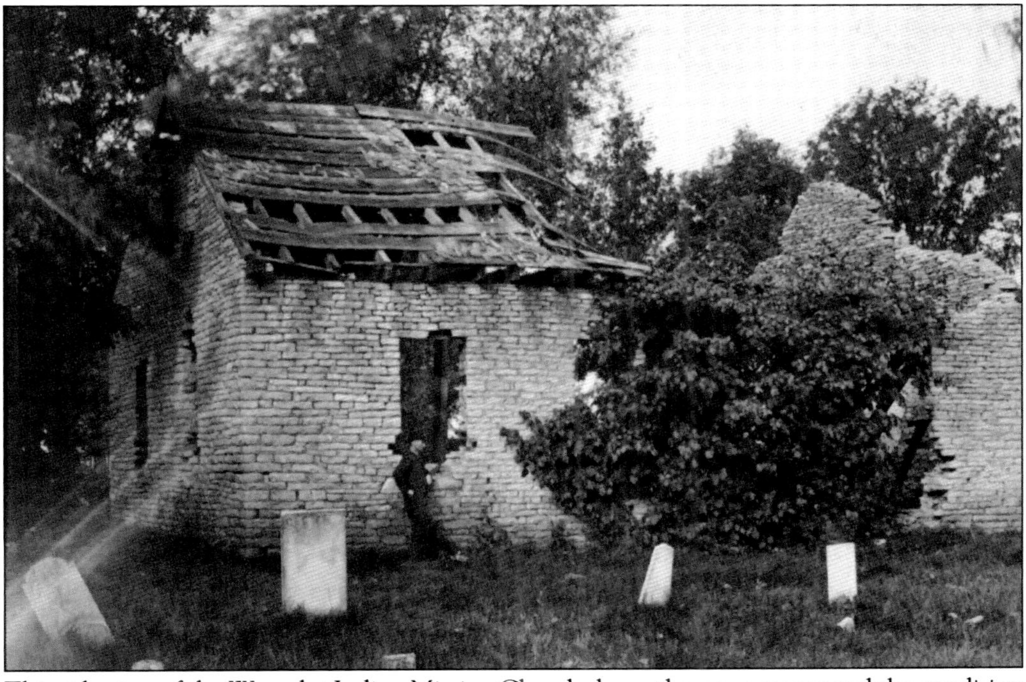

This side view of the Wyandot Indian Mission Church shows the grave stones and the condition the mission was in before being restored. The church is the first officially recognized mission of the Methodist Episcopal Church in America.

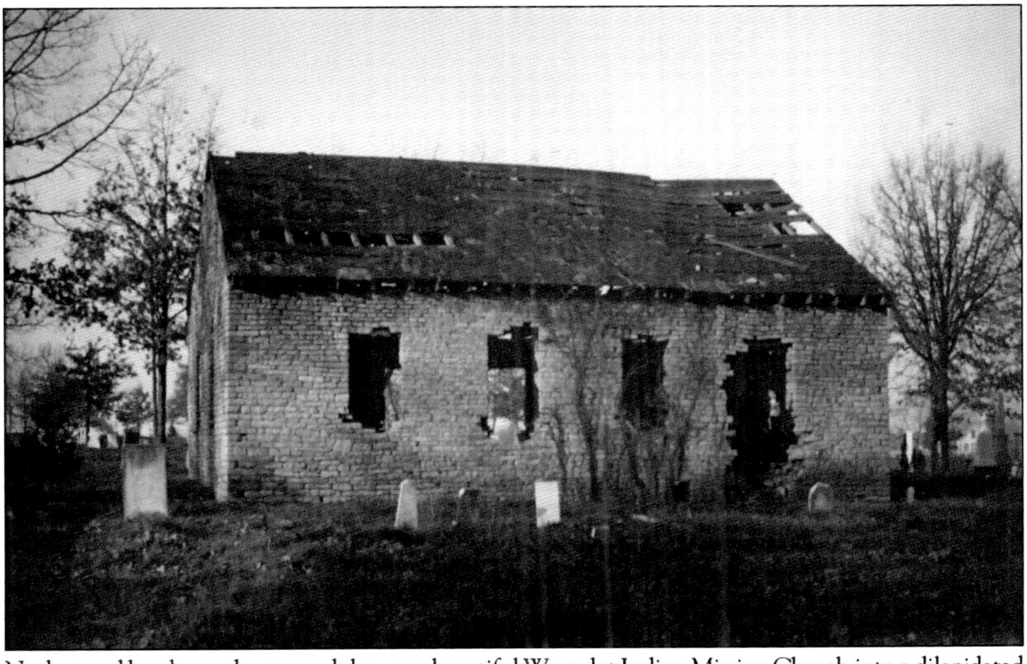

Neglect and harsh weather turned the once beautiful Wyandot Indian Mission Church into a dilapidated ruin until Reverend N. B. C. Love started renovation work on it in the 1880s. The Wyandot tribe kept the mission in good repair. They would have been heartbroken to see it in this condition.

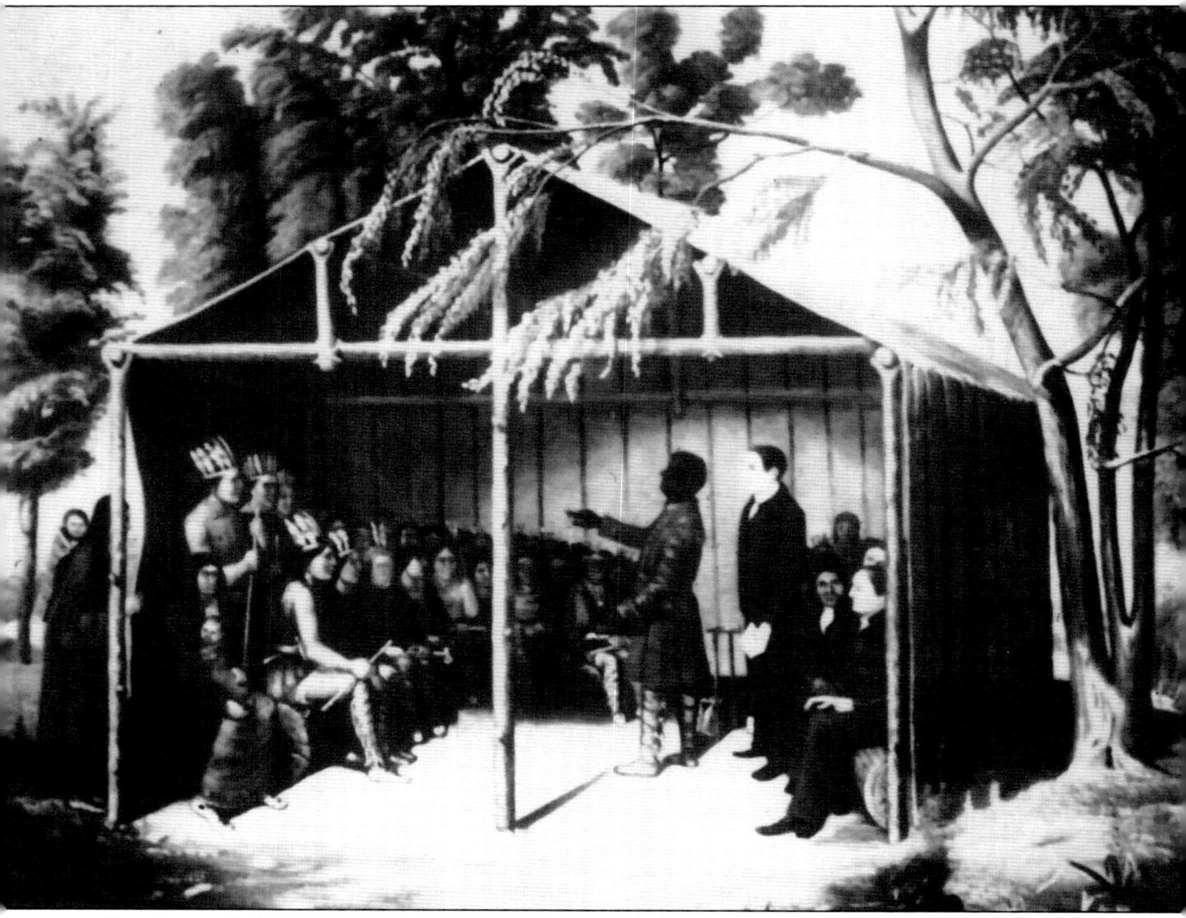

Rev. James B. Finley preaches to Indians with the help of interpreter Jonathan Pointer. The Rev. John Stewart is seated on the log behind Finley. Many of the tribe were skeptical of the white man's religion, but several members were converted to Christianity. This painting was completed in 1880 by Rev. N. B. C. Love.

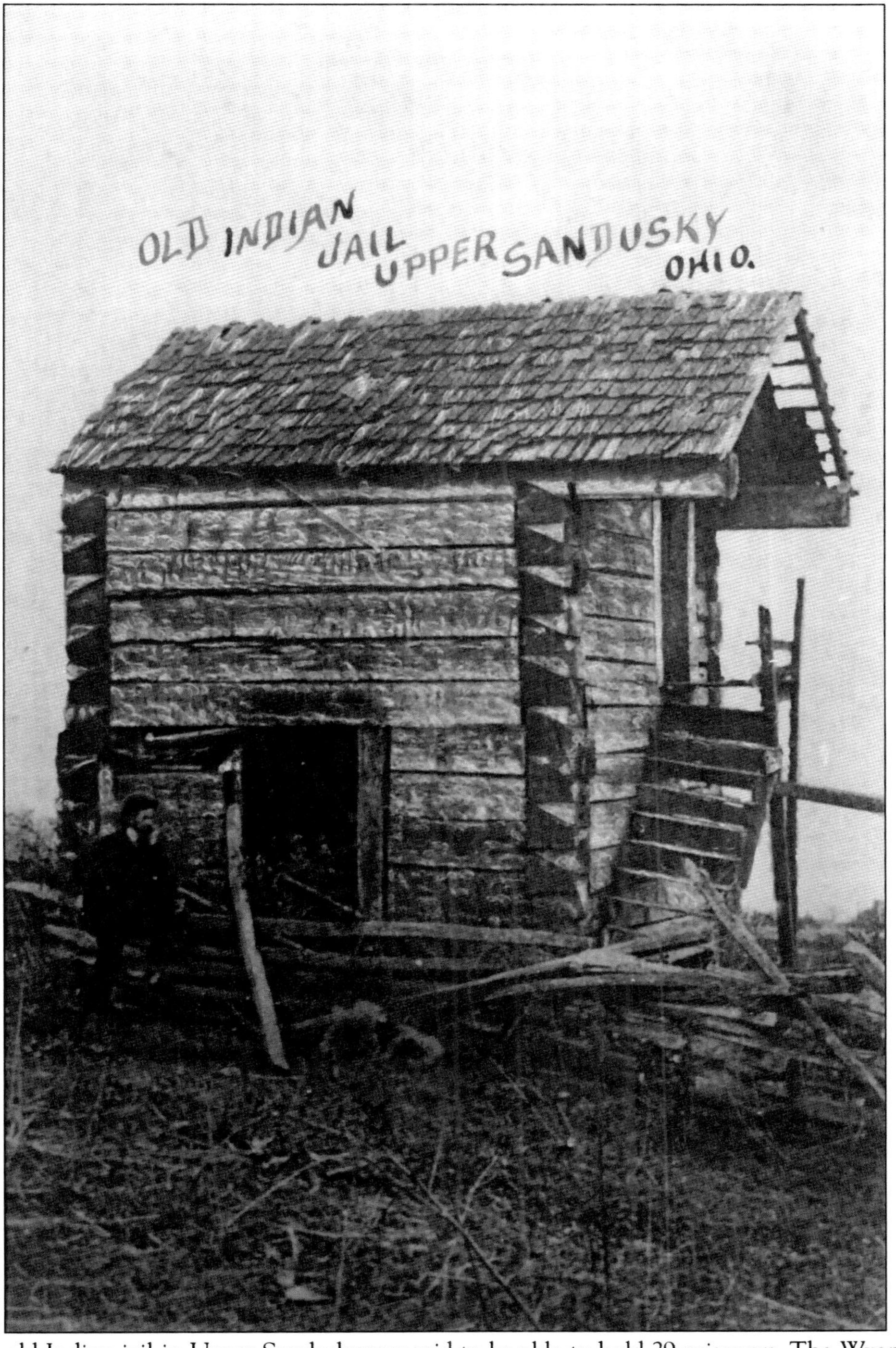

The old Indian jail in Upper Sandusky was said to be able to hold 29 prisoners. The Wyandot County Museum has the key on display. Situated close to Fort Ferree, the jail measured 12 by 14 feet and was a two-story building. It was located on the west line of 3rd Street and was used until 1848. (Photograph from the collection of Tom and Marnie Hill.)

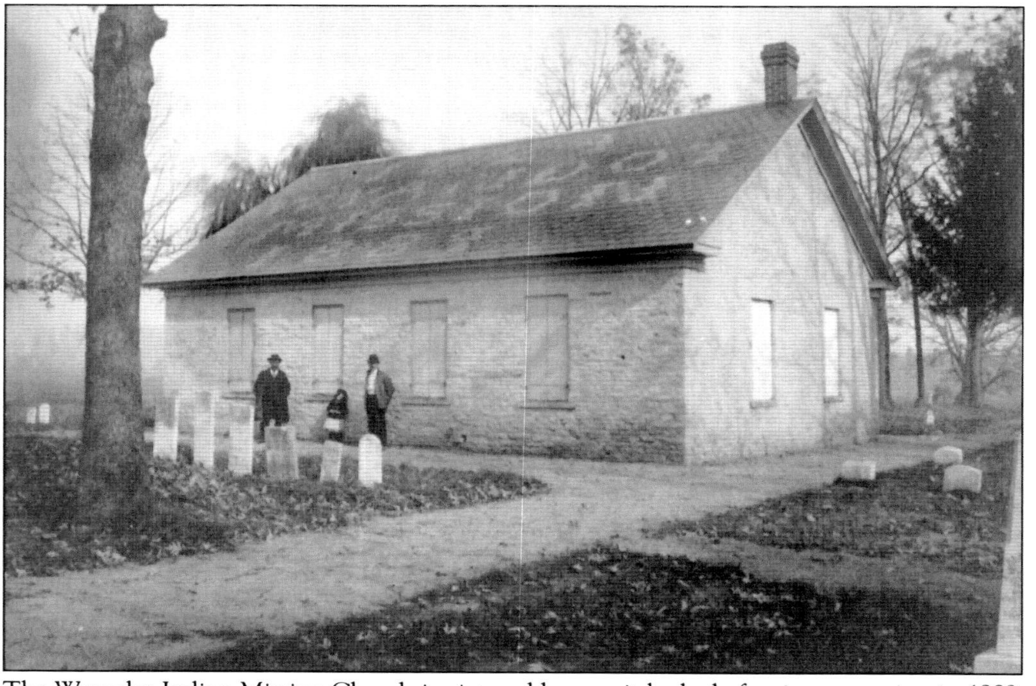

The Wyandot Indian Mission Church is pictured here as it looked after its restoration in 1889. Services are still held at the church in the summertime.

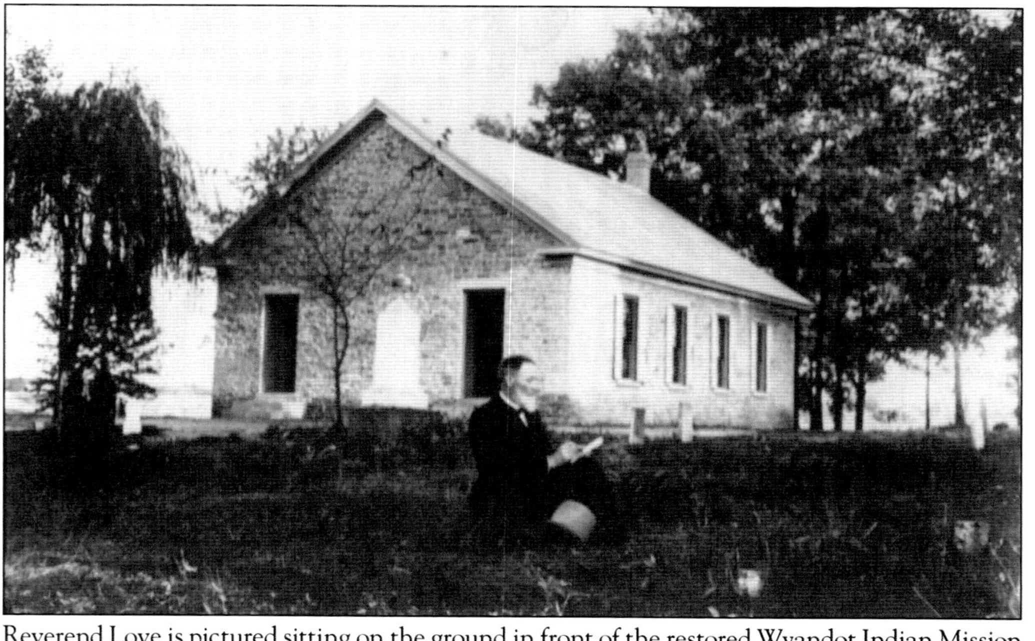

Reverend Love is pictured sitting on the ground in front of the restored Wyandot Indian Mission Church. Love was the pastor of the Methodist Episcopal Church in Upper Sandusky. He received his license to preach in 1852, and also served as a circuit rider and elder. He was a well known lecturer and teacher. Love was also a talented artist. He died on December 29, 1922 and is buried along with his wife Eliza Ginn at Fort Meigs Cemetery in Perrysburg, Ohio.

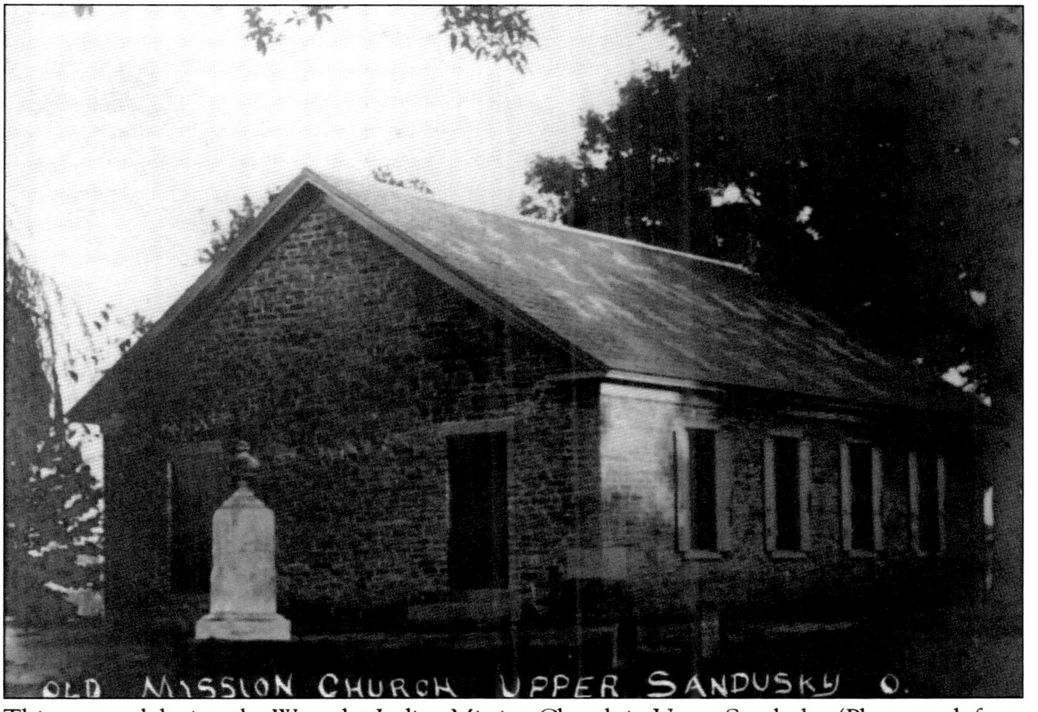

This postcard depicts the Wyandot Indian Mission Church in Upper Sandusky. (Photograph from the collection of Tom and Marnie Hill.)

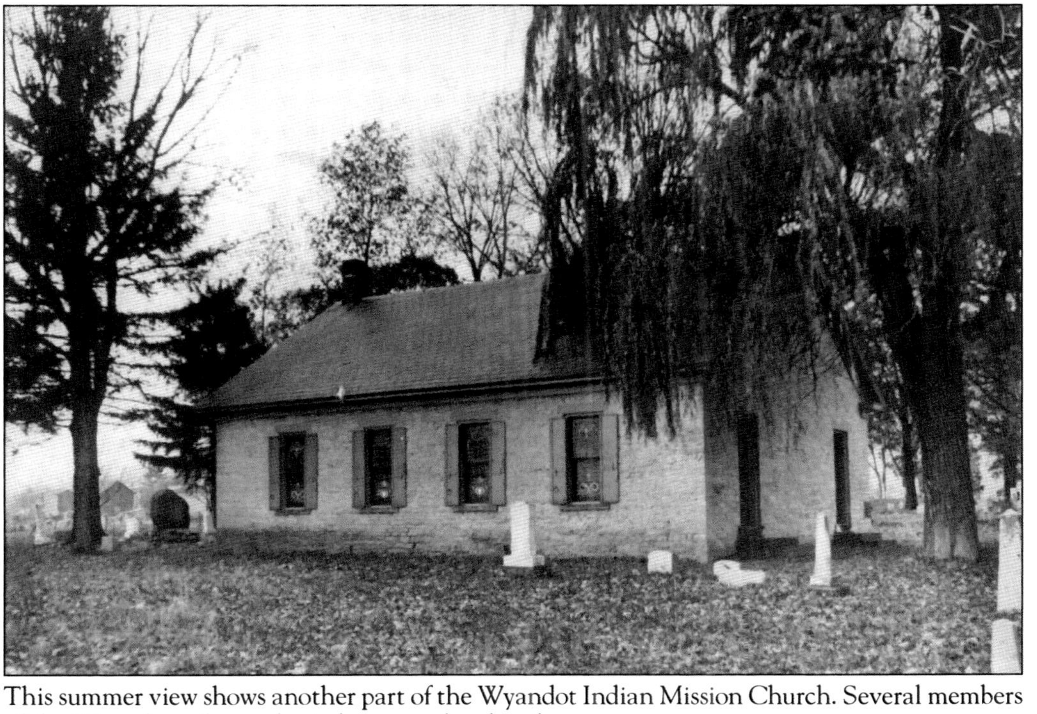
This summer view shows another part of the Wyandot Indian Mission Church. Several members of the Wyandot tribe are buried next to the church.

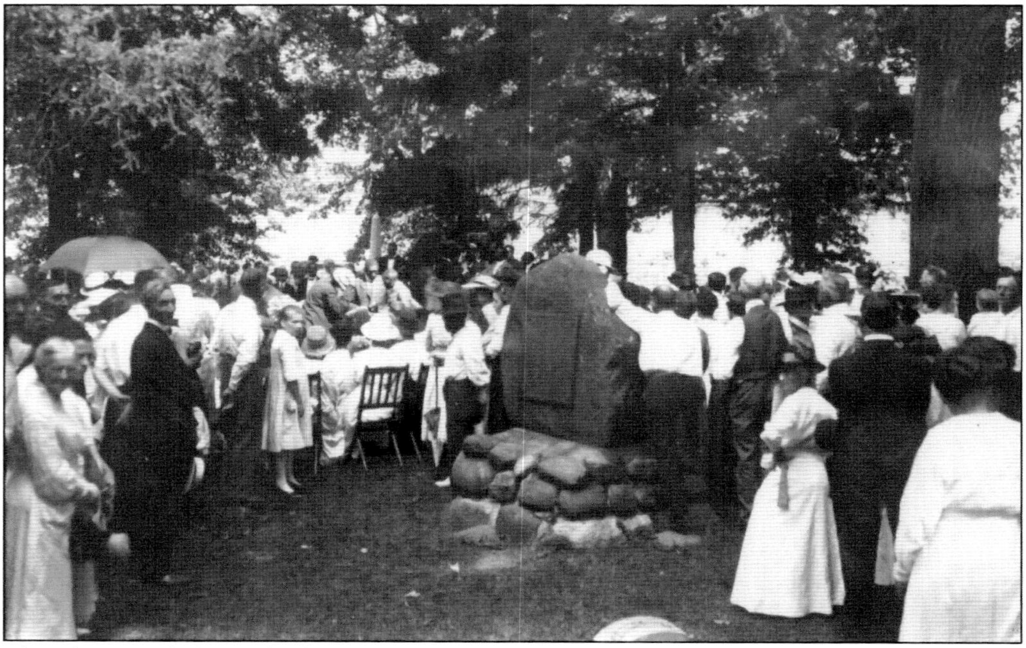

This photograph shows the dedication of the John Stewart memorial monument at the Wyandot Indian Mission Church cemetery. The stone was from the area where Col. William Crawford met his fate at the hands of Captain Pipe, a Delaware chief. Gov. Frank B. Willis dedicated the memorial on October 12, 1916.

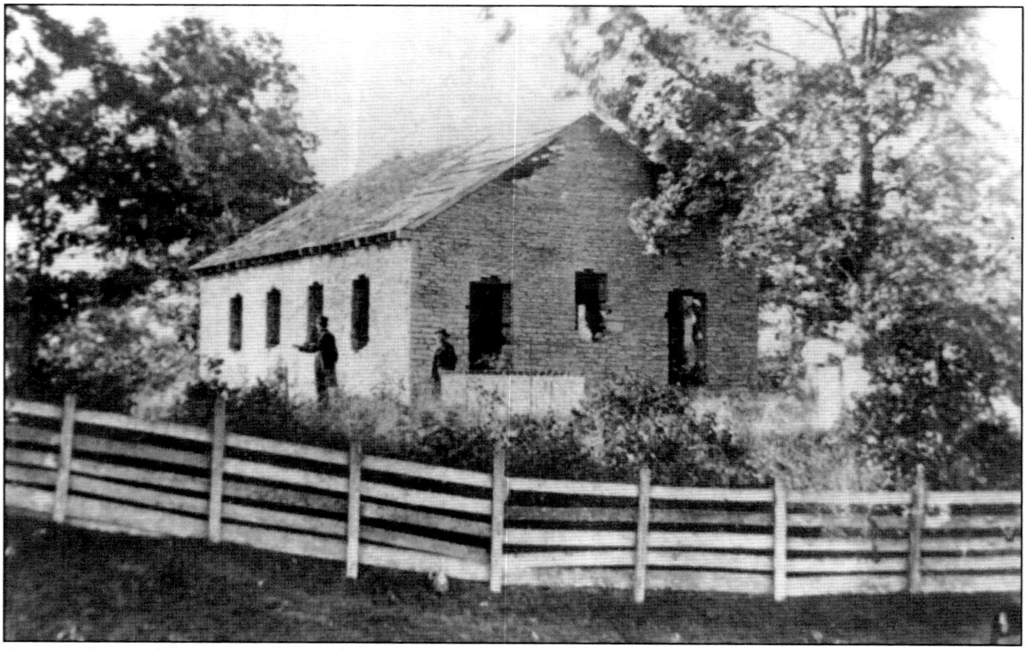

Some of the deterioration of the Wyandot Indian Mission Church is starting to show here. Notice that boards are starting to fall from the once white fence surrounding the mission and that undergrowth is taking over the area.

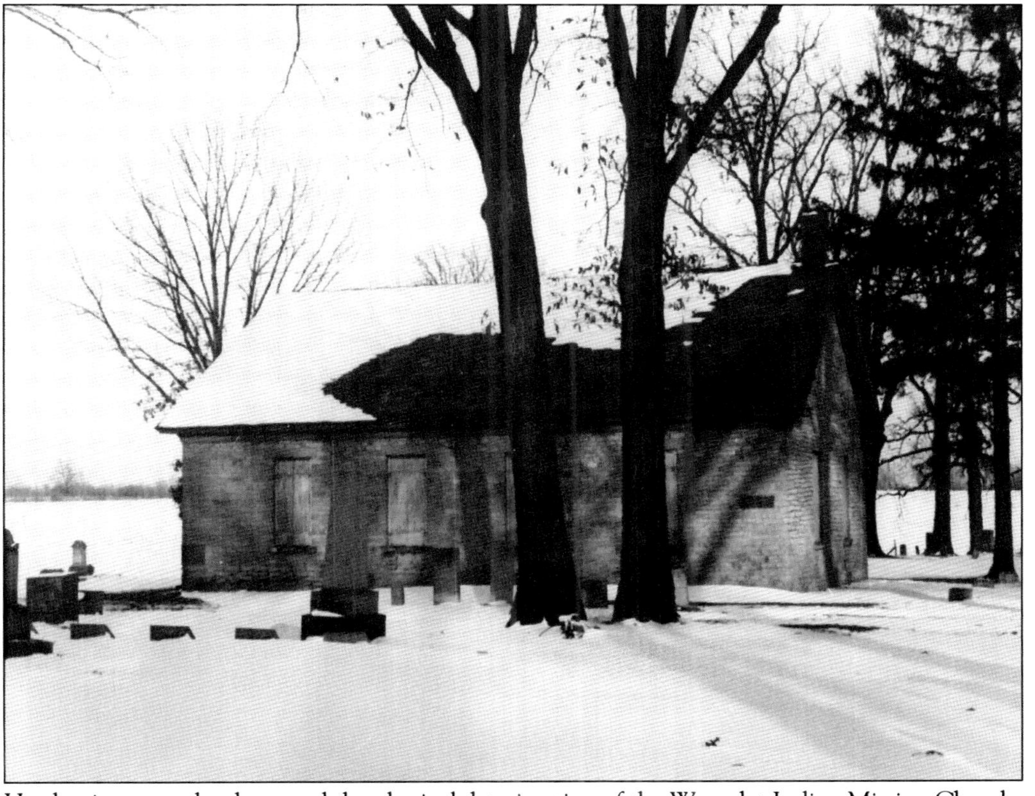

Harsh winter weather hastened the physical deterioration of the Wyandot Indian Mission Church.

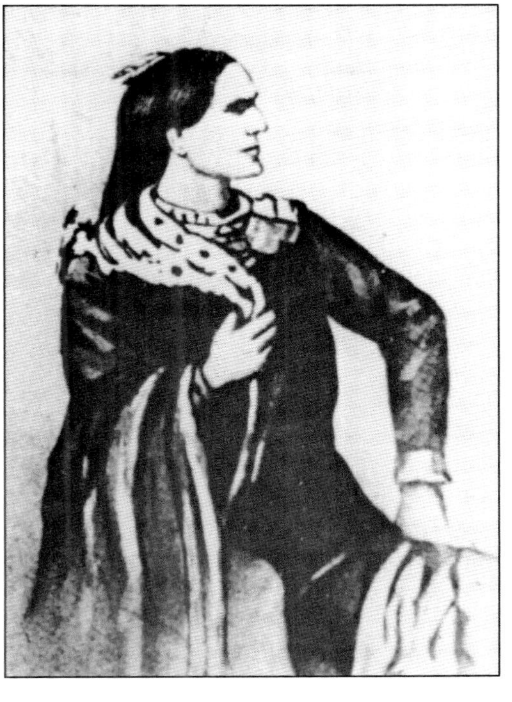

Chief Tarhe "The Crane" was born into the Porcupine clan near Detroit. Tarhe lived in several locations, including Upper Sandusky and Cranetown. During the Battle of Fallen Timbers, he was severely wounded. Tarhe decided to make peace with the Americans after that. He led all Indian tribes at the Treaty of Greenville. He participated in the War of 1812 on the American side. Tarhe's funeral was the largest ever known for an Indian chief.

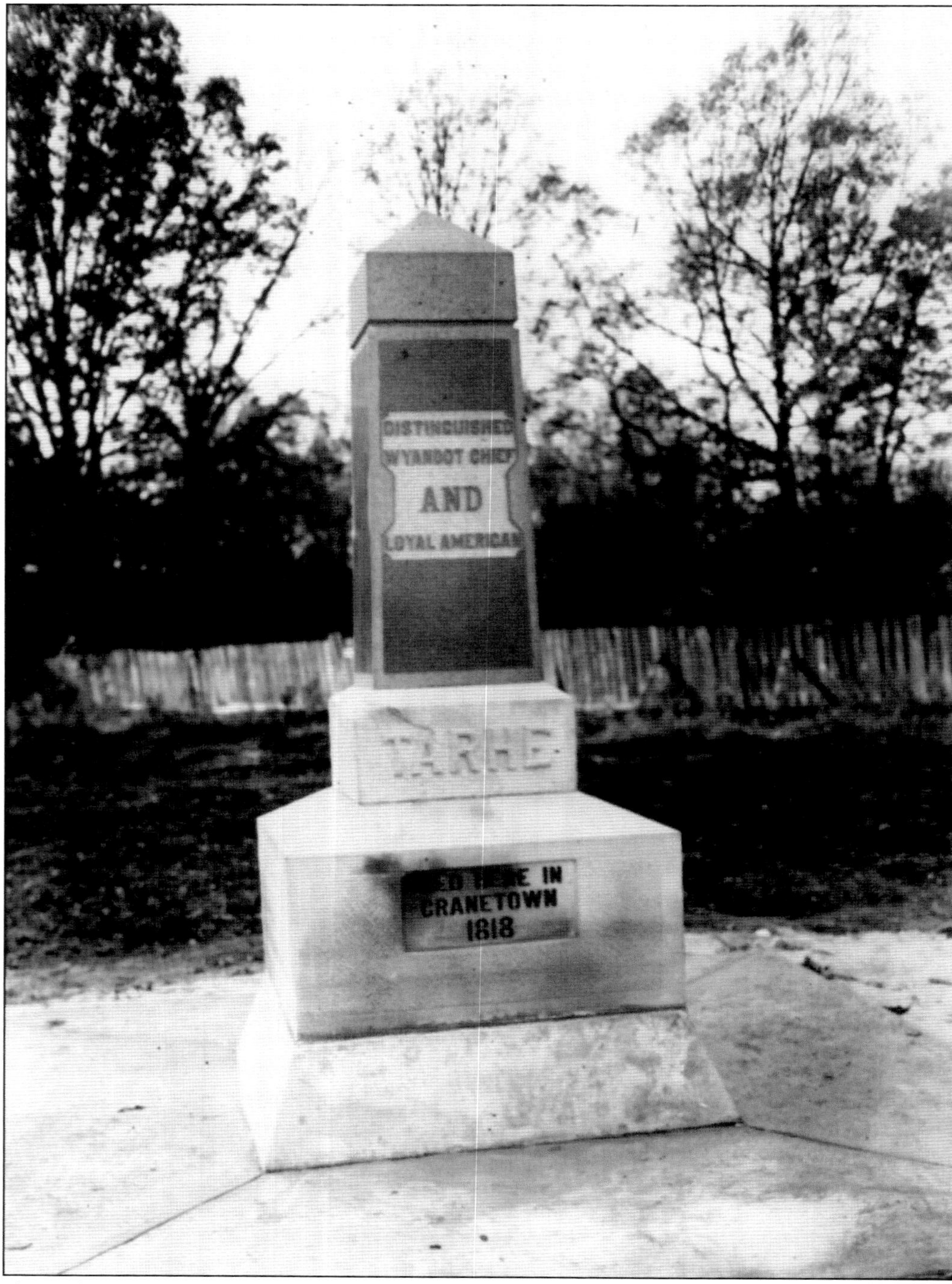

Shown here is the Chief Tarhe monument near Cranetown, the village named after him. Tarhe lived out his days well respected by whites and Indians. The monument is said to be seated at the spot where he died. It overlooks a valley where the Indian village of Cranetown is believed to have been. Just west of the monument is where two gauntlet grounds were used by the Indians.

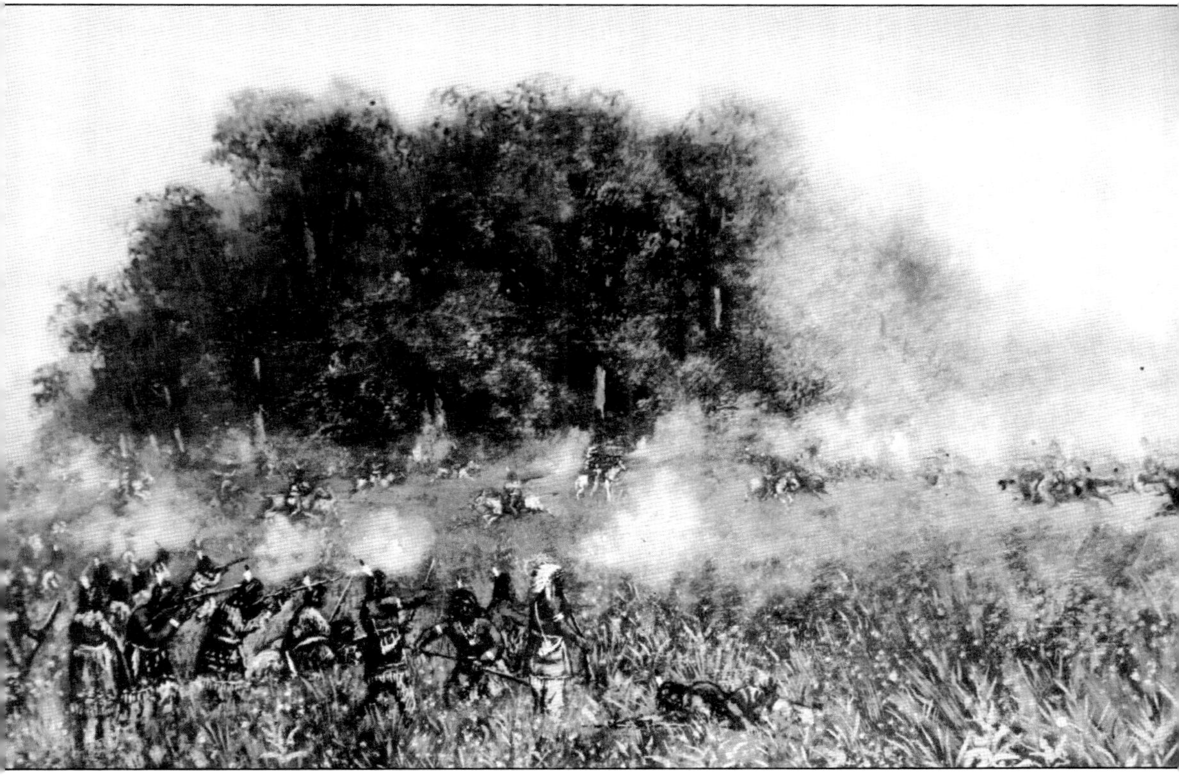

This painting shows Col. William Crawford's defeat at Battle Island on June 4–5, 1782. Colonel Crawford's troops were winning the battle the first day, but when more Indian tribes arrived and British Capt. William Caldwell of Butler's Rangers joined the Indians with a company of mounted rangers and a couple of grasshopper cannons (small cannons that jumped backward after firing three-pound balls), Crawford, being surrounded by hostile troops and Indians, had a council of war with his officers. They decided to retreat during the night, which resulted in confusion. Colonel Crawford and Dr. Knight were eventually captured. Crawford was tortured and killed at the hands of Delaware war chief Captain Pipe in retaliation for the Moravian massacre earlier in 1782 at Gnadenhutten, Ohio. The Moravian massacre was committed by troops of Col. David Williamson, Crawford's second in command at the Battle of Sandusky Plains in Upper Sandusky.

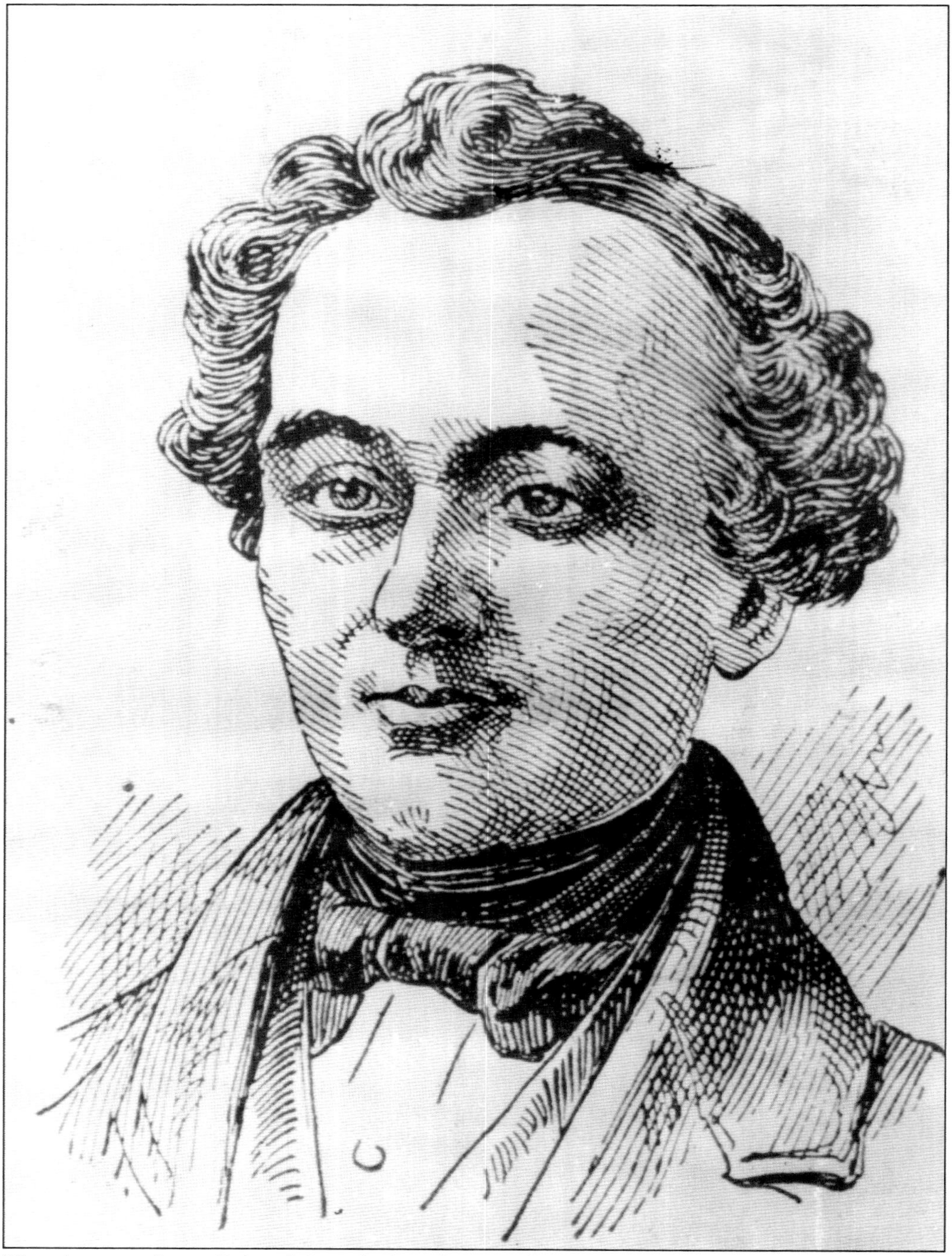

This drawing shows Colonel Crawford at the age of 40. He would suffer a horrendous death within 10 years at the hands of Delaware war chief Captain Pipe after the Battle of Sandusky Plains. Crawford had his will made out before leaving for the expedition because he had a bad premonition. It would turn out to come true for the unfortunate Crawford, his son-in-law, and a nephew.

Two

THE LIFE OF A WARRIOR

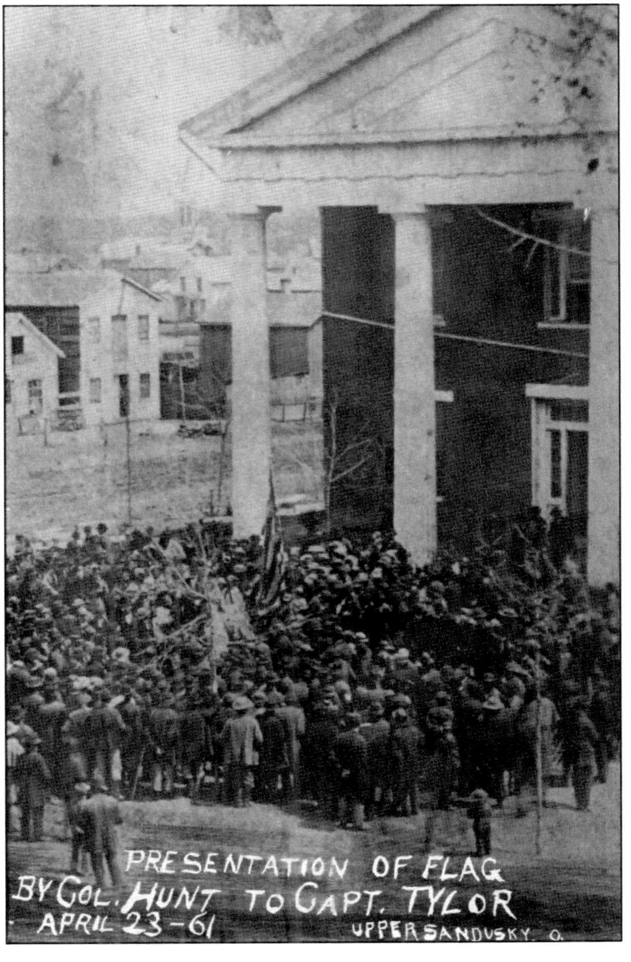

Here Capt. Peter Austva Tyler receives the American flag from Colonel Hunt in 1861. Hunt was adjutant for the 81st Ohio Volunteer Infantry (OVI). Tyler was commissioned captain before returning to Upper Sandusky to form Company D 81st OVI. Tyler lost his commission because of a letter he wrote during the war. He served as a representative in the 51st General Assembly from 1854 to 1856. He was elected mayor of Upper Sandusky in October 1863. Tyler died on June 15, 1864, after being shot in Bucyrus.

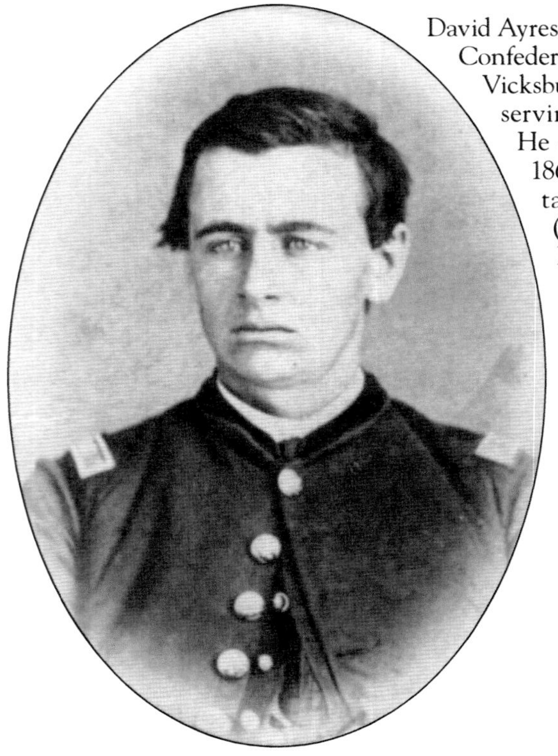

David Ayres received the Medal of Honor for storming a Confederate stronghold with a group of volunteers in Vicksburg, Mississippi, during the Civil War while serving with the 57th Ohio Volunteer Infantry. He enlisted in the 57th OVI on September 2, 1861, at Upper Sandusky. The photograph was taken in Upper Sandusky by F. L. Merrill. (Photograph from the collection of Tom and Marnie Hill.)

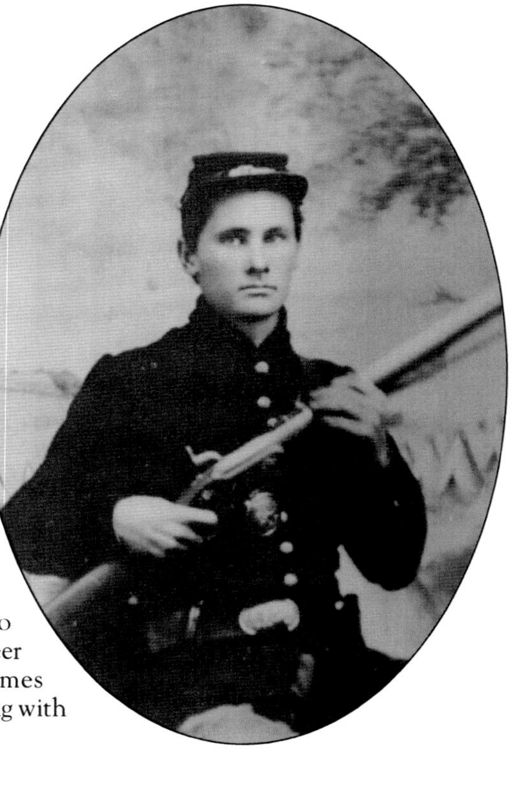

This photograph shows Joseph Chadwick, who served with company I of the 82nd Ohio Volunteer Infantry in the Civil War. A grandson, James Chadwick, would be killed in action while serving with the U.S. Marines in 1965 in Vietnam.

This photograph shows John and Lydia Ann (Burson) Davis holding their son, William Myron Davis, in 1870. John Davis enlisted in Company A of the 123rd Ohio Volunteer Infantry along with his brother Alexander. They were captured and held in Belle Isle as prisoners of war. John survived a neck wound at Snickers Gap, Virginia, during the war. Alexander died of consumption while serving. (Photograph from the collection of Tom and Marnie Hill.)

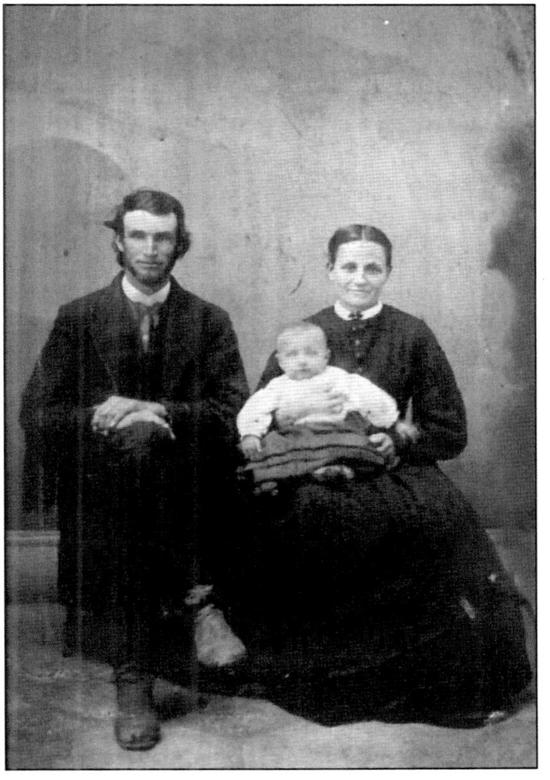

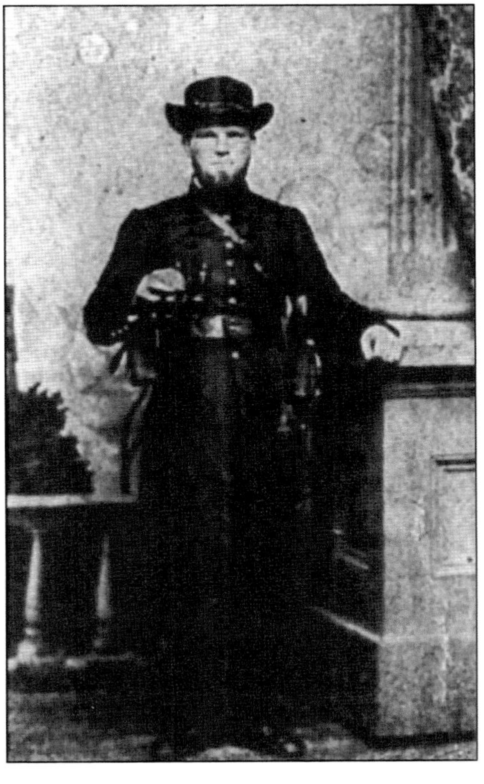

This is a photograph of Cyrus Sears as a first lieutenant with the 11th Ohio Independent Battery in 1861. He was severely wounded at the battle of Iuka, Mississippi, on September 19, 1862. He would later command the 49th United States Colored Infantry Volunteers, originally the 11th Regiment Louisiana Volunteers. Lieutenant Colonel Sears fought the rest of the war under the threat of immediate execution by Confederate forces for commanding an African American regiment.

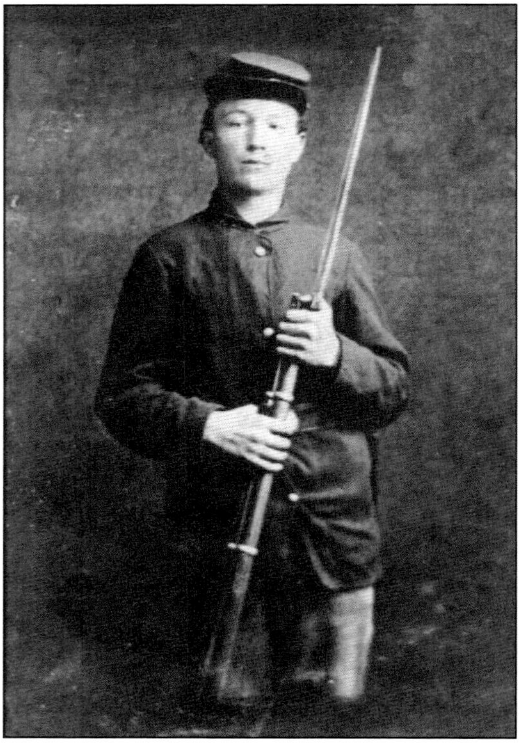

Francis M. Leith enlisted at age 16 in Company K, 55th Ohio Volunteer Infantry on December 10, 1862. He was captured at Chancellorsville. After he was paroled, he was captured again in North Carolina and subsequently killed by guerrillas.

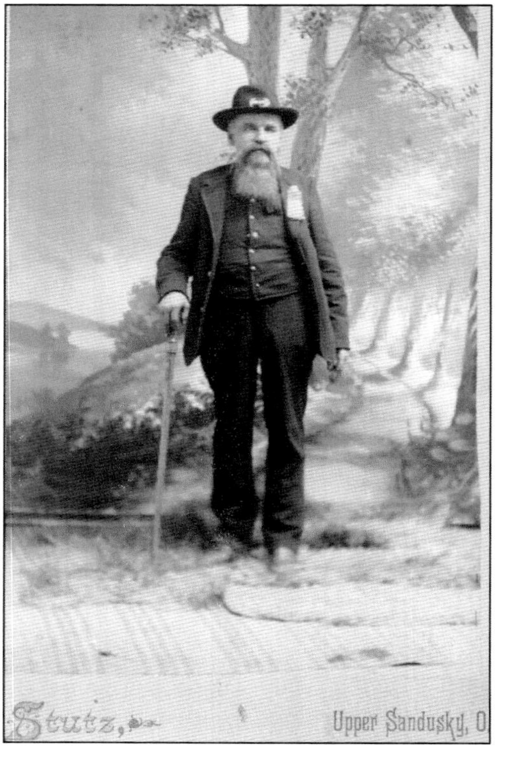

This is a photograph of a Grand Army of the Republic veteran in Upper Sandusky by Stutz photography. Note the G. A. R. emblem on his hat and the ribbon on his chest. (Photograph from the collection of Tom and Marnie Hill.)

Harkness K. Inman enlisted on October 23, 1863, and served in Company F, 9th Ohio Volunteer Calvary. Inman was born in 1833 and died in 1908. This photograph was taken by A. E. Turnbull between 1868 and 1870. (Photograph from the collection of Tom and Marnie Hill.)

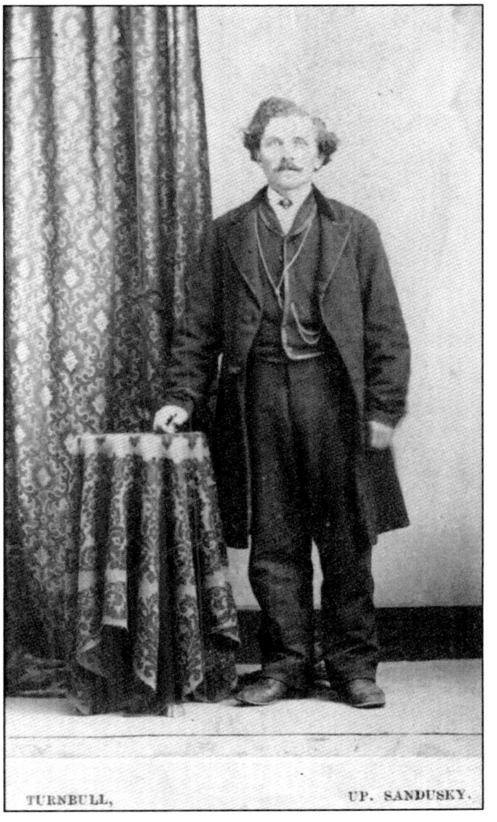

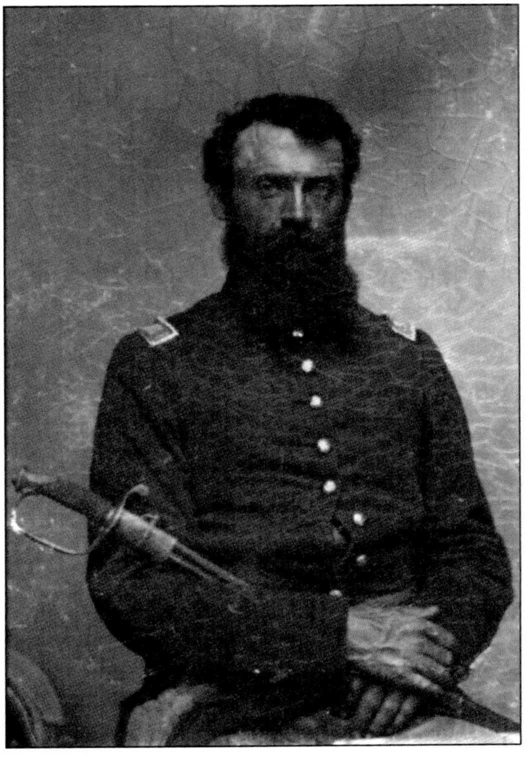

J. Steele Leith enlisted on May 2, 1864, in Company A, 144th Ohio Volunteer Infantry. He was a first lieutenant and was discharged with the regiment.

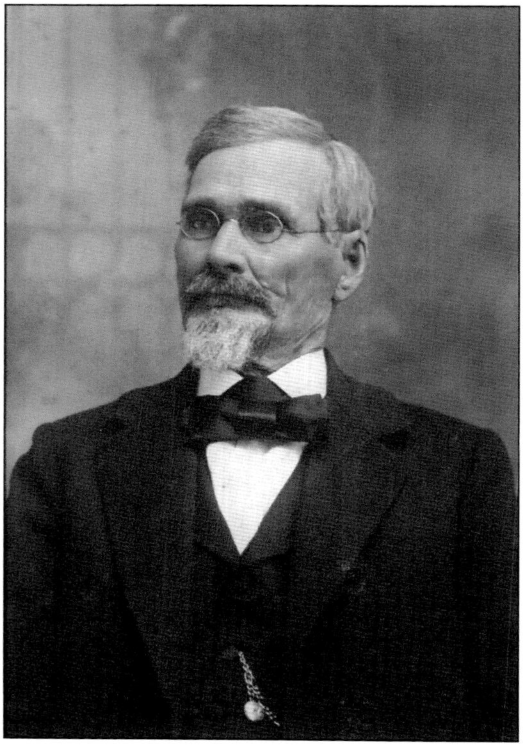

Jesse James Hollingshead served in the 1st Regiment Ohio Volunteer, Heavy Artillery, from 1863 to 1865. This photograph was taken in Upper Sandusky during the 1890s. (Photograph from the collection of Tom and Marnie Hill.)

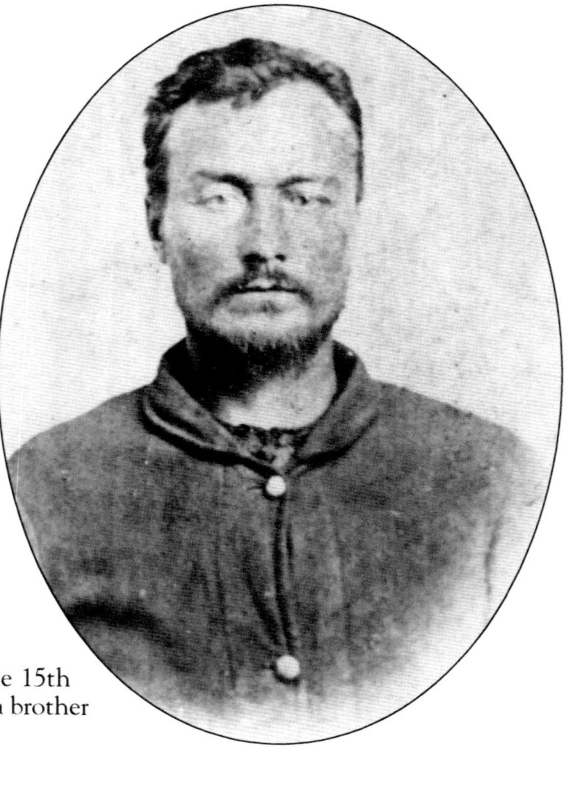

Lowery Leith served in Company D of the 15th Ohio Infantry as a third corporal. He was a brother of J. Steele and Owen Leith.

Owen W. Leith enlisted for a three-month period in Company E of the 11th Illinois Infantry and was killed at Fort Donelson.

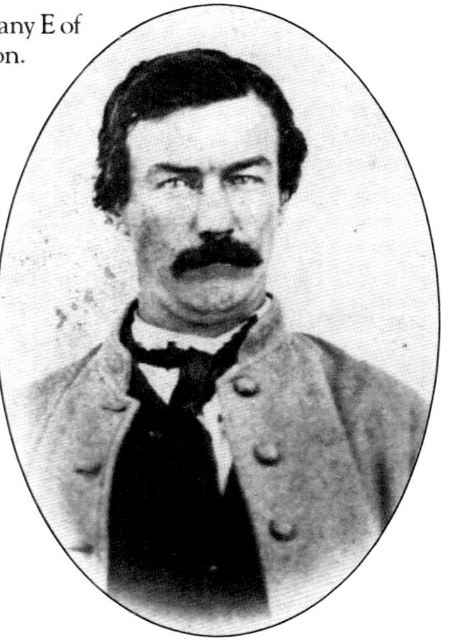

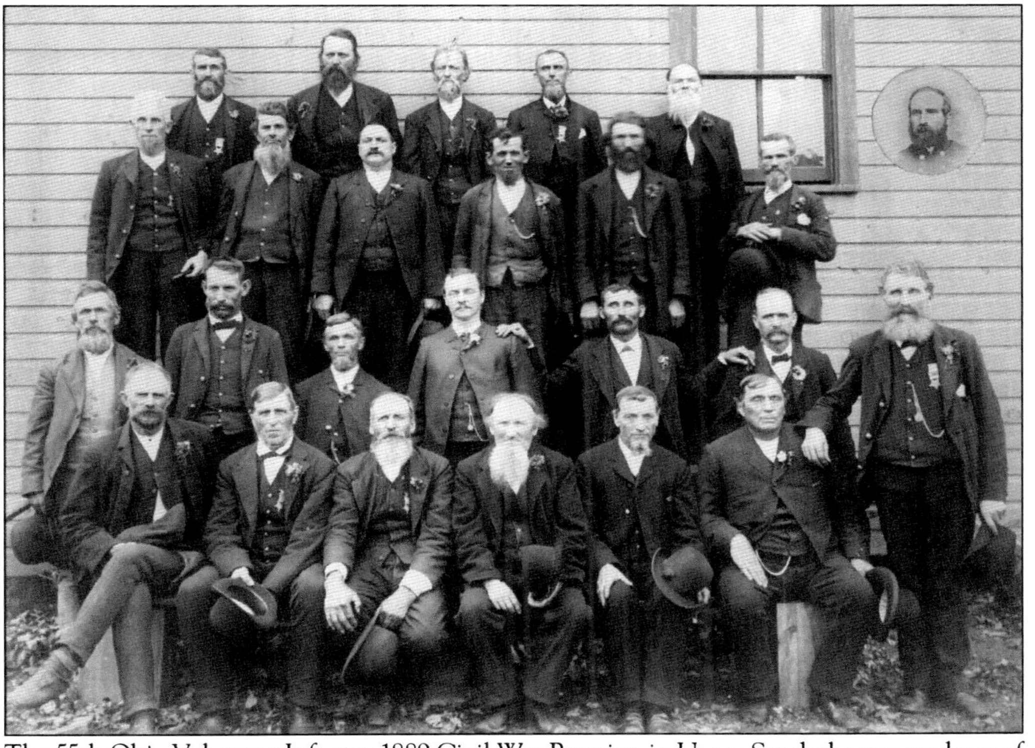

The 55th Ohio Volunteer Infantry 1889 Civil War Reunion in Upper Sandusky was made up of mostly Company K members. The inset shows Maj. Rudolphus Robbins, who was killed in action at Resaca, Georgia, on May 14, 1864. His wife, Kate, pinned a buttonhole bouquet on the lapel of each man's coat. The bouquets are visible in the photograph. The 55th's reunion headquarters were in the courtroom of the Wyandot County Courthouse.

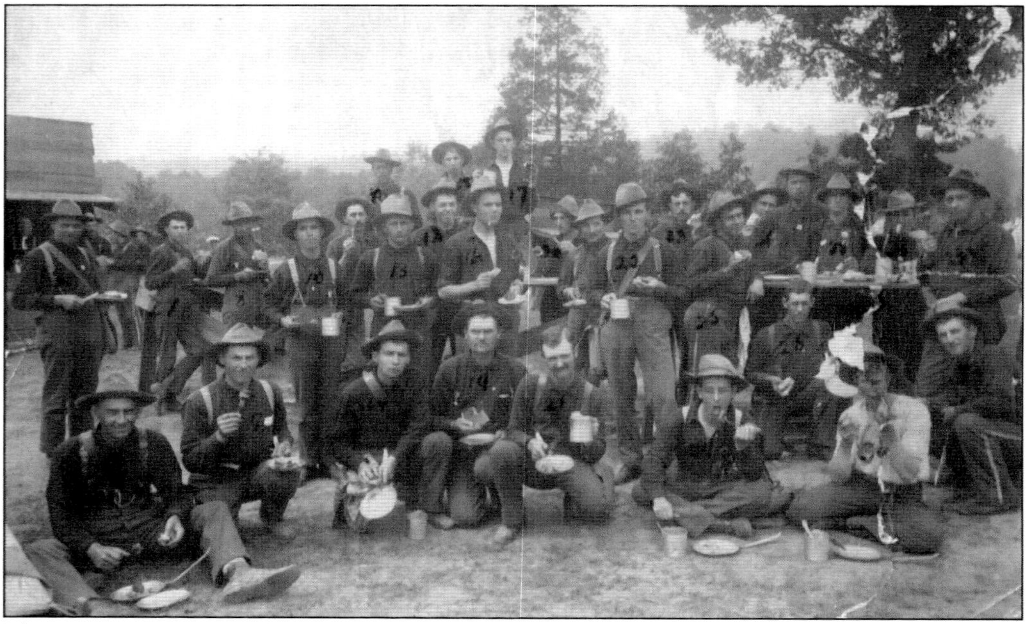

This is Company B, 2nd Regiment during the Spanish American War. Those identified are: (1) Marston, (2) Stoneburner, (3) Oldfield, (4) Halbedel, (5) Ritter, (6) Kalb, (7) Emptage, (8) Grundtisch, (9) Slemmer, (10) Earp, (11) Layton, (12) Pontius, (13) McEvoy, (14) Haskin, (15) Phelps, (16) Hoover, (17) Kimmel, (18) Harper, (19) Harman, (20) Zimmerman, (21) Lindsey, (22) Holmes, (23) Hornby, (24) Mohr, (25) Ragon, (26) Trimble, (27) Taylor, (28) Summers, (29) Metz, (30) Stoner, (31) Cammarn, (32) Pool, (33) G. Greek, (34) Forney, and (SP) unidentified, probably I. P. Cameron, who donated the photograph to the museum.

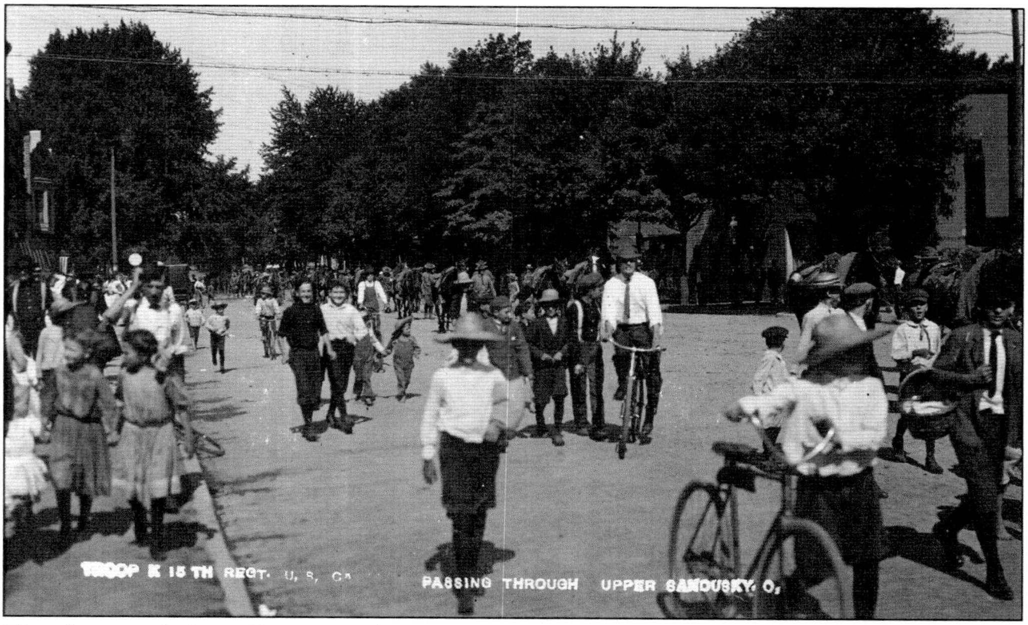

This photograph shows Troop K, 15th Regiment, 8th U.S. Calvary passing through Upper Sandusky in the late 1890s (Photograph from the collection of Tom and Marnie Hill.)

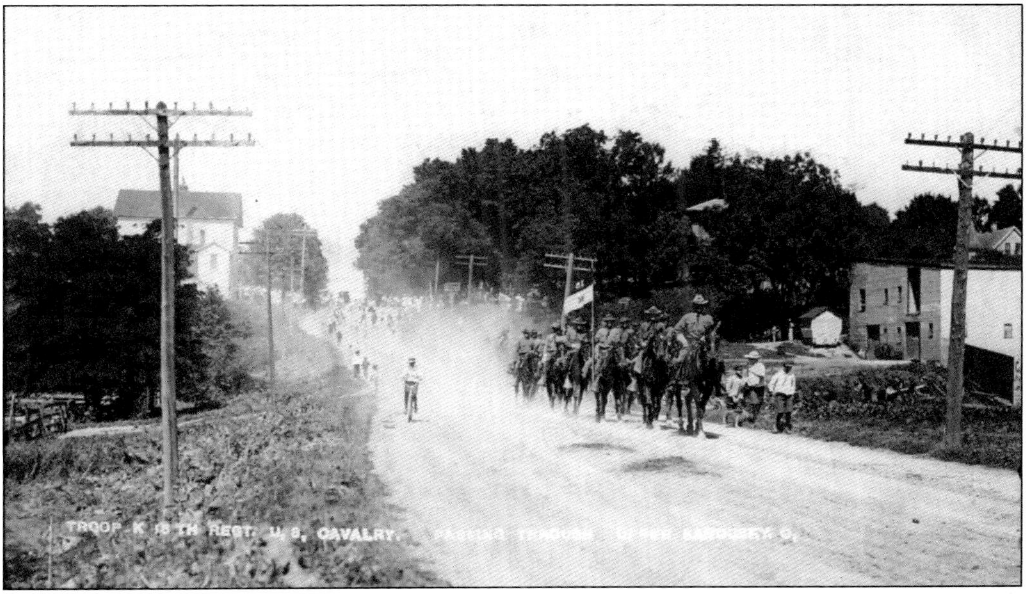

Troop K, 15th Regiment, 8th U.S. Calvary is seen here riding down Kirby Hill by Harrison Smith Park in Upper Sandusky. (Photograph from the collection of Tom and Marnie Hill.)

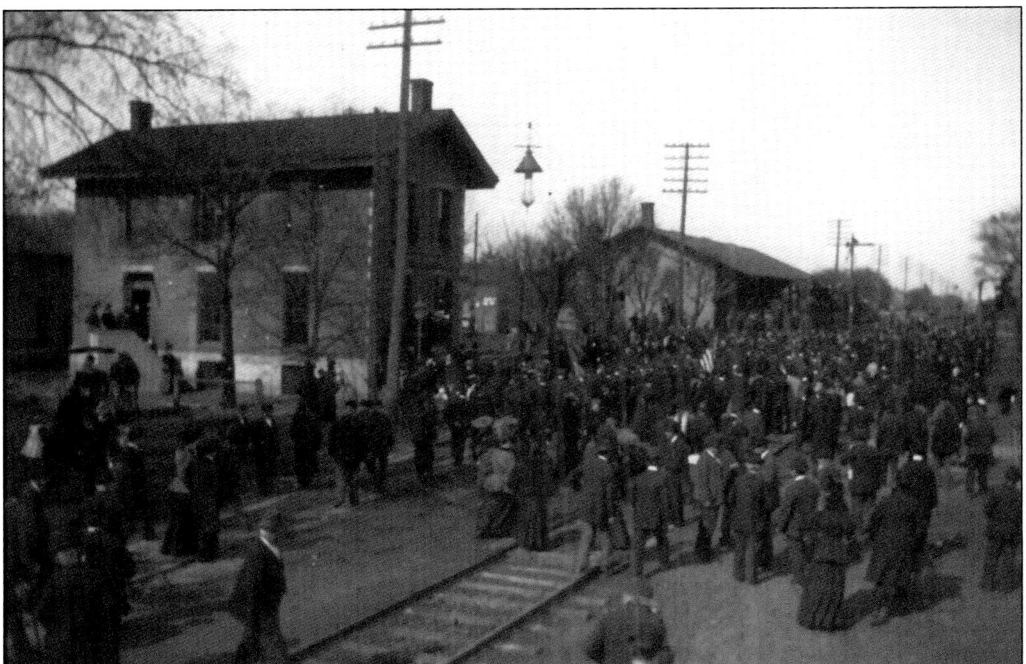

Company B is seen here at a railroad depot in 1898. The soldiers are getting ready to depart Upper Sandusky during the Spanish American War.

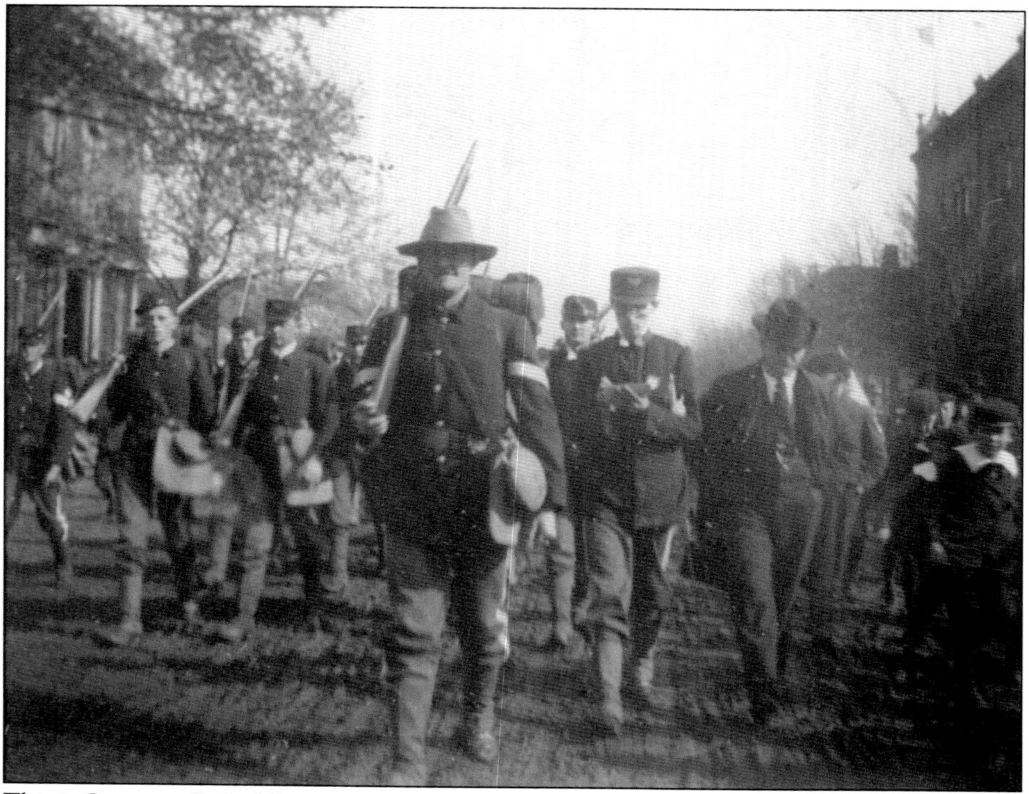

This is Company B, 2nd Regiment, seen coming home from the Spanish American War. Avery Peters is marching in the front of the column.

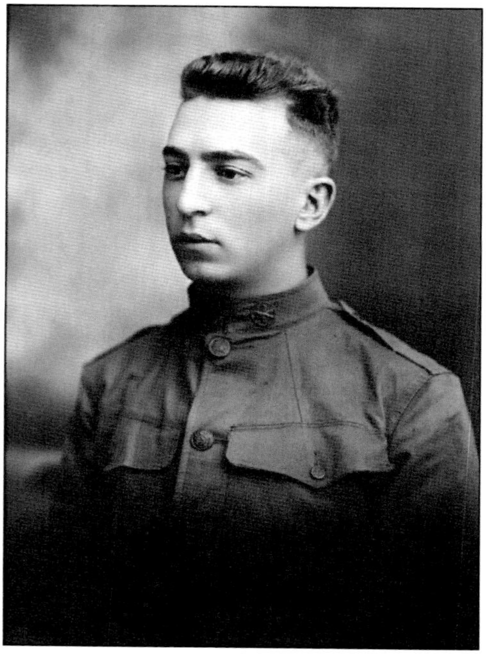

Harold William Shock enlisted in the Ohio National Guard on July 16, 1917, in Carey, Ohio. He was promoted to the rank of corporal on September 17, 1917. He received an honorable discharge on August 25, 1918, to accept a commission as a second lieutenant in the infantry. He served in Company L, 1st Provisional Regiment, Camp Sevier, 156th Depot Brigade, until his honorable discharge on March 20, 1919 at Camp Jackson in Columbia, South Carolina. (Photograph from the collection of Tom and Marnie Hill.)

Pictured from left to right are Donald Skivers, James Corfman, and Robert Shock. Skivers served in Europe and Africa with the U.S. Army. Corfman attended Gyro school at the Brooklyn Naval Yard and served aboard the U.S.S. *Biloxi*. Shock was on Kwajalein with VMB 613 that flew B25 Mitchells. He transferred to Voler (from the French word "to fly") Marine Fighter Group 618 in China. John Glenn, a marine pilot, also served with this unit. (Photograph from the collection of Tom and Marnie Hill.)

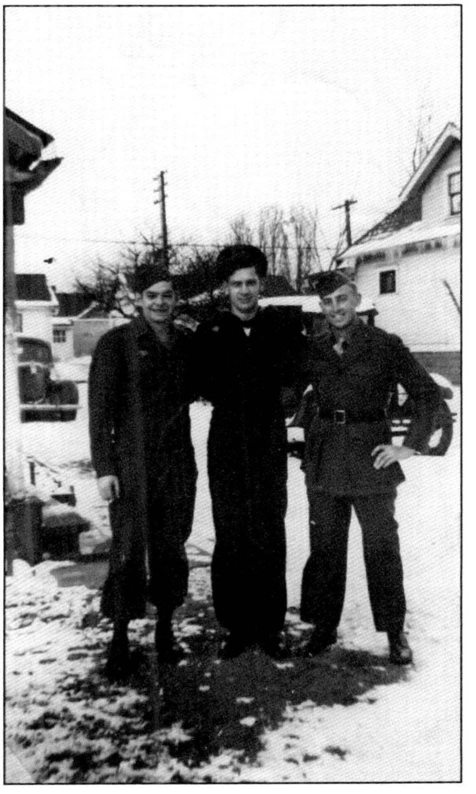

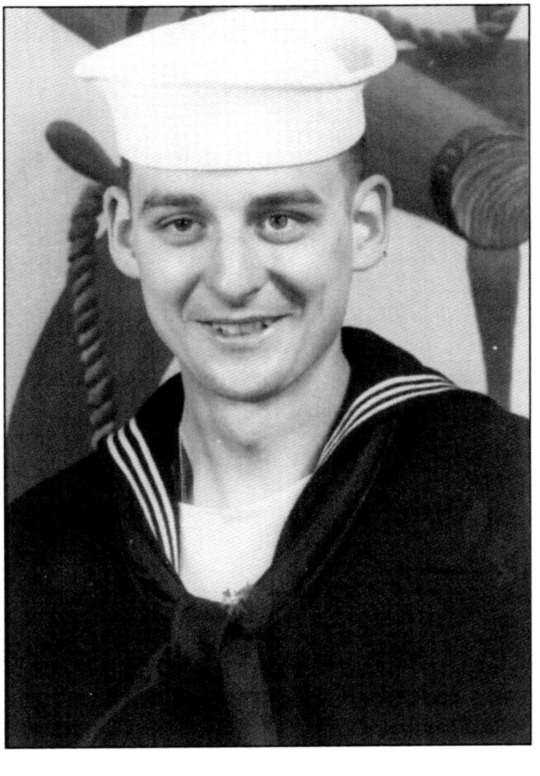

Ronald H. Klink enlisted on January 3, 1957 and served in Bethesda, Maryland as a hospital corpsman, second class. He was selected to serve with the White House staff as a physical therapist for Pres. John F. Kennedy. After the Kennedy assassination, Klink briefly stayed on in the same position for Pres. Lyndon B. Johnson. He received his honorable discharge on December 14, 1964. (Photograph from the collection of Bonnie Klink.)

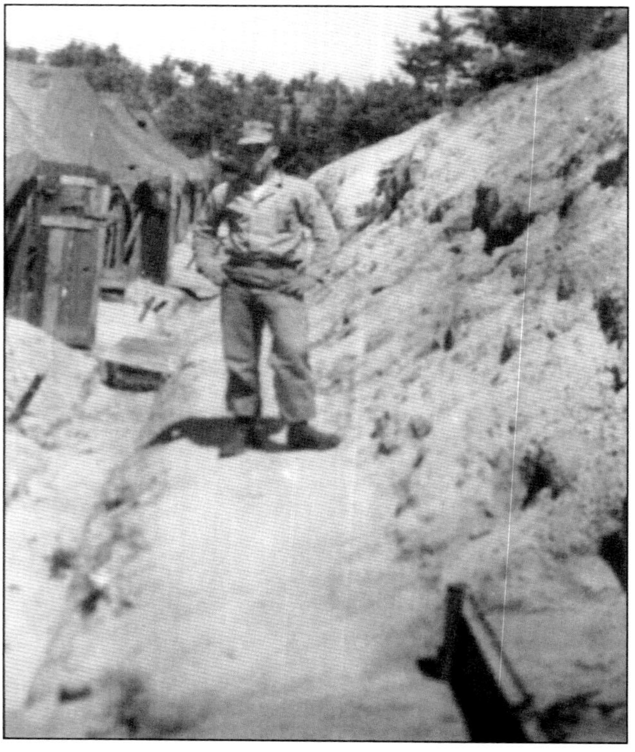

Pictured is Jerry Hill with the 1st U.S. Marine division in Korea. Hill had two bothers in the service at the same time. Richard Hill, with the 24th Infantry division, was briefly held as a prisoner of war by North Koreans. Ronnie Hill, in the U.S. Navy during the Korean War, was aboard the USS *Patapsco* gasoline tanker when it was exposed to radiation after the atomic bomb test on Enewetak Atoll on March 1, 1954. (Photograph from collection of Tom and Marnie Hill.)

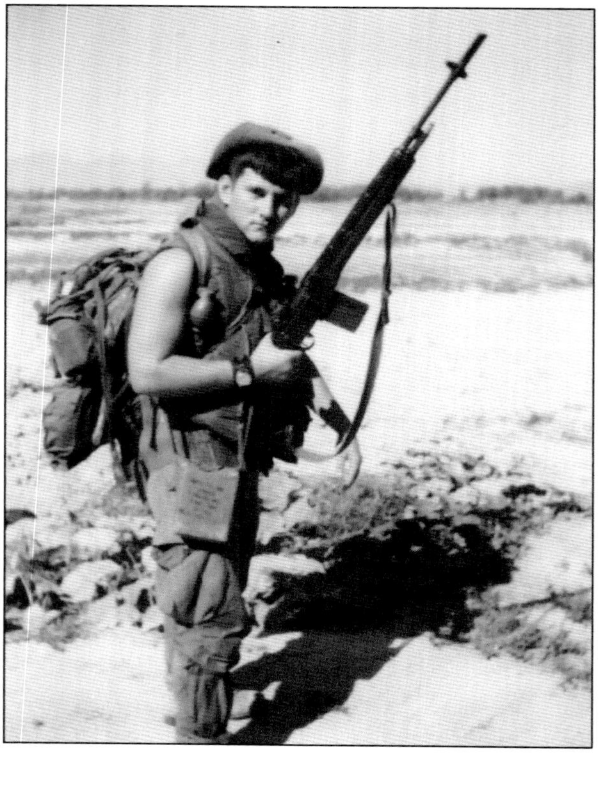

Tom Hill is getting ready for patrol with Combined Action Platoon (CAP) 143 in Chu Lai, South Vietnam, in 1969. Ties around his legs were to keep leeches, snakes, and centipedes from crawling up his legs and biting. The backpack could weigh up to 60 pounds with extra canteens and c-rations. Note the M26 hand grenade hanging from his flak jacket and the extra ammunition on his side. The rifle is an M-14. (Photograph from the collection of Tom and Marnie Hill.)

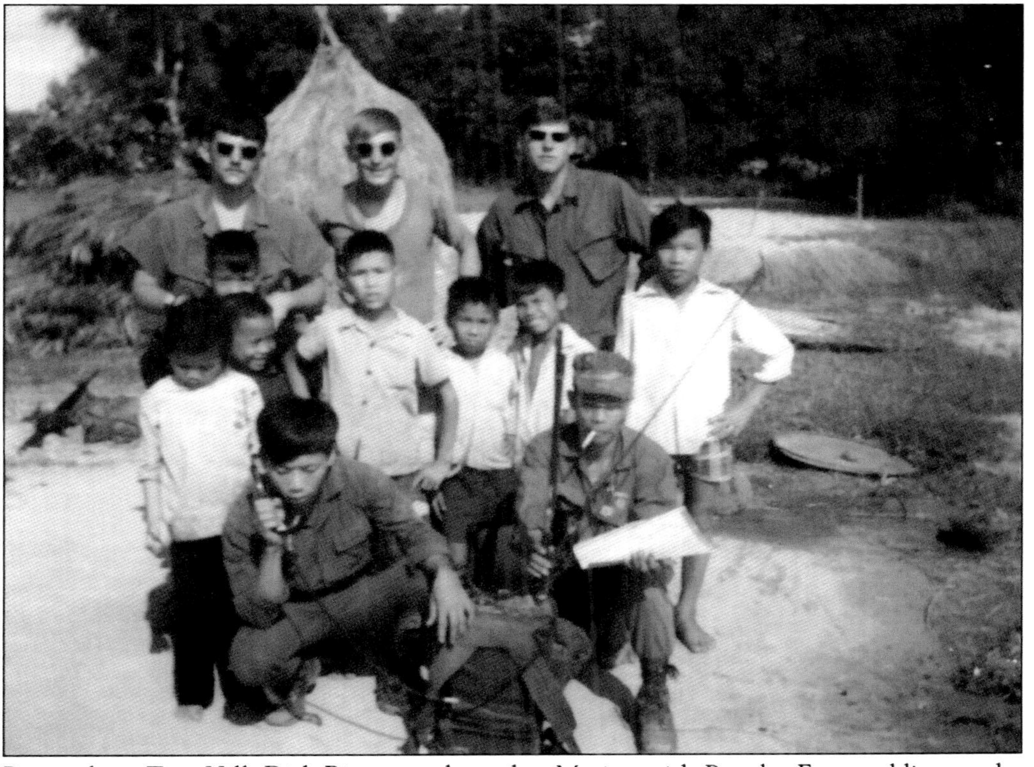

Pictured are Tom Hill, Dick Risner, and another Marine with Popular Force soldiers at the Combined Action Platoon 141 compound. CAP units were supposed to have 12 men including a Navy corpsman. They lived in the villages and performed civic action duties. They taught military tactics to the Popular Force soldiers during the day, and at night, the Marines set out ambushes along with Vietnamese Popular Force soldiers (PFs). (Photograph from the collection of Tom and Marnie Hill.)

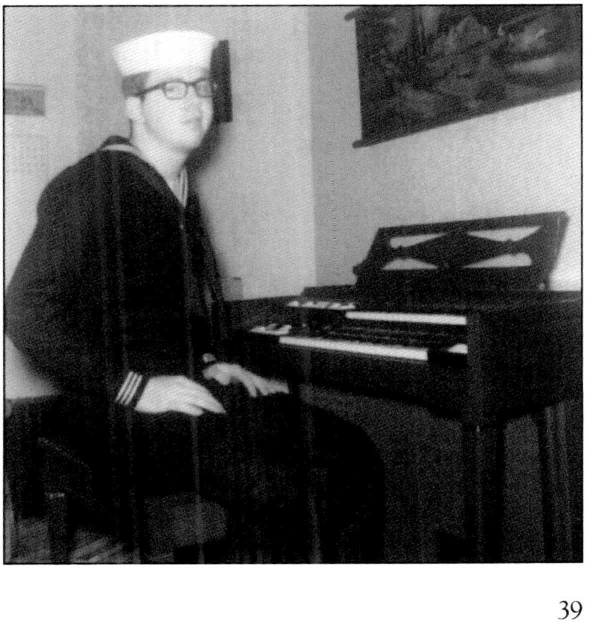

Nelson E. Spitler served in the U.S. Navy. While aboard the USS *Forrestal* on July 29, 1967, an explosion was set off by a Zuni rocket discharging from an F-4 Phantom. The rocket struck a fuel tank on an A-4 Skyhawk, causing fuel to ignite. The fire killed 134 sailors and injured 161. Spitler was one of the fatalities. The *Forrestal* was engaged in combat operations off the coast of Vietnam. (Photograph from the collection of Bill and Karen Spitler.)

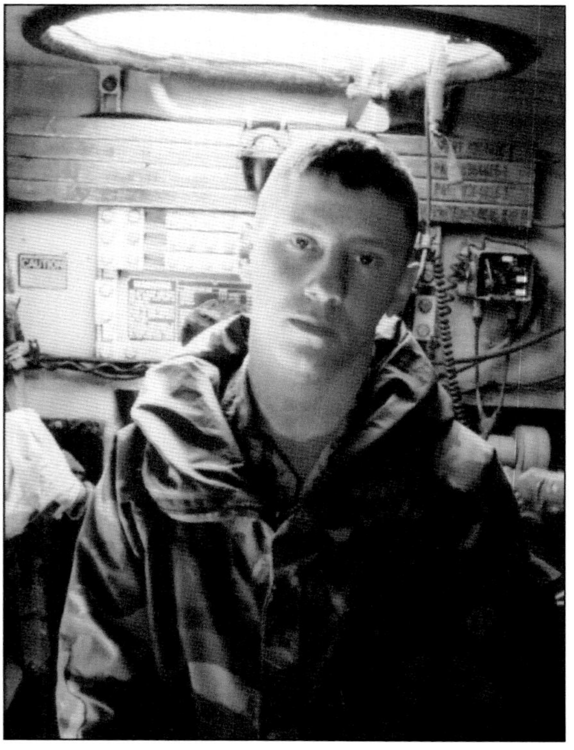

Steve Hill is shown inside his M113 tracked vehicle during Operation Desert Storm. The vehicle was almost targeted by friendly fire during the major advance of coalition forces into Iraq. Hill enlisted in the Army in 1988. After he was discharged in 1991, he received a bachelor's degree from Ohio State University as a registered dietician. He reenlisted into the U.S. Army Reserves as a second lieutenant in 2001. At the present time, Hill is a captain in the reserves. (Photograph from the collection of Steve Hill.)

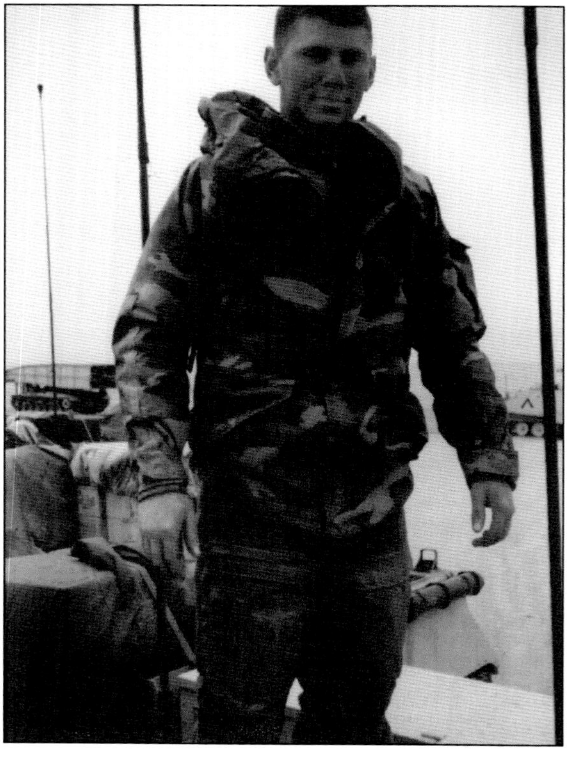

Steve Hill was a forward observer with HHB 2/1 Field Artillery, 1st Armored Division, and 7th Corps in Iraq during Operation Desert Storm. He was a specialist E4 and was assigned to an M113 tracked vehicle. The black soot on his face was from burning oil wells set on fire by Iraqi troops to slow down the coalition advance. (Photograph from the collection of Steve Hill.)

Three

Expansion and Enterprise

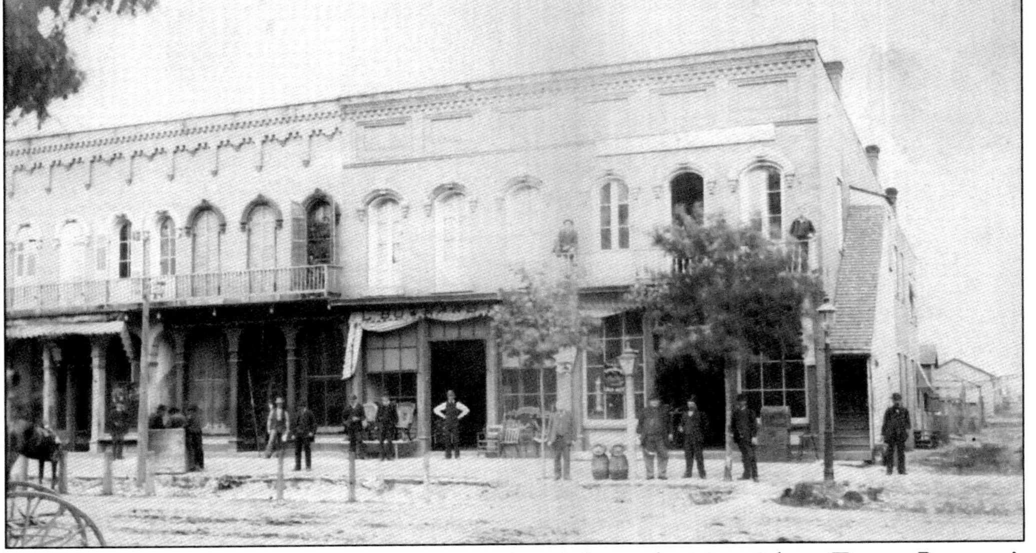

Bottle Row on East Wyandot Avenue included, from left to right, Mart Gibson Tavern, Bowman's Furniture and Undertaking, and the Jake Schaeffer Tavern operated by Fatty Abers.

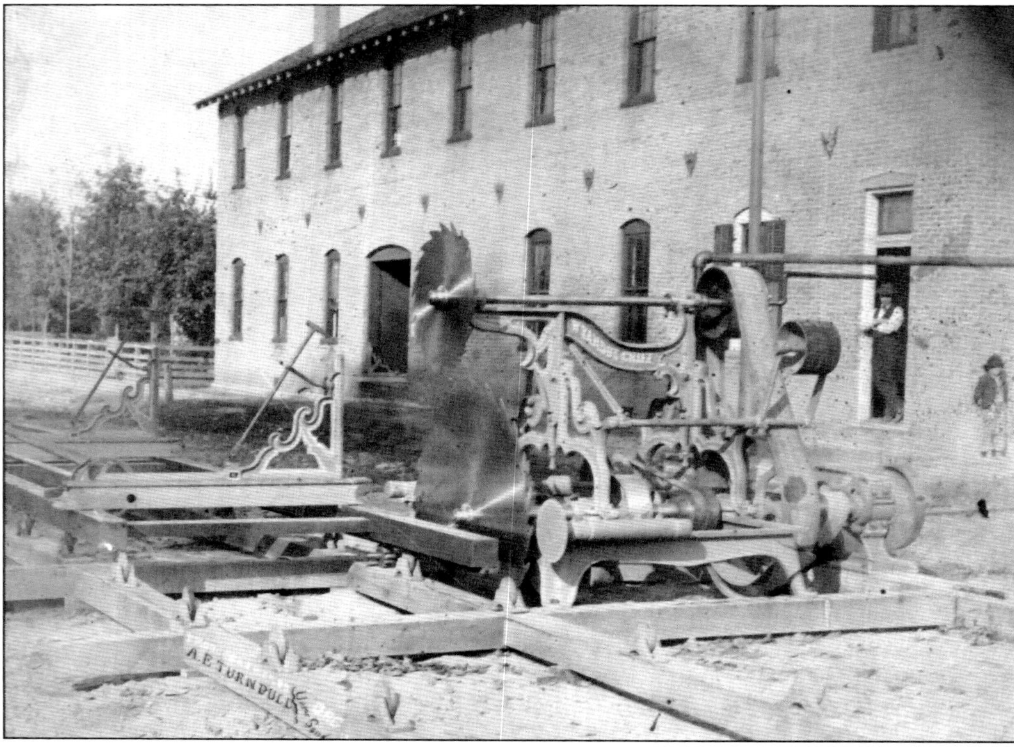

This machinery was used to print the *Wyandot Chief* newspaper in Upper Sandusky. The paper's editor was H. A. Tracht. The paper operated as the *Weekly Chief* from 1879 to 1887 and the *Daily Chief* from 1896 to 1938.

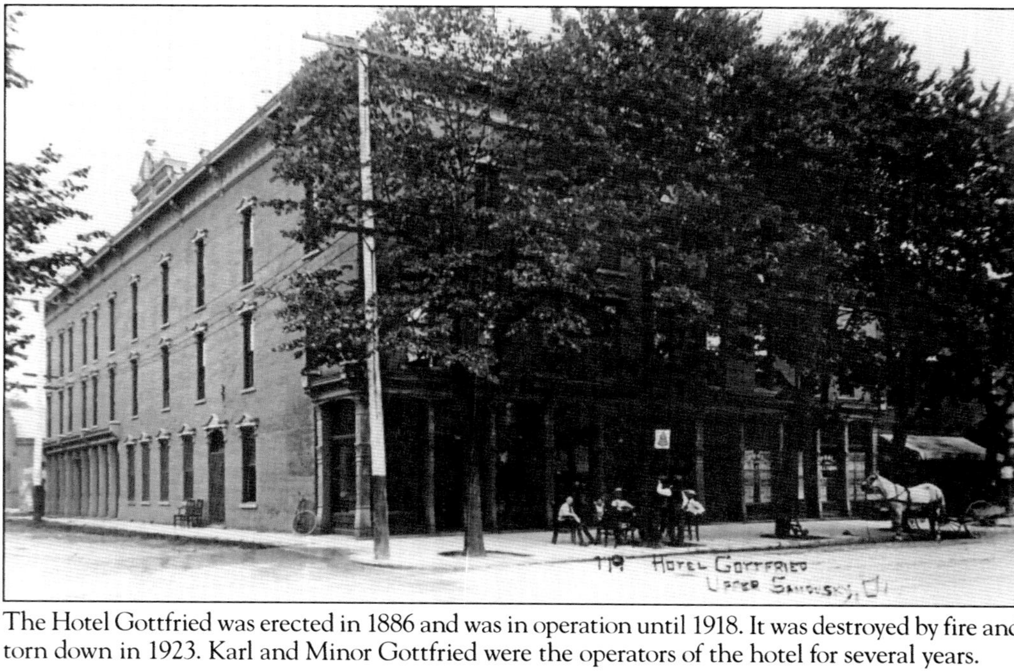

The Hotel Gottfried was erected in 1886 and was in operation until 1918. It was destroyed by fire and torn down in 1923. Karl and Minor Gottfried were the operators of the hotel for several years.

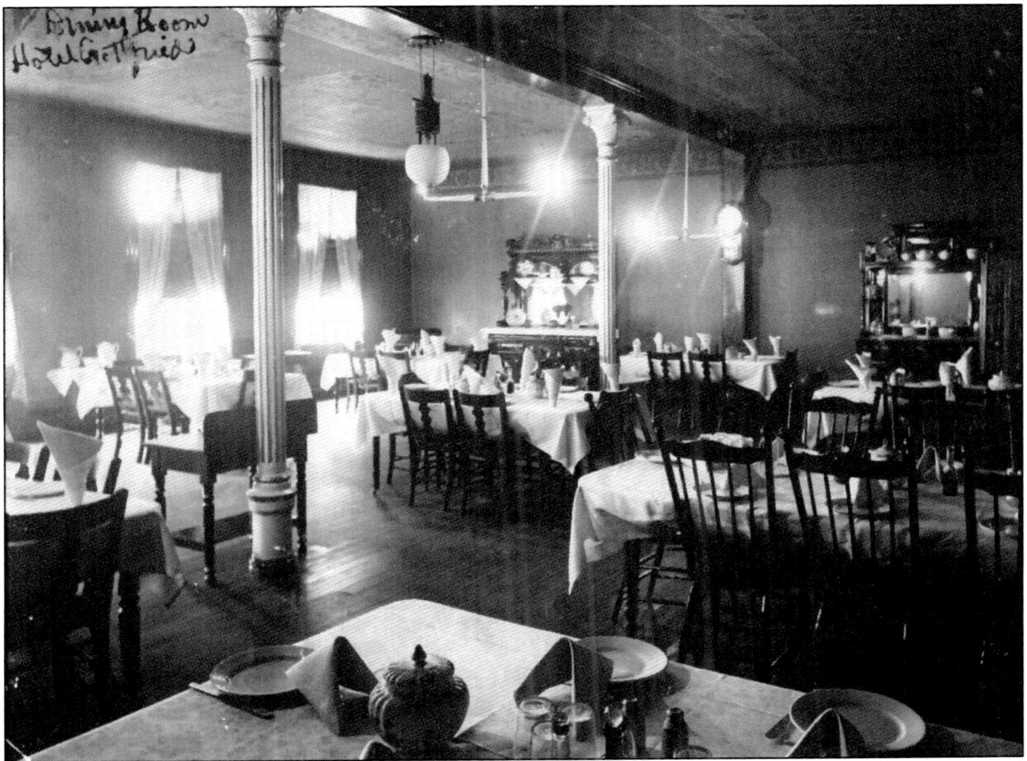

The dining room of Hotel Gottfried is pictured here. Note the elegant china dinnerware and shaped napkins laid out on the tables. The floor was made of hardwood, and ornate chairs graced the dinner tables as guests sat down to have their meal.

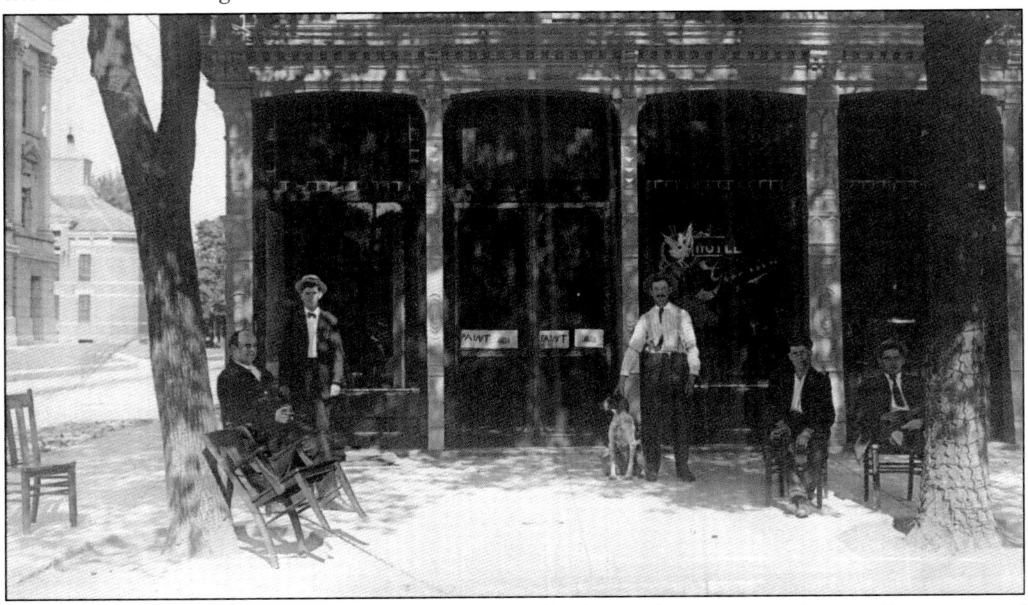

This 1908 view shows the front of the Hotel Gottfried. The hotel was built in 1886 at a cost of $23,000. Five hundred thousand bricks were needed to complete the building.

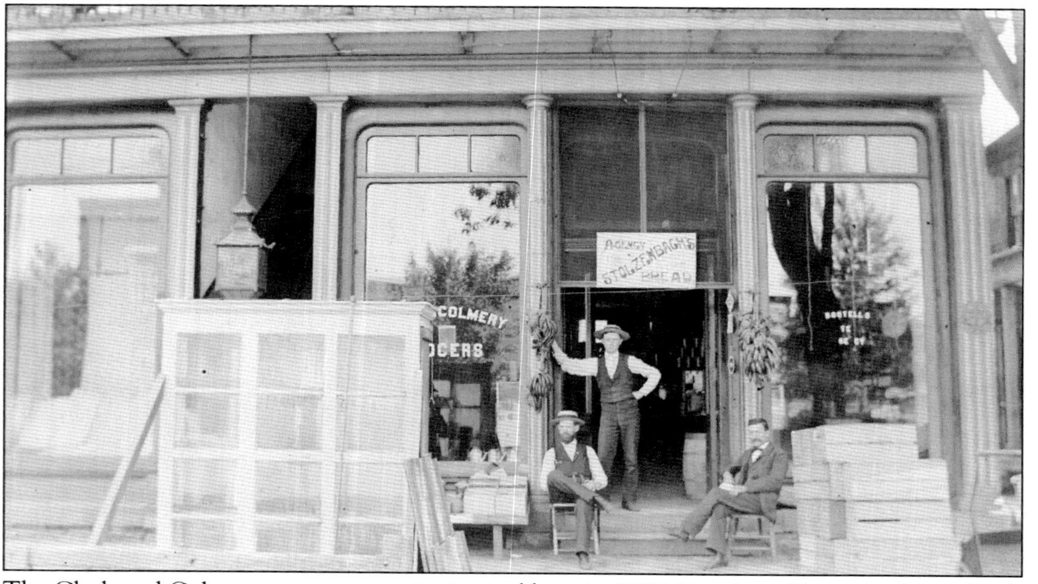

The Clark and Colmery grocery store is pictured here in 1880. Bunches of bananas hang above the gentlemen sitting in the chairs. The sign above the door advertises that the store was an agency for Stolzenbach's "famous steam bread."

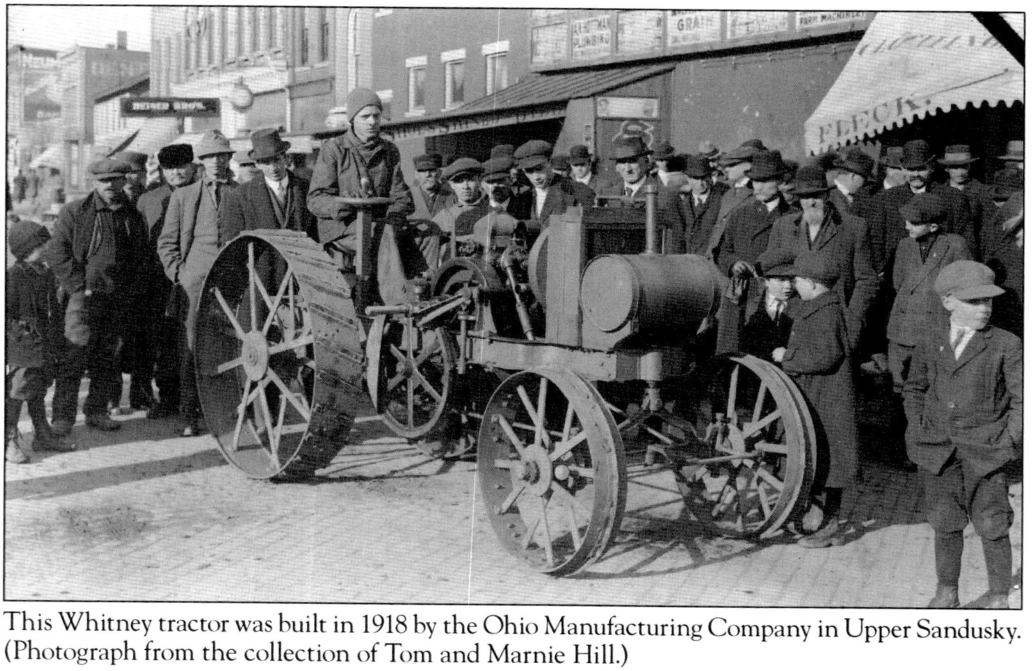

This Whitney tractor was built in 1918 by the Ohio Manufacturing Company in Upper Sandusky. (Photograph from the collection of Tom and Marnie Hill.)

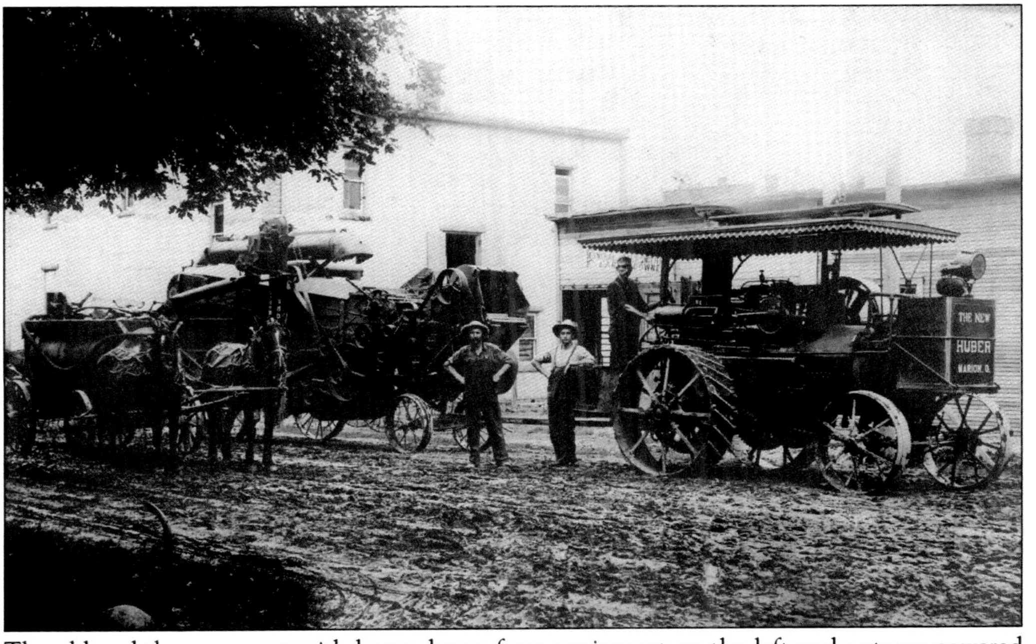

The old and the new meet with horse drawn farm equipment on the left and a steam powered Huber tractor on the right. (Photograph from the collection of Tom & Marnie Hill.)

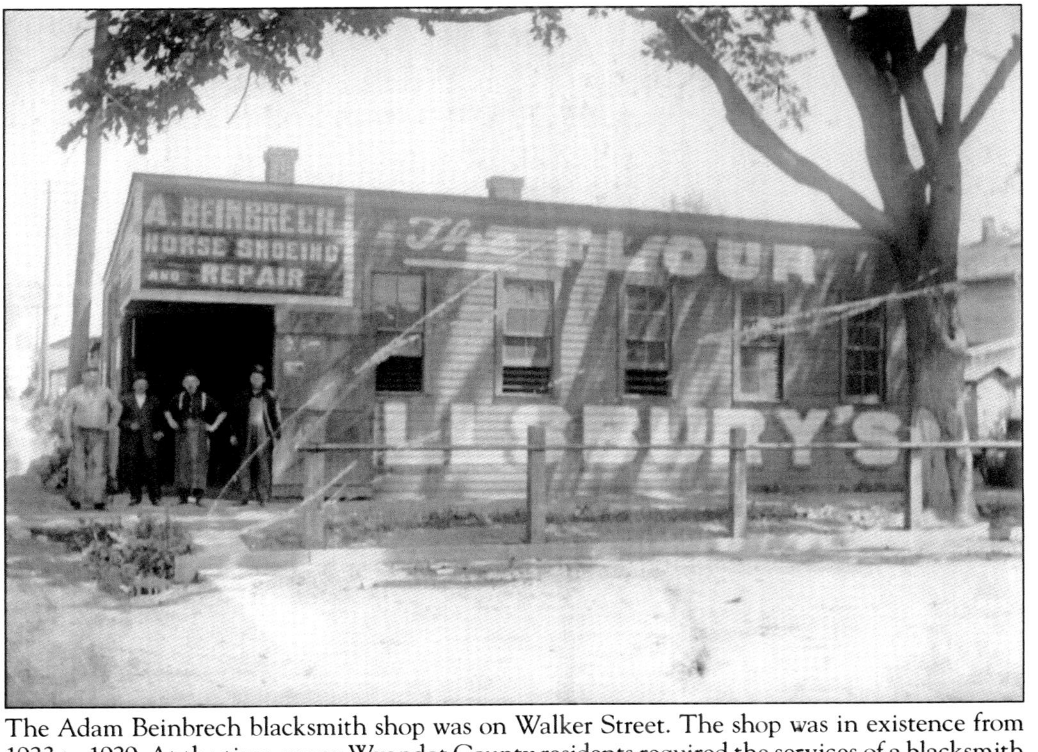

The Adam Beinbrech blacksmith shop was on Walker Street. The shop was in existence from 1923 to 1929. At the time, many Wyandot County residents required the services of a blacksmith to shoe their horses and to fix iron tools.

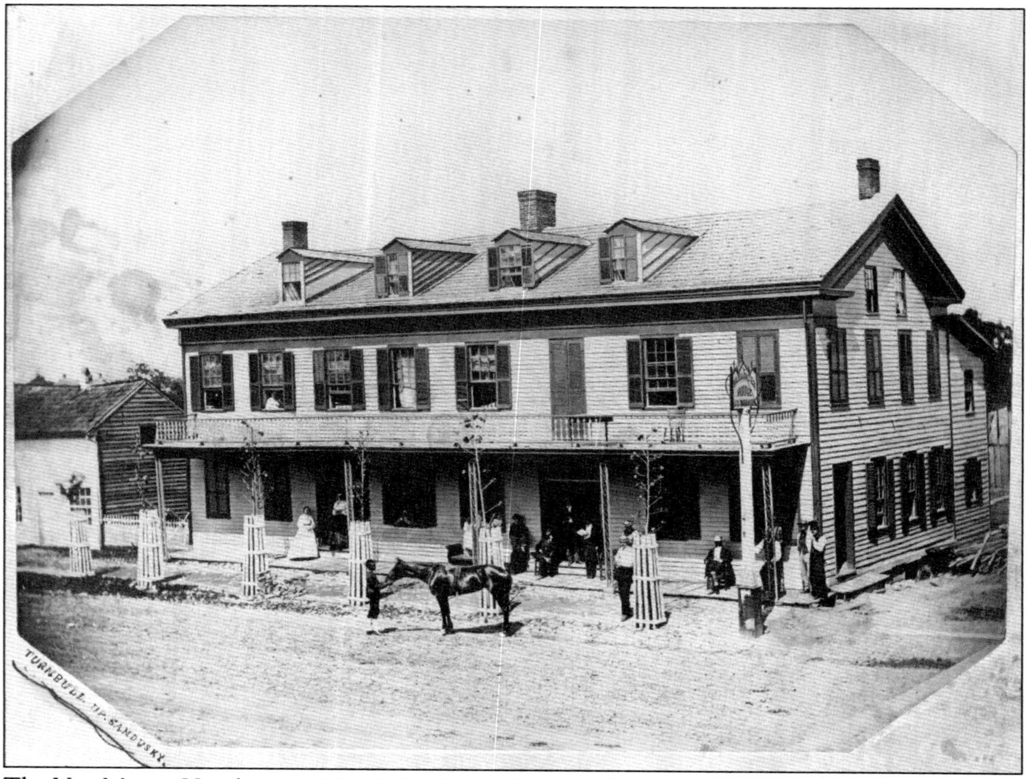

The Van Marter Hotel was on North Sandusky Street in the area where the VFW, Rosebud Café, and Doctor Hoover are located today. The Indian Agent Building is to the left of the hotel and was operated by Purdy McElvain in the 1840s.

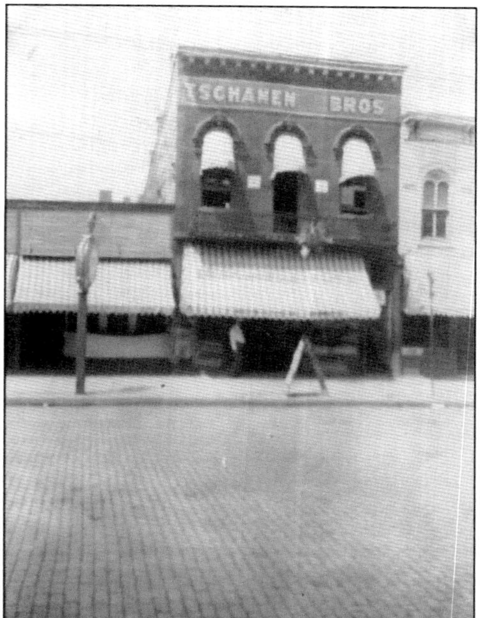

The Tschanen Brothers' drug store at 128 South Sandusky Avenue operated from 1880 to 1921 in Upper Sandusky. Charles F. Tschanen also operated a photography business from 1896 to 1899 in a shop above the Bon Ton restaurant until the fire of 1918.

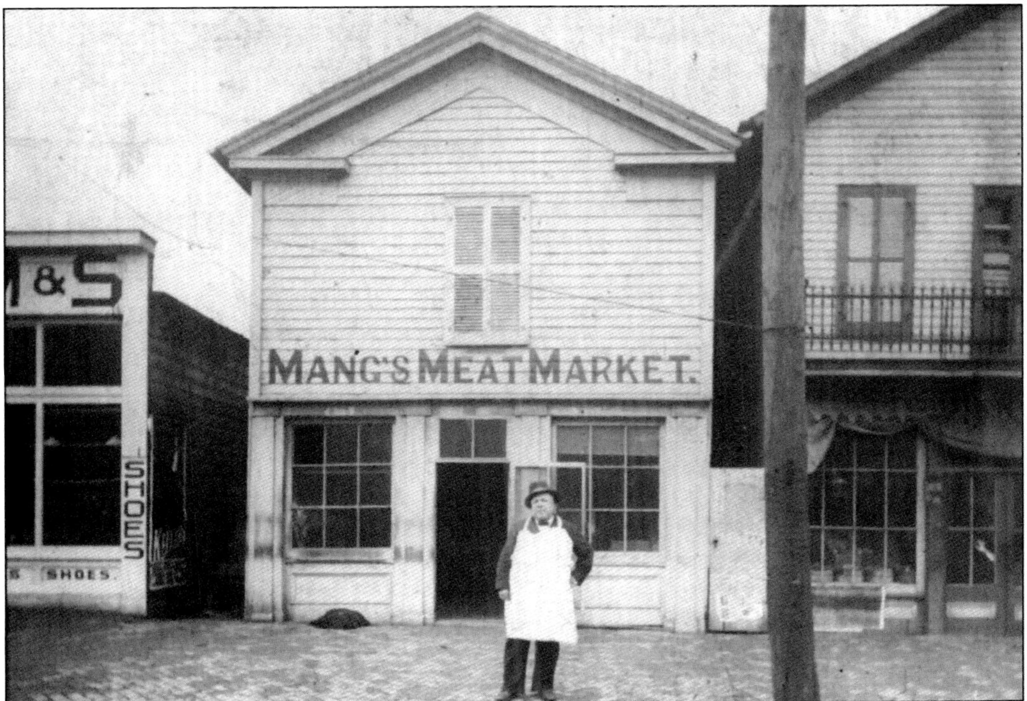

Mang's Meat Market started operating at 107 North Sandusky Avenue in 1875 and was run by Joseph Mang. He is standing in front of his store in this photograph.

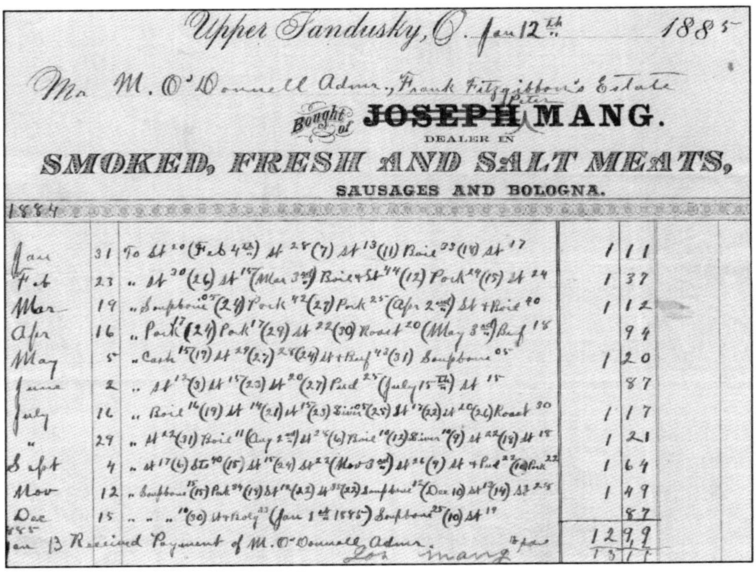

Upper Sandusky, O. Jan 12th 1885

Mr M. O'Donnell Adm., Frank Fitzgibbon's Estate

Bought of ~~JOSEPH~~ Peter MANG.

DEALER IN

SMOKED, FRESH AND SALT MEATS,

SAUSAGES AND BOLOGNA.

1884

Jan	31	To St 20 (Feb 4th) St 28 (7) St 13 (11) Boil 33 (18) St 17	1	11
Feb	23	" St 30 (26) St 15 (Mar 3rd) Boil & St 44 (12) Pork 29 (15) St 24	1	37
Mar	19	" Soupbone 05 (24) Pork 42 (27) Pork 25 (Apr 2nd) St + Boil 40	1	12
Apr	16	" Pork 17 (24) Pork 17 (29) St 22 (30) Roast 20 (May 3rd) Beef 18		94
May	5	" Cash 15 (17) St 29 (27) 28 (24) St + Beef 43 (31) Soupbone 05	1	20
June	2	" St 13 (3) St 15 (23) St 20 (27) Paid 25 (July 15th) St 15		87
July	16	" Boil 16 (19) St 14 (21) St 15 (23) Liver 05 (25) St 17 (22) St 20 (26) Roast 30	1	17
"	29	" St 22 (31) Boil 11 (Aug 2nd) St 28 (6) Boil 16 (12) Liver 16 (9) St 22 (18) St 18	1	21
Sept	4	" St 17 (6) St 40 (15) St 15 (24) St 22 (Nov 3rd) St 26 (9) St + Paid 22 (10) Pork 22	1	64
Nov	12	" Soupbone 15 (15) Pork 34 (19) St 12 (22) St 35 (22) Soupbone 12 (Dec 10) St 12 (14) St 28	1	49
Dec	15	" " " 16 (30) St + Boly 33 (Jan 1st 1885) Soupbone 25 (10) St 19		87
			12	99
1885 Jan	13	Received Payment of M. O'Donnell Adm. 12 pa	13	11

Jos Mang

This Mang's Meat Market bill is from 1885, with "Joseph" scratched out and "Peter" written above it.

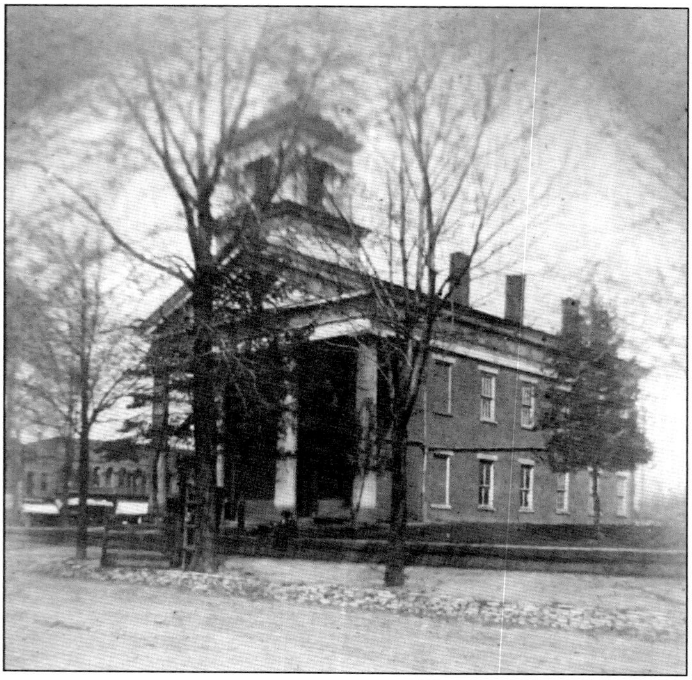

The first courthouse in Upper Sandusky was built around 1846 for the sum of $12,000. Before it was completed, the county commissioners held their first meeting in the council house of the Wyandot tribe on April 16, 1845.

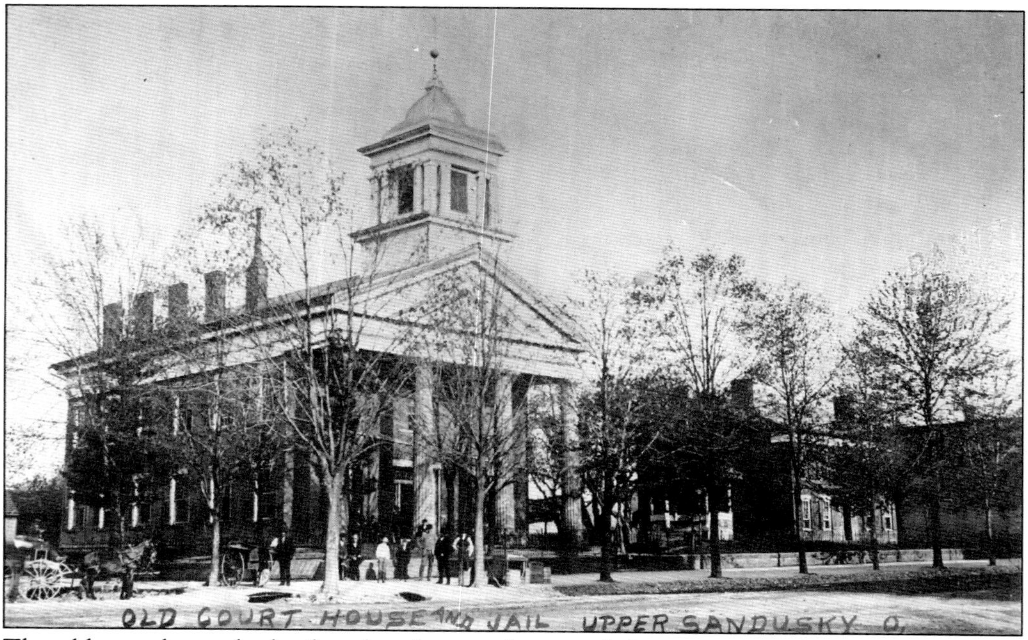

The old courthouse had a fire that destroyed some of the county's early records. The new courthouse was built on the site of the old one in 1900. It was said to be "vault safe" and had two Columbiad cannons on the lawn that were donated by Rhode Island to the Robbins Post No. 91 Grand Army of the Republic lodge.

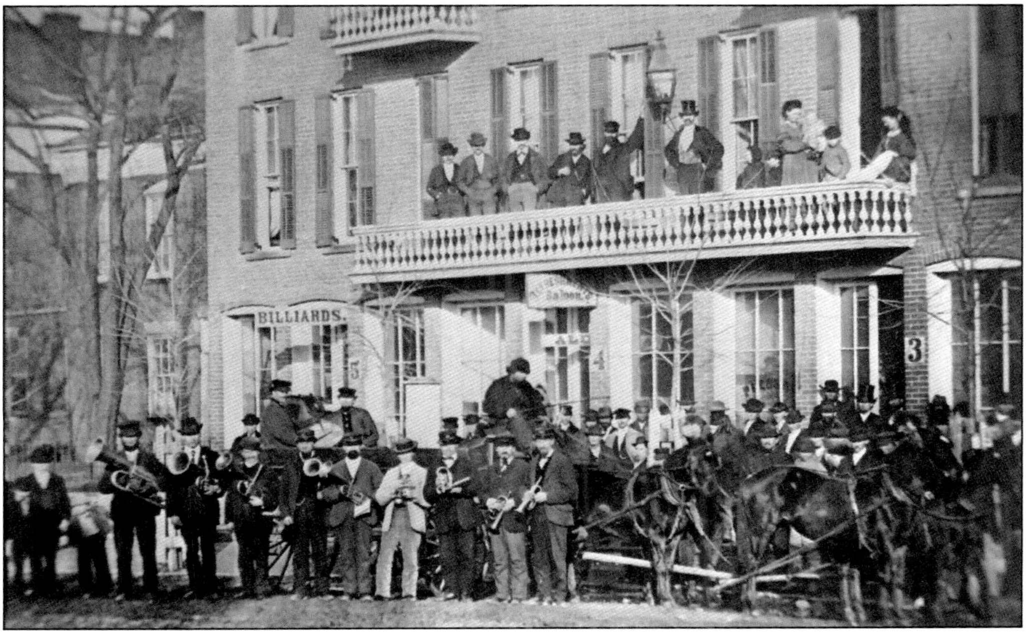

The Pierson House Hotel in Upper Sandusky was built in 1847 and torn down by 1884. The Hotel Gottfried was built on the same site in 1886. The photograph shows several men with their instruments in hand, apparently watching a parade go by. Up on the balcony on the right hand side stands a woman with a baby in her arms.

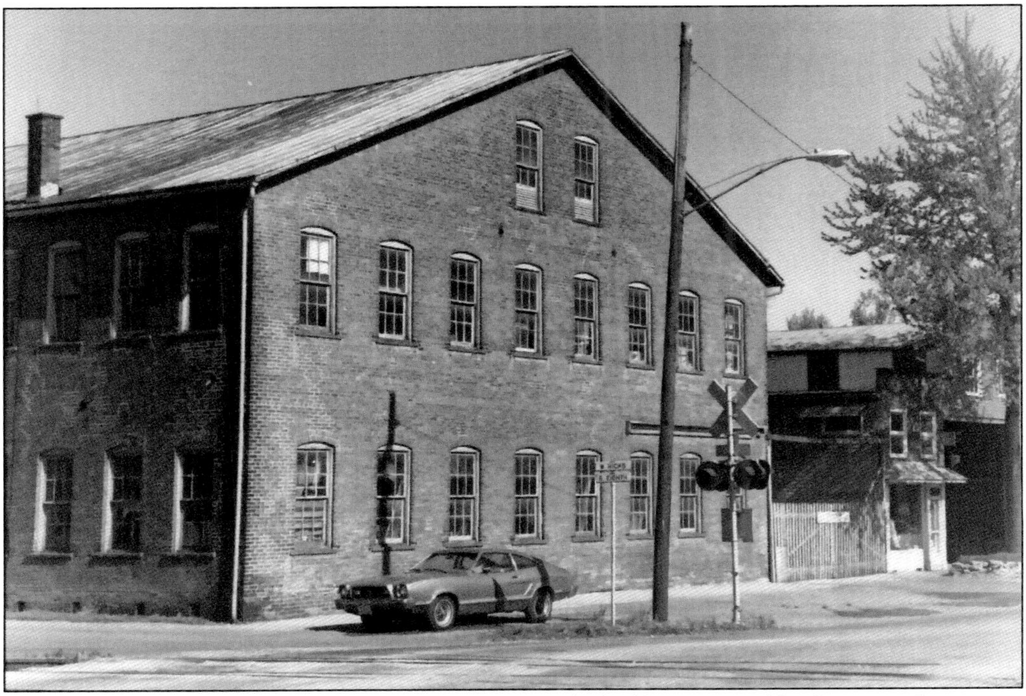

This view shows the Stephan Lumber Company. In 1994, the building was used for the prison shop scenes for the movie *The Shawshank Redemption*. (Photograph courtesy of John and Mary Jane Constien.)

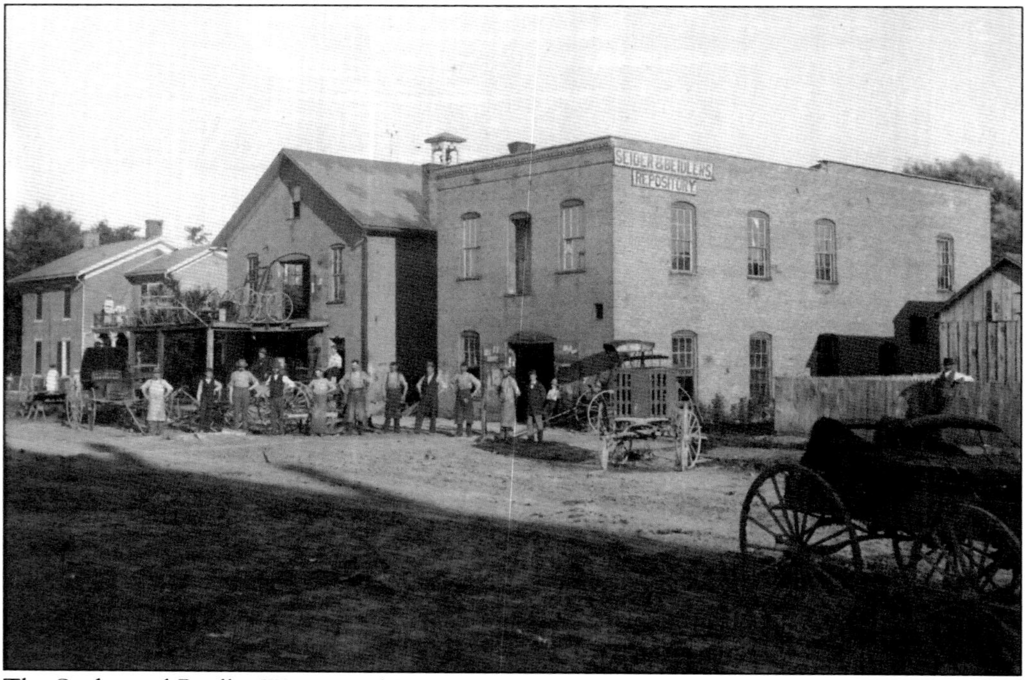

The Seider and Beidler Wagon and Buggy Factory on Walker Street was built in 1857 by John Seider. He operated the business until Frank Beidler became partner in 1871. The two ran the shop together until 1880.

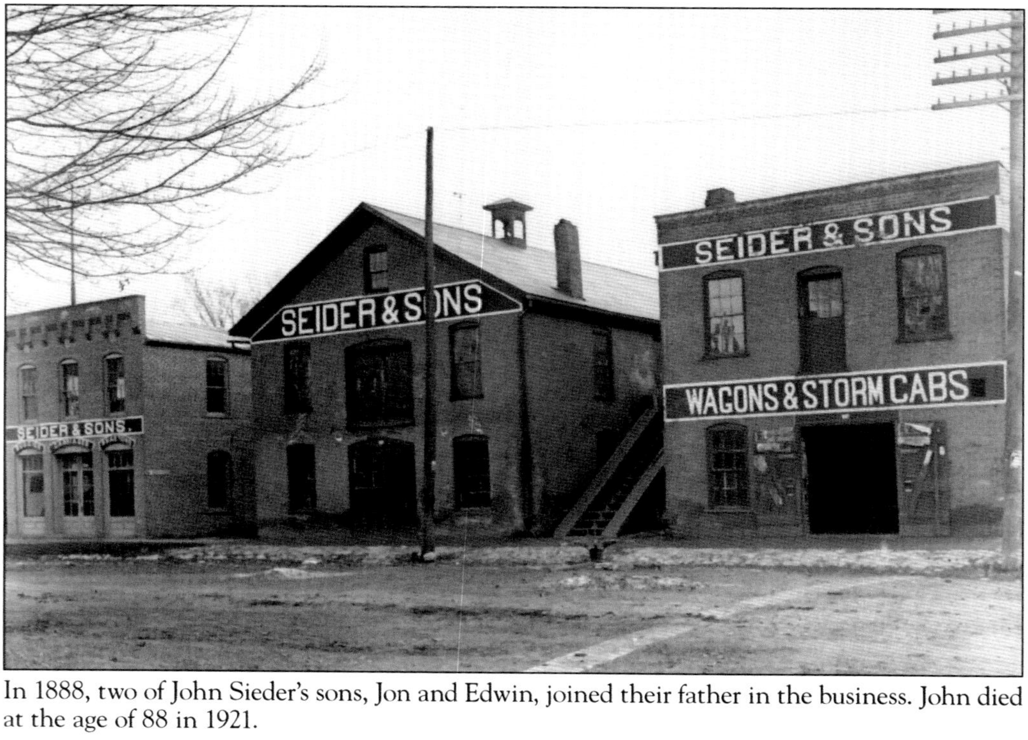

In 1888, two of John Sieder's sons, Jon and Edwin, joined their father in the business. John died at the age of 88 in 1921.

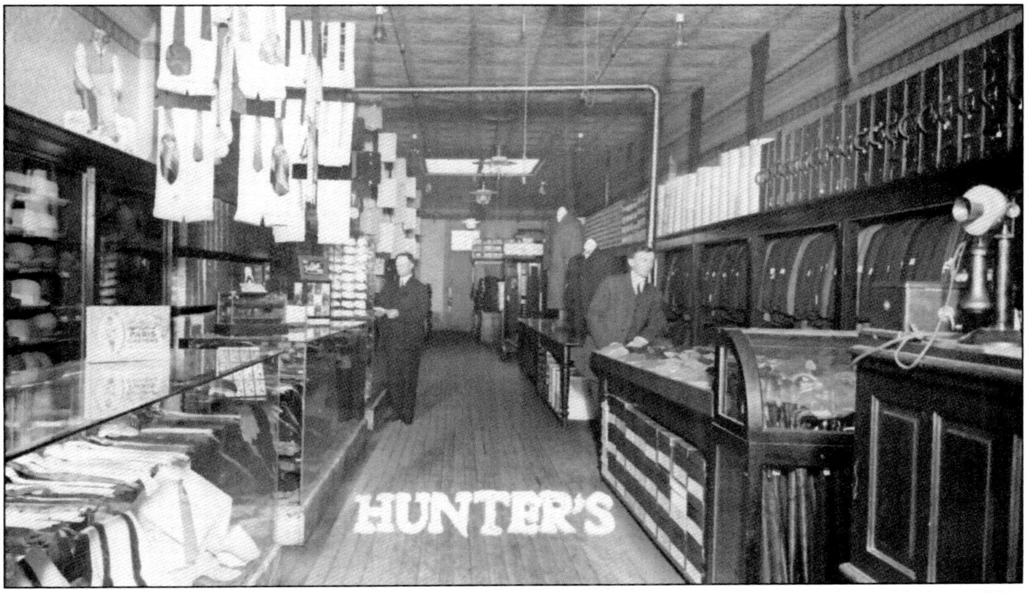

Hunter's Store was located at 102 South Sandusky Avenue. It was in business from 1911 to 1921. Notice the gas lights on the ceiling. The store sold everything from men's garters to suits and ties. (Photograph from the collection of Tom and Marnie Hill.)

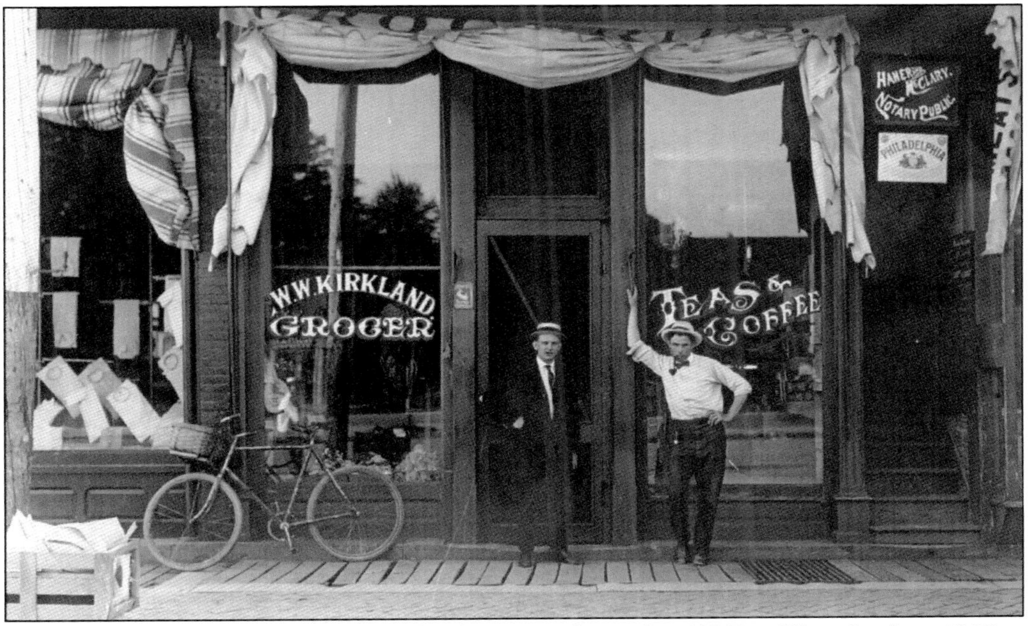

This is a storefront view of W. W. Kirkland Grocery, located at 102 East Wyandot from 1907 to 1910. This is the present site of Gottfried Electric.

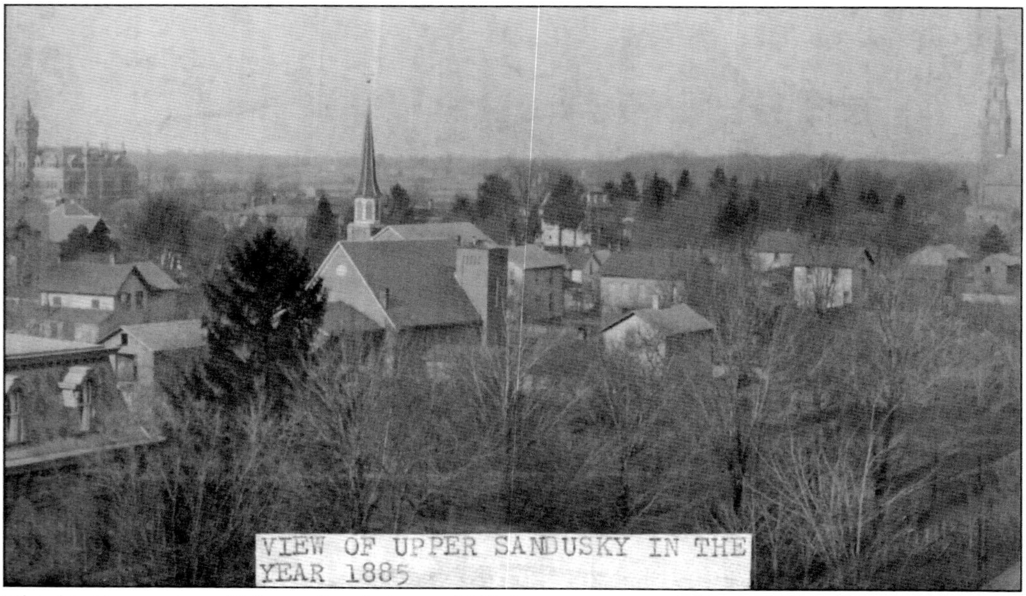

This bird's-eye view of Upper Sandusky in 1885 shows a corner of the roof of the house that would become the county museum. At the top left is a view of the Upper Sandusky High School. On the right is Saint Peters Catholic Church, with the 200-foot steeple that was lost on May 30, 1887, during a heavy storm. Lighting struck the steeple, causing it to fall across Finley Street.

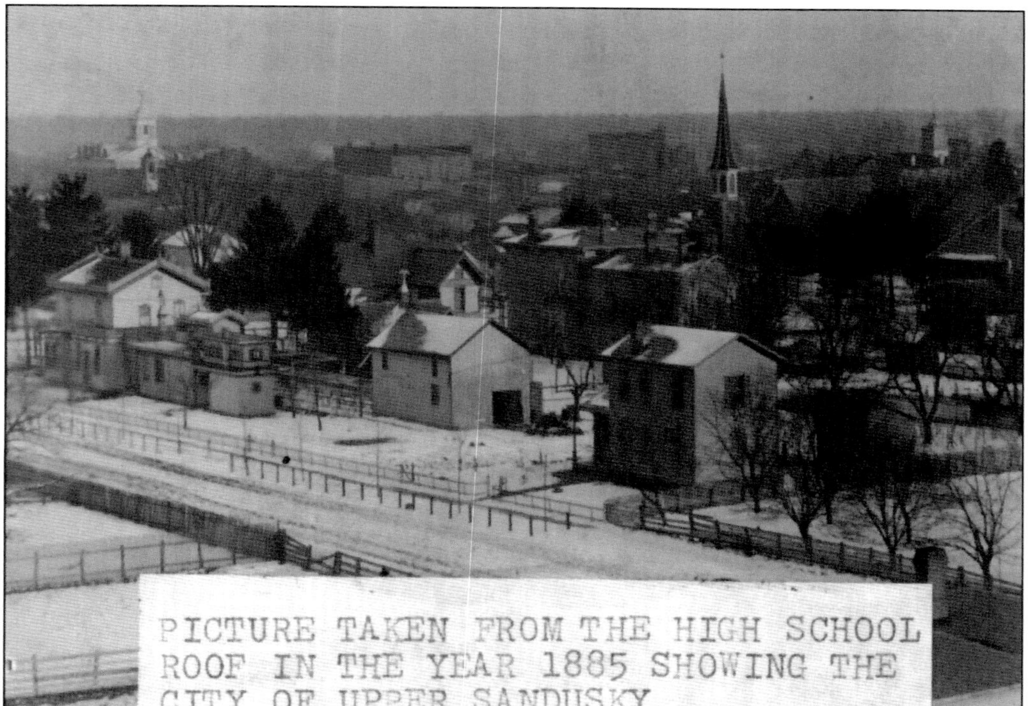

This view of Upper Sandusky was taken from the roof of the high school in 1885. The old courthouse is visible at the upper left.

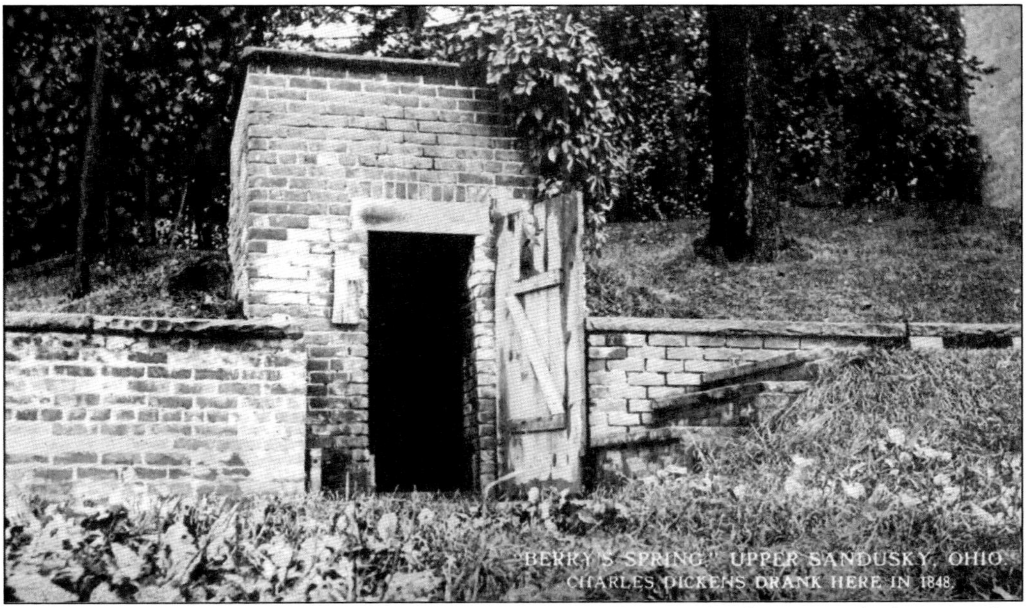

Charles Dickens drank from Beery's Spring while en route from Columbus to Sandusky to catch a steamer to Buffalo. According to his *American Notes*, Dickens spent a restless night at the tavern near the spring in 1842.

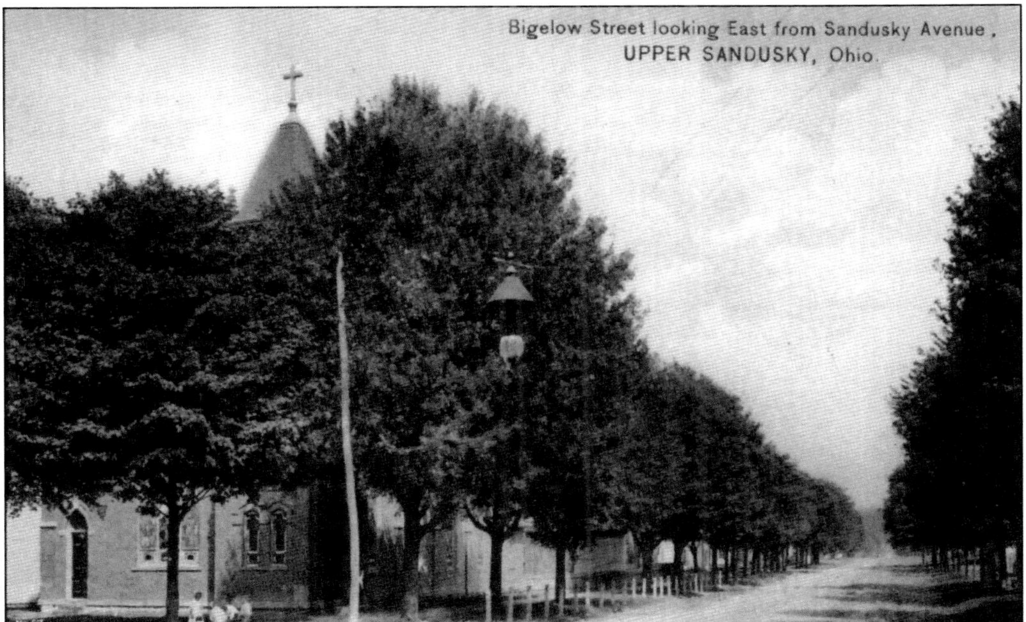

This photograph shows Bigelow Street in Upper Sandusky. The Lutheran church was built there around 1867. In 1910, the First Ward School was built three blocks east of the church. Today the school is known as East School. (Photograph from the collection of Tom and Marnie Hill.)

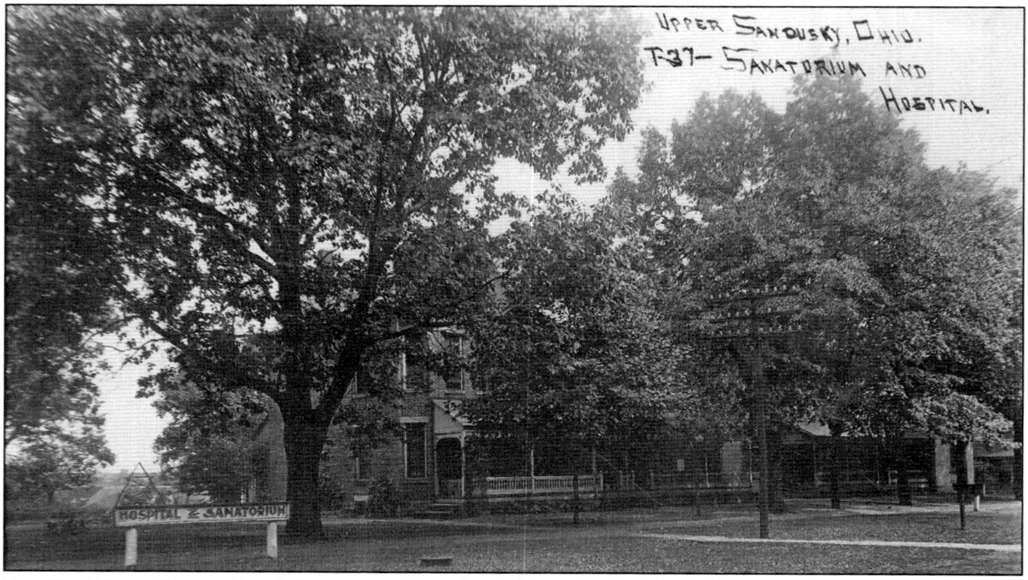

Smalley Naus Hospital and Sanatorium was built from parts of the old Union School. Dr. L. Walter Naus graduated from medical school in Cincinnati in 1899. He came to Upper Sandusky to start a general practice. After three years, he formed a partnership with Dr. C. L. Shepard, and together they operated the hospital and sanitarium. He specialized in the treatment of cancers, tumors, and blood and chronic diseases. (Photograph from the collection of Tom and Marnie Hill.)

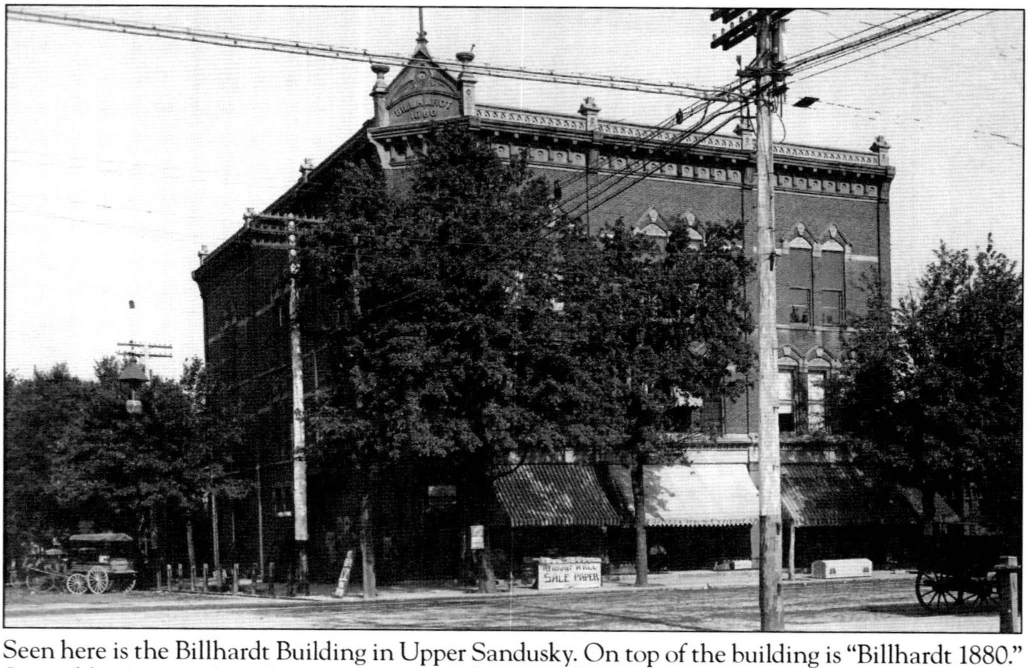

Seen here is the Billhardt Building in Upper Sandusky. On top of the building is "Billhardt 1880." Several businesses shared space in this building at different times. In front is a sign advertising a wallpaper remnant sale. On the left is a horse and wagon. The building was built by Dr. A. Billhardt in 1886. Billhardt and his sons opened the Billhardt Drug Store. In the 1890s, he was appointed as American consul to Russia by President Cleveland.

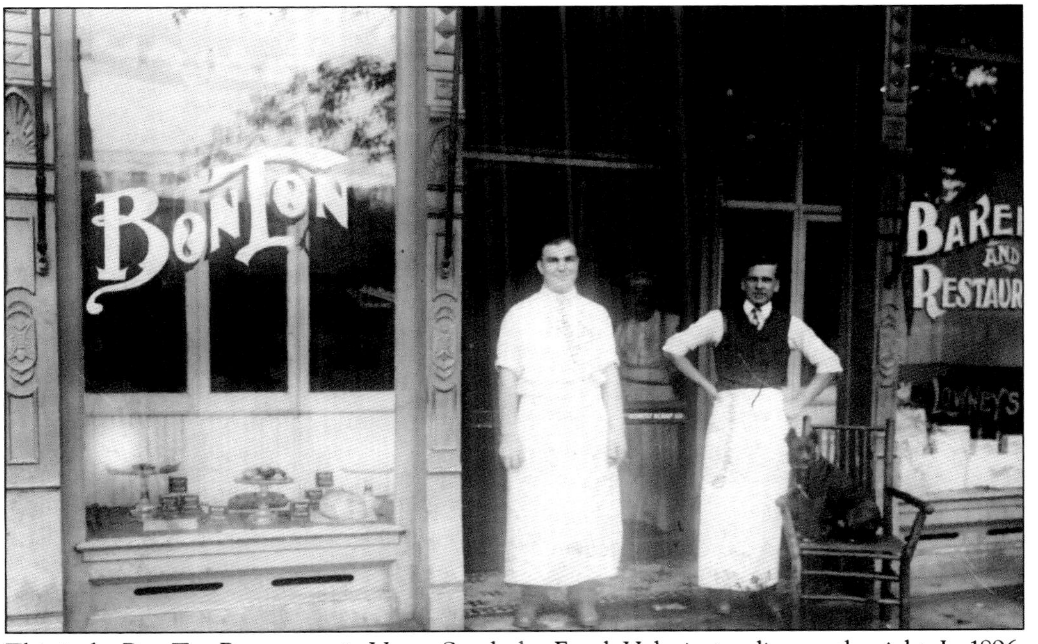

This is the Bon Ton Restaurant in Upper Sandusky. Frank Hehr is standing on the right. In 1896, the restaurant was run by Edwin Stephan. In 1918, the restaurant's bakery had a fire that destroyed half a city block. The restaurant was later bought by Wilfred Pearl Osborn (Fred or Ossie Green) who played major and minor league baseball from 1905 until 1909. Fred was born on November 28, 1883, in Nevada, Ohio, and died on September 2, 1954, in Upper Sandusky.

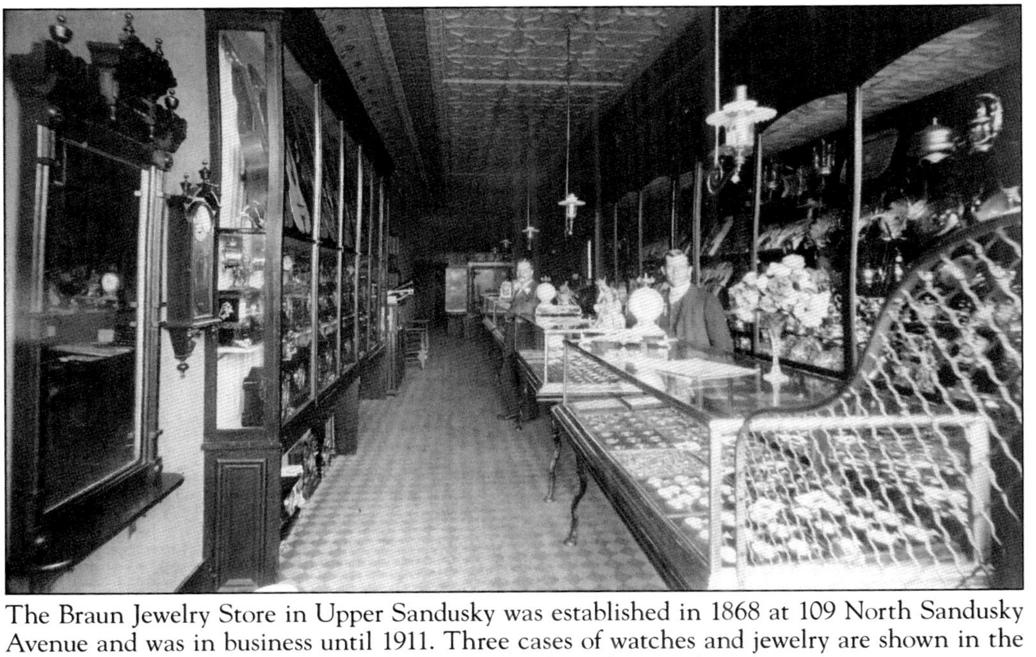

The Braun Jewelry Store in Upper Sandusky was established in 1868 at 109 North Sandusky Avenue and was in business until 1911. Three cases of watches and jewelry are shown in the photograph. The first case on the right is filled with pocket watches.

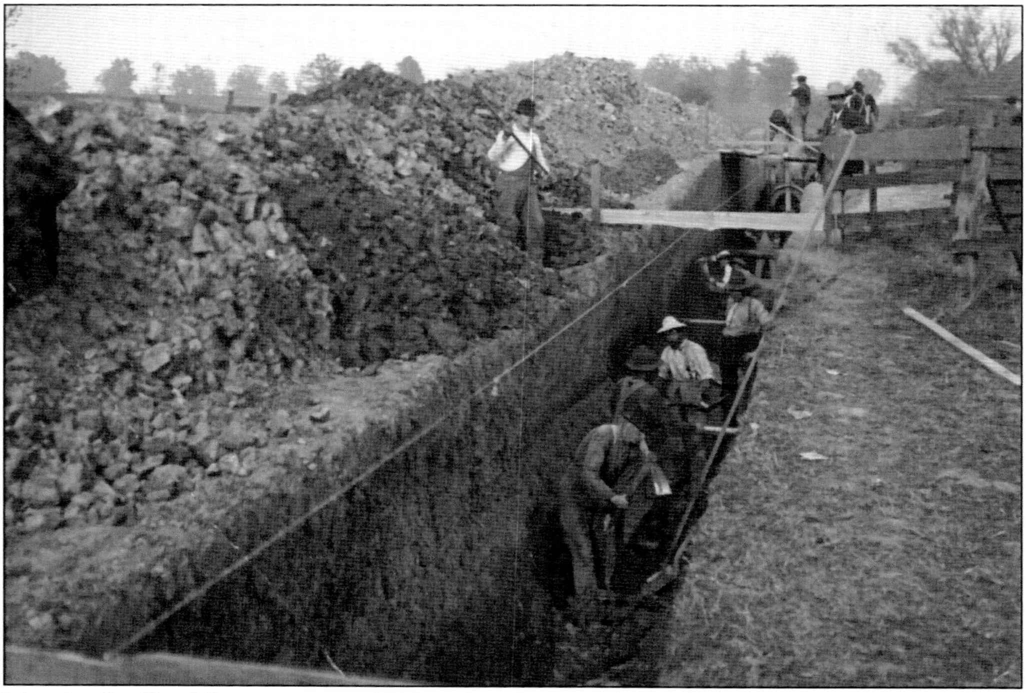

Men dig the Hazel Street sewer in 1908 in this photograph. Work of this type was backbreaking and took considerable time to complete without the use of machinery.

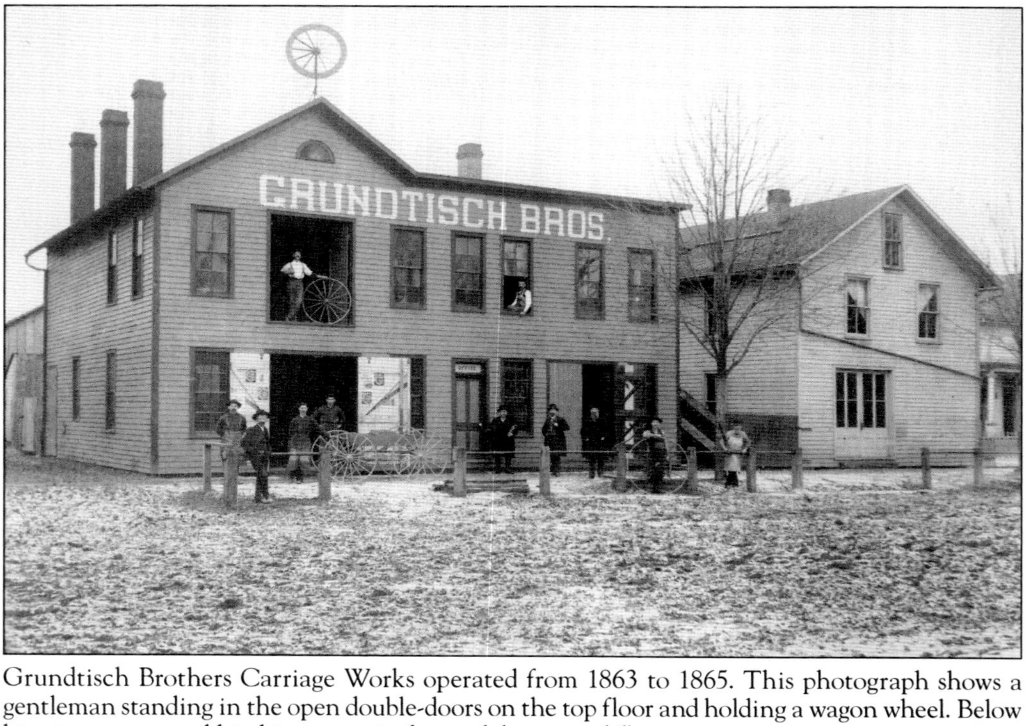

Grundtisch Brothers Carriage Works operated from 1863 to 1865. This photograph shows a gentleman standing in the open double-doors on the top floor and holding a wagon wheel. Below him is a wagon and hitching posts in front of the ground floor.

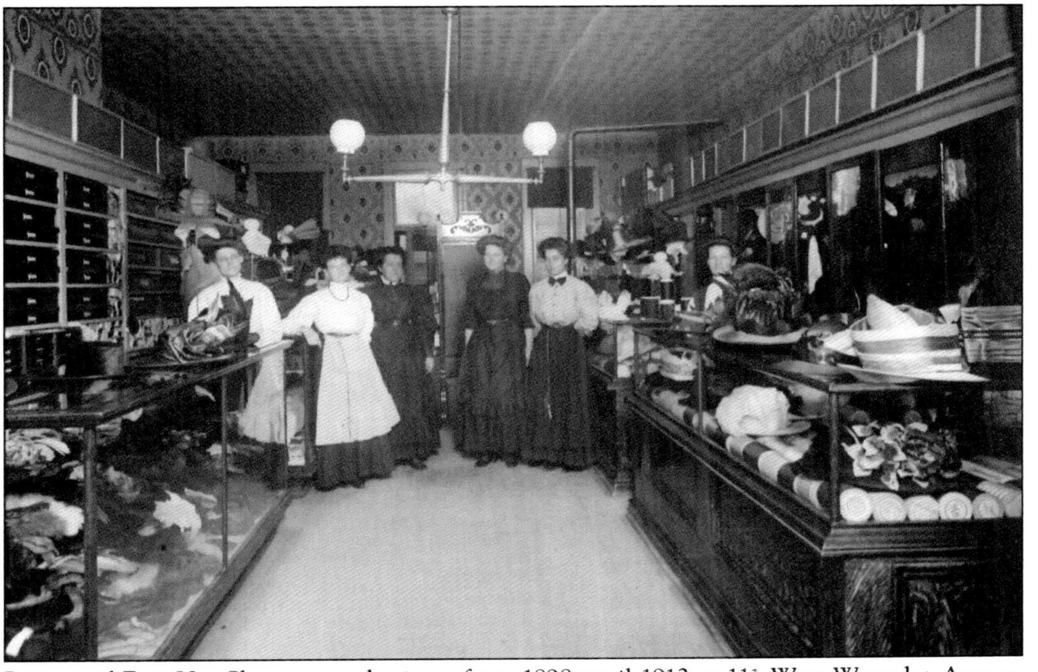

Baum and Frey Hat Shop was in business from 1898 until 1913 at 111 West Wyandot Avenue in Upper Sandusky. Six women posed for this photograph. The second and fifth women have scissors hanging from their waists

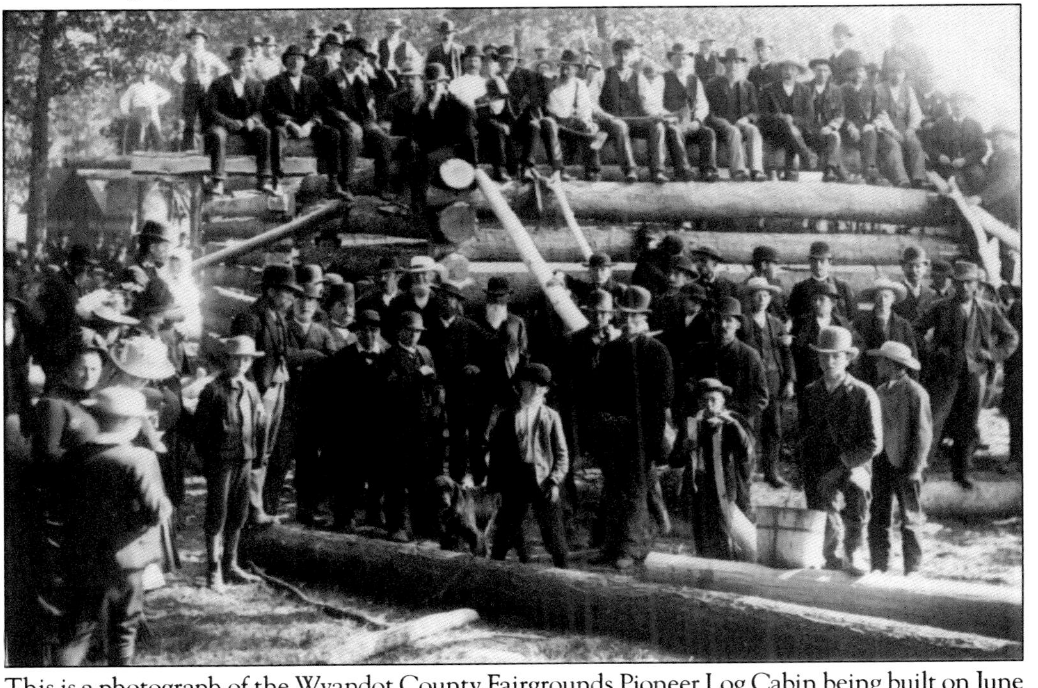

This is a photograph of the Wyandot County Fairgrounds Pioneer Log Cabin being built on June 11, 1888. The crew tried to complete it by this date for the 106th anniversary of the burning of Colonel Crawford.

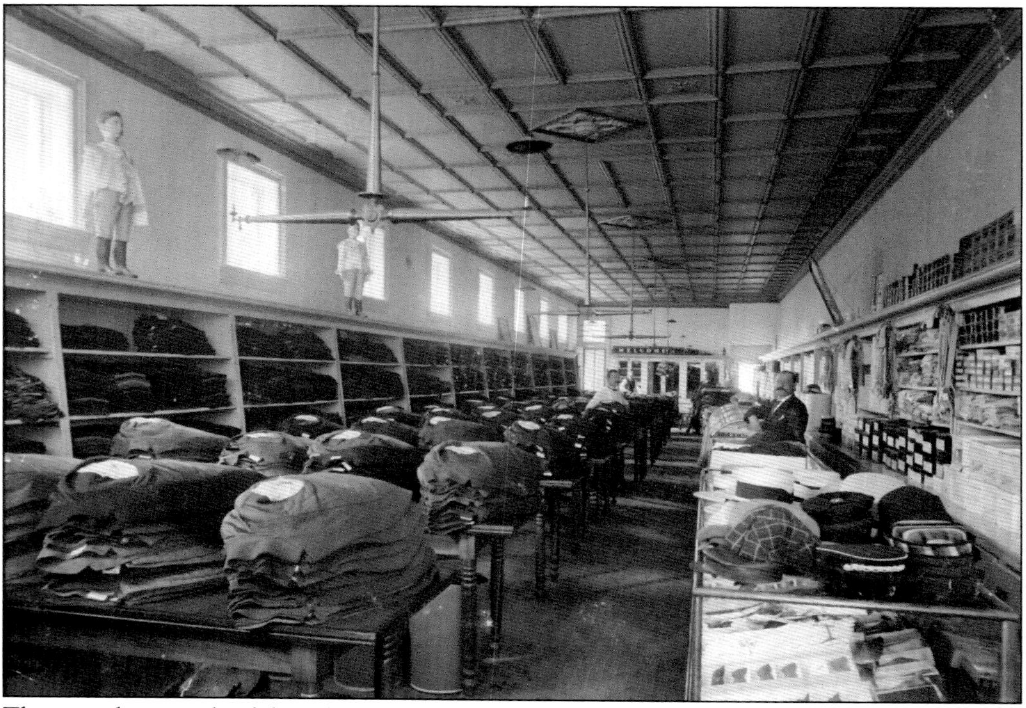

This is a photograph of the John Vogel Clothing Store in Upper Sandusky. The store was here from 1861 until 1870, when a new building was built. They were in business until 1874.

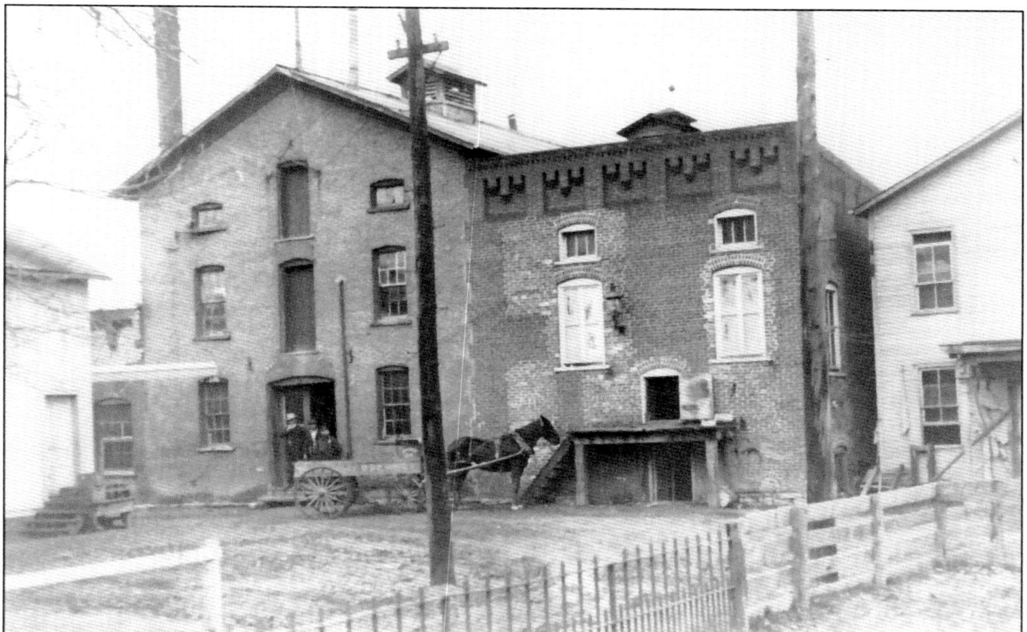

Upper Sandusky Brewery, located between 3rd and 4th Streets, started making ice in 1906. In this photograph, Old Bob, the horse, is getting loaded for a delivery. (Photograph courtesy of John and Mary Jane Constien.)

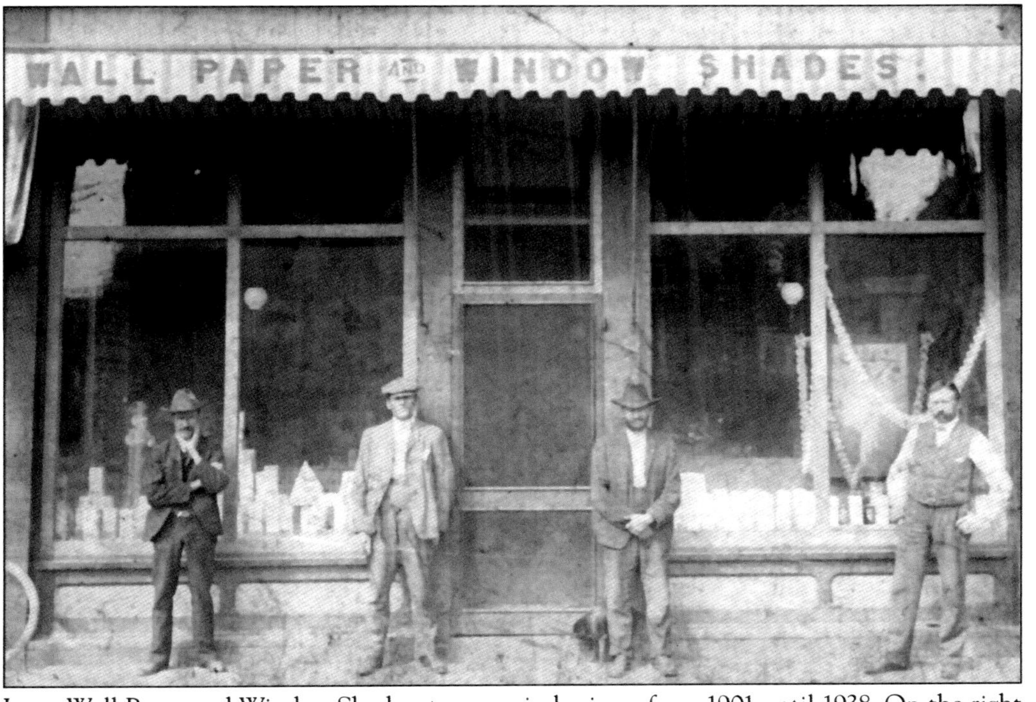

Leser Wall Paper and Window Shades store was in business from 1901 until 1938. On the right is Albert "Doc" Leser.

The Lincoln Highway Restaurant was in business briefly from 1915 until 1916 at 108 East Wyandot Avenue. The poster in the window advertises a train excursion on the Hocking Valley Railroad to the Ohio State Fair in Columbus. (Photograph from the collection of Tom and Marnie Hill.)

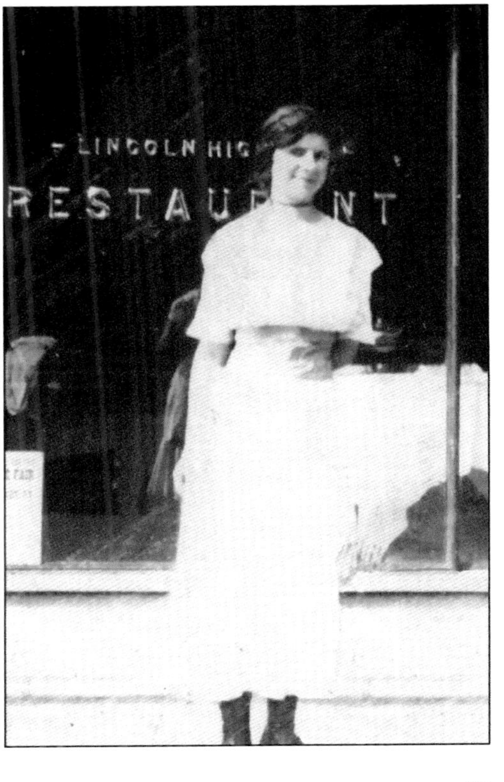

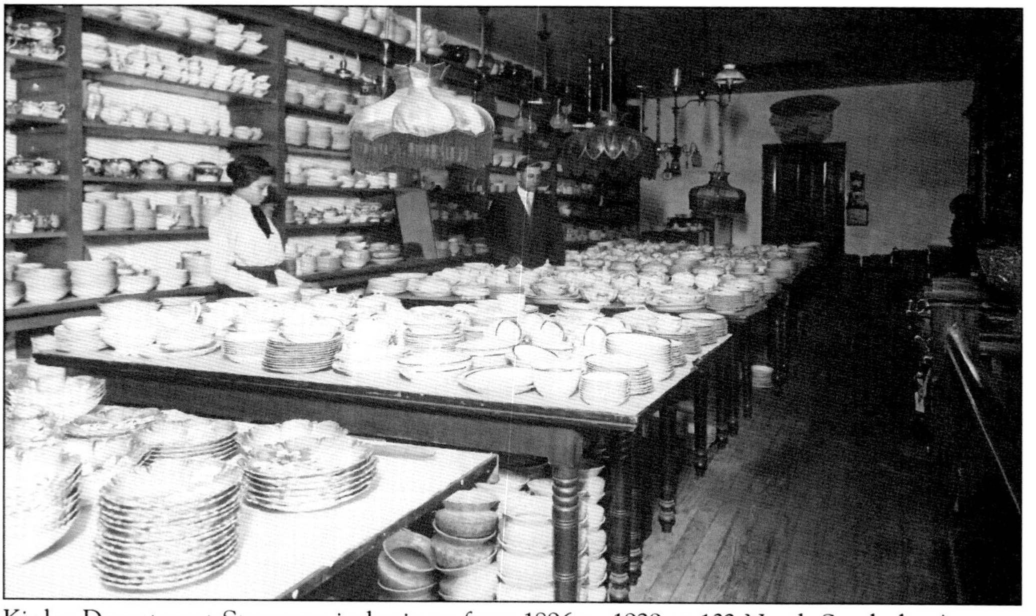

Kinley Department Store was in business from 1896 to 1929 at 132 North Sandusky Avenue. The second floor displayed a variety of glass and dinnerware. The store also sold postcards that are sought by today's collectors. Woods Antiques, owned by Irv and Janice Woods, currently occupies this building.

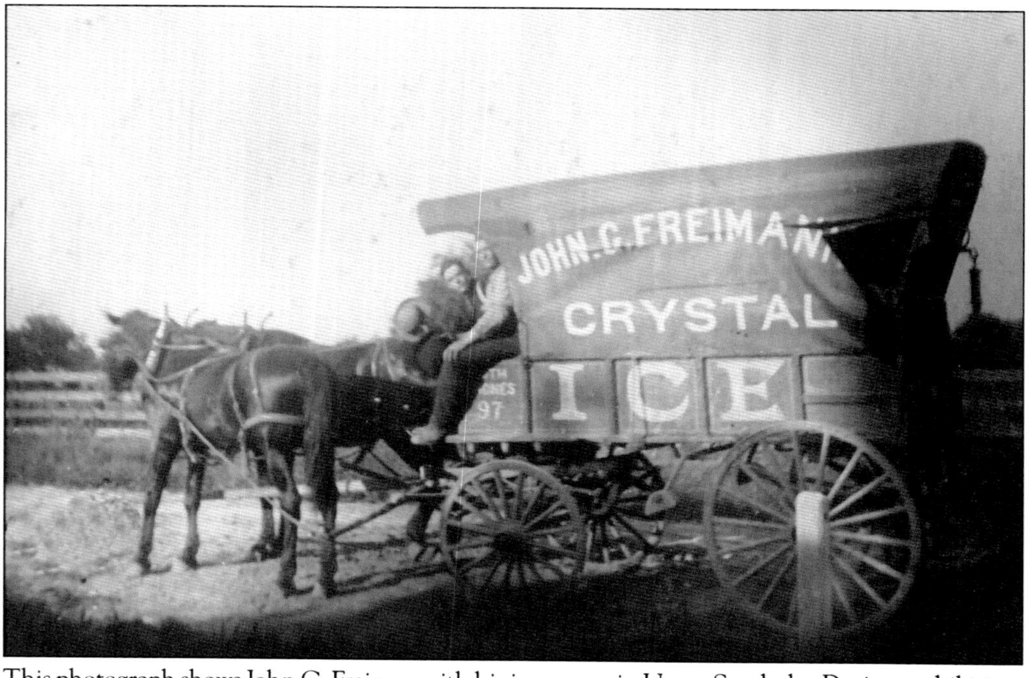

This photograph shows John G. Freiman with his ice wagon in Upper Sandusky. During prohibition, the John Freiman Brewery became the John Freiman Beverage and Ice Company. The building was located at 121 North Fourth Street. The wagon in the photograph is being pulled by two horses and both men in the wagon are posing for the camera.

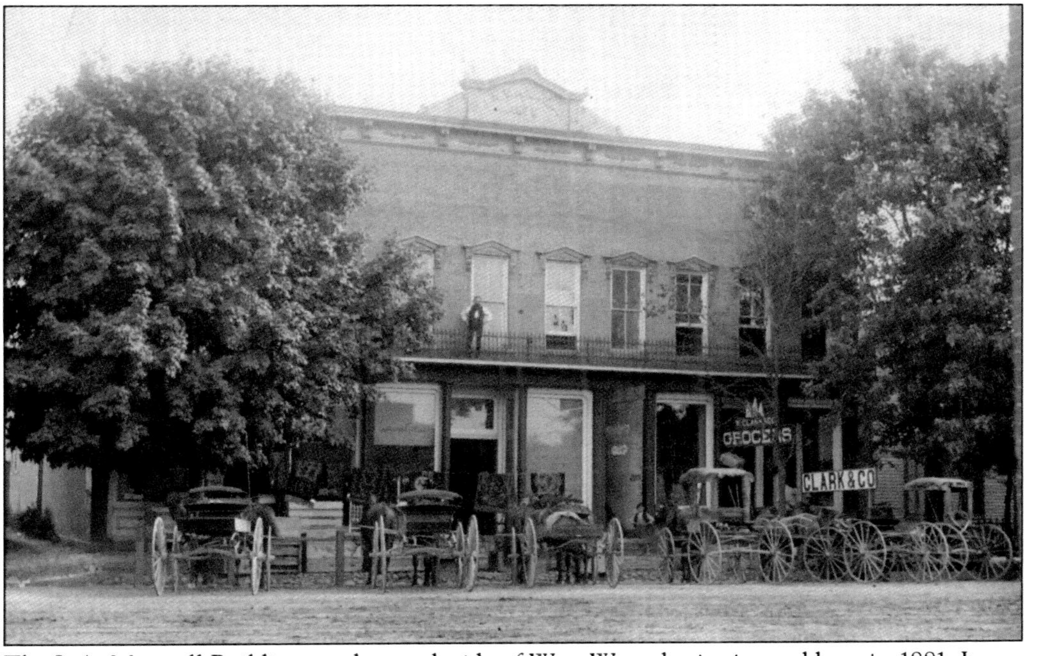

The J. A. Maxwell Building on the south side of West Wyandot is pictured here in 1881. It was built in 1876. August Muller, a tailor, is standing on the balcony. There are nine horses and six carriages in the photograph. Also shown is the W. Clark and Company Grocery store on the right, and to the left, there are several rugs hanging on a line in front of Maxwell's storefront.

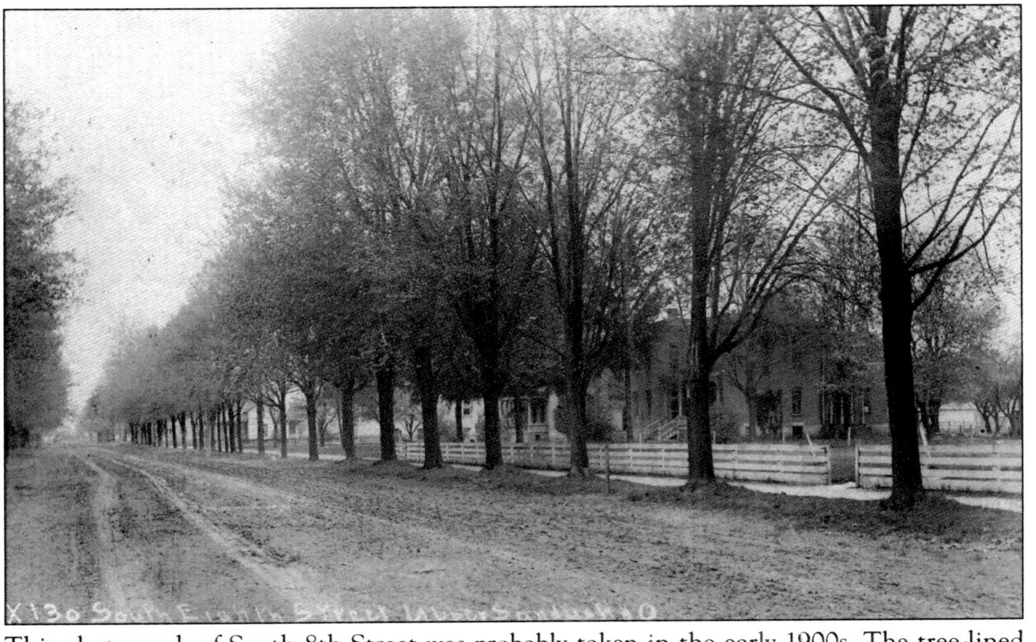

This photograph of South 8th Street was probably taken in the early 1900s. The tree-lined street is unpaved, and there are fences in front of several of the residences. (Photograph from the collection of Tom and Marnie Hill.)

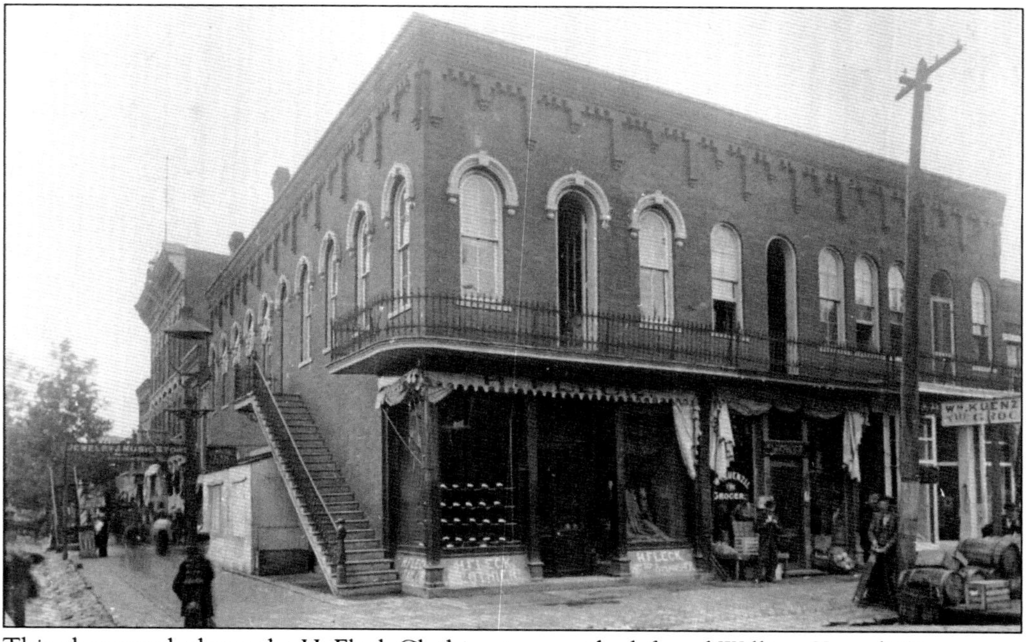

This photograph shows the H. Fleck Clothier store on the left and William Kuenzli Grocery on the right. The building had a long history of businesses from 1848 until 1870 when a new building was erected. The new building has endured from 1870 to the present.

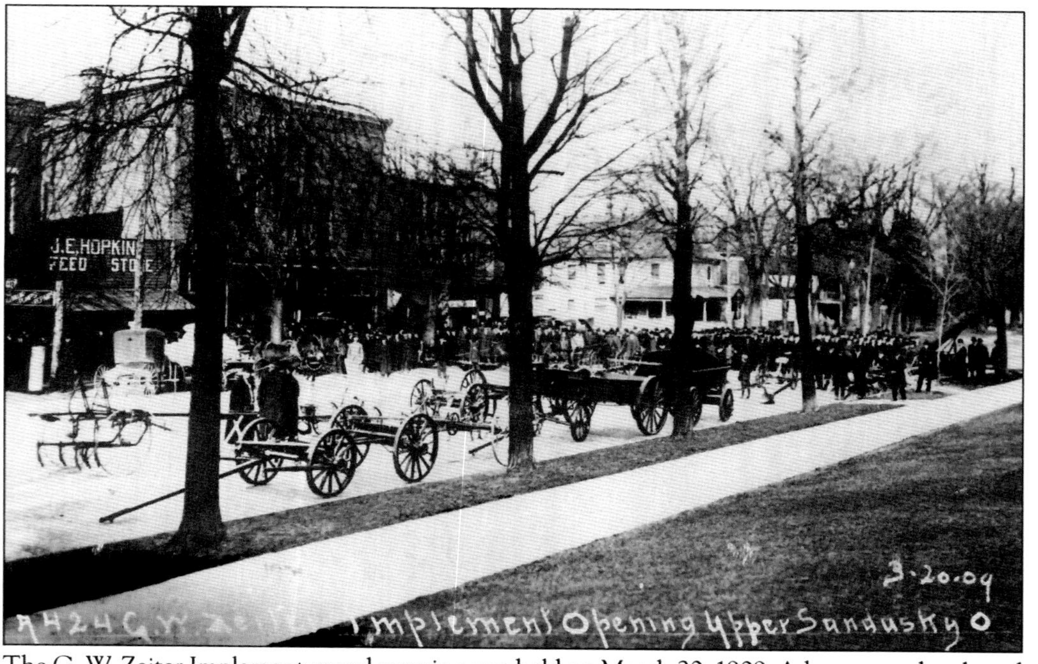

The G. W. Zeiter Implement grand opening was held on March 20, 1909. A large crowd gathered to see the new implements that were offered. The store was located at 130 East Wyandot Avenue from 1905 until 1922. The site is occupied by Domino's Pizza and Dining today.

The canopy on the storefront says "Frank Vogel's Sons." They were in business from 1881 until 1899. At the top of the building is written "John Vogel 1894." A sign above the canopy advertises L. R. Seaman Real Estate and Loan Agent Office upstairs. The business to the right of Vogel's says "M. A. Brukaw."

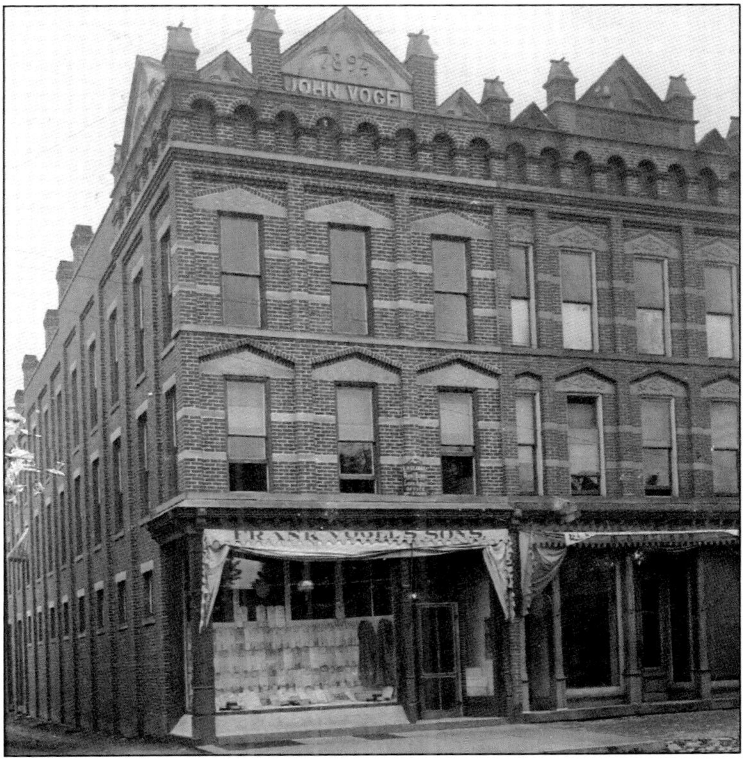

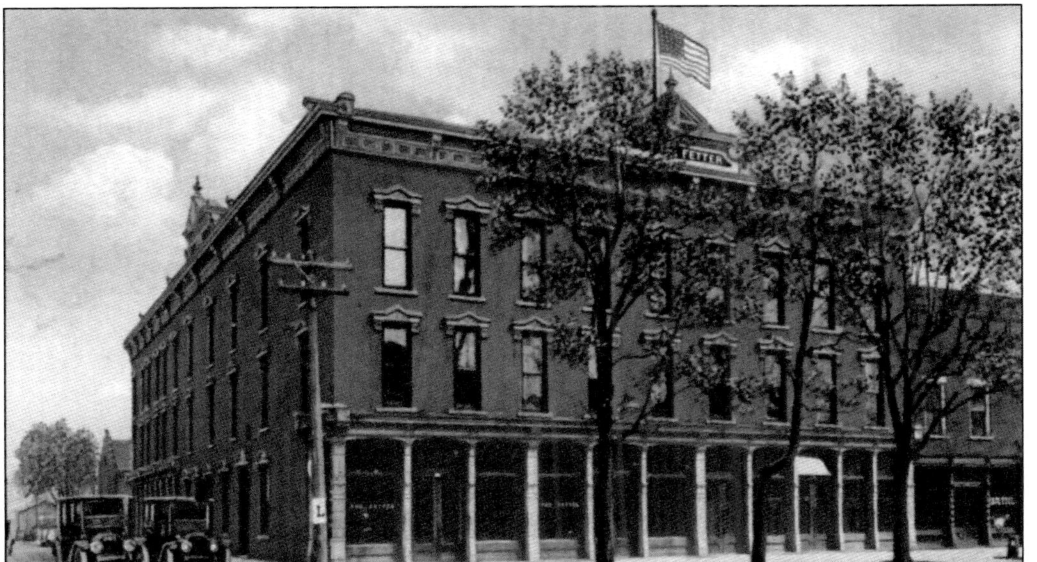

Shown here is the Fetter Hotel in Upper Sandusky. Signs in the front window read, "The Fetter." On the telephone pole to the left of the building is a Lincoln Highway sign. (Photograph from the collection of Tom and Marnie Hill.)

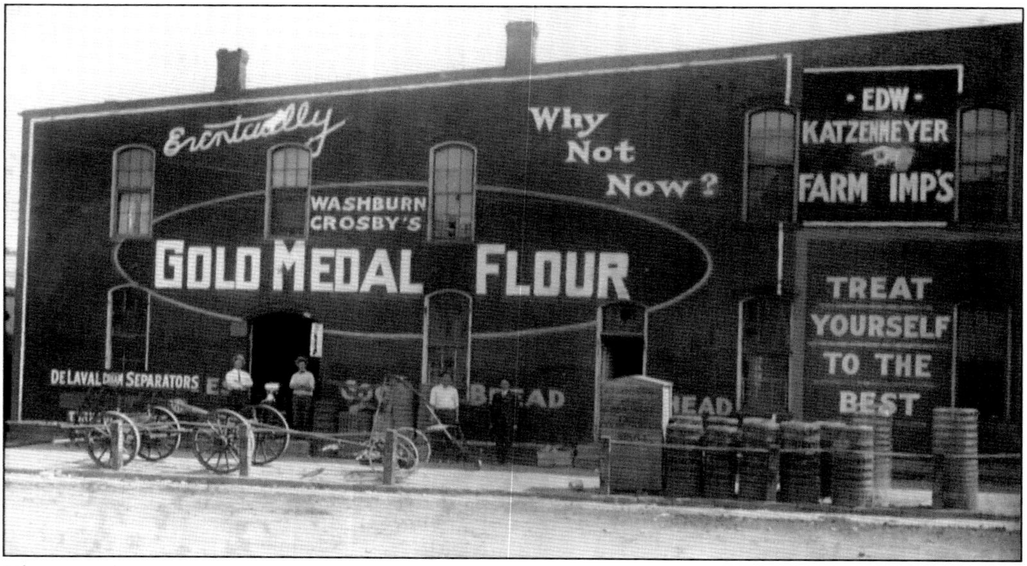

This is a photograph of Edwin Katzenmeyer Farm Implements Building. The Katzenmeyer name was involved in several different ventures including Katzenmeyer and Marlow Harness (1861 to 1871 at 120 South Sandusky Avenue), Katzenmeyer footwear and Harness shop (1872 to 1915 at 130 South Sandusky Avenue), Tracht Katzenmeyer Shoes (1856 and 1857), Katzenmeyer Shoes (1858 and 1859), Katzenmeyer and Drunkmiller Shoes (1864 and 1865), Katzenmeyer and Marlow Shoes (1866), and Katzenmeyer Shoes (1867 to 1873).

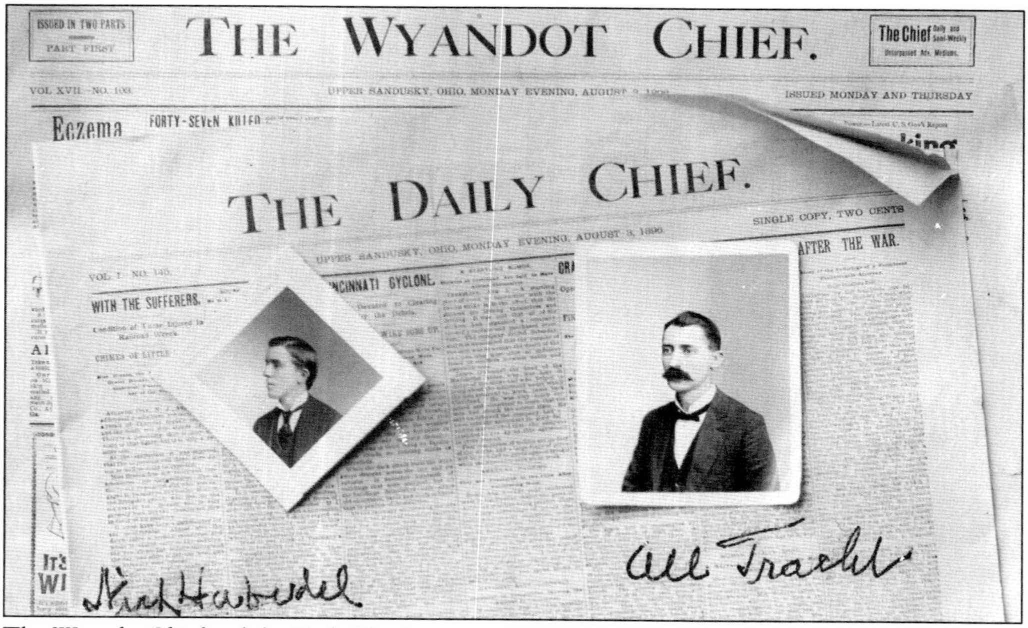

The *Wyandot Chief* and the *Daily Chief* newspapers' August 3, 1896 editions are pictured here along with photographs of Nick Habedel and H. A. Tracht. Tracht was born on August 26, 1862, in Upper Sandusky. He quit school at the age of 14 because of an eye problem, and with $5 from selling rabbits, he bought a small hand press and started a printing office in 1876. It grew into the *Daily Chief*, which is still in existence as the *Daily Chief-Union*. Jeff Barnes is the owner-publisher.

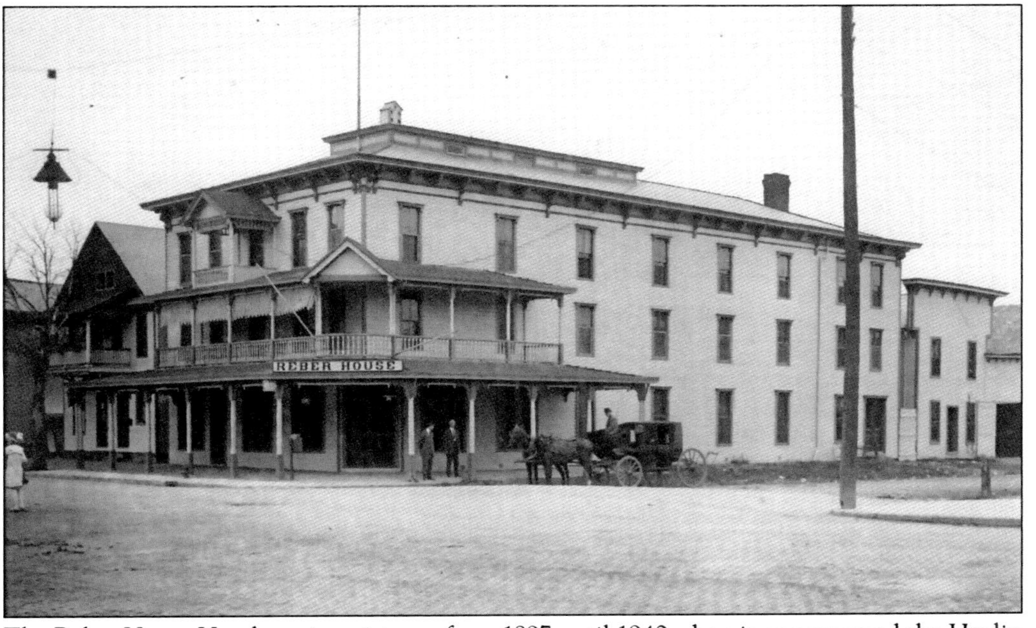

The Reber House Hotel was in existence from 1897 until 1940 when it was renamed the Havlin Hotel. The building was built in 1848 by W. W. Bates and was originally called the American Hotel. There were five different hotels in the building until it was torn down in 1991. The Am Vets Park now occupies the space.

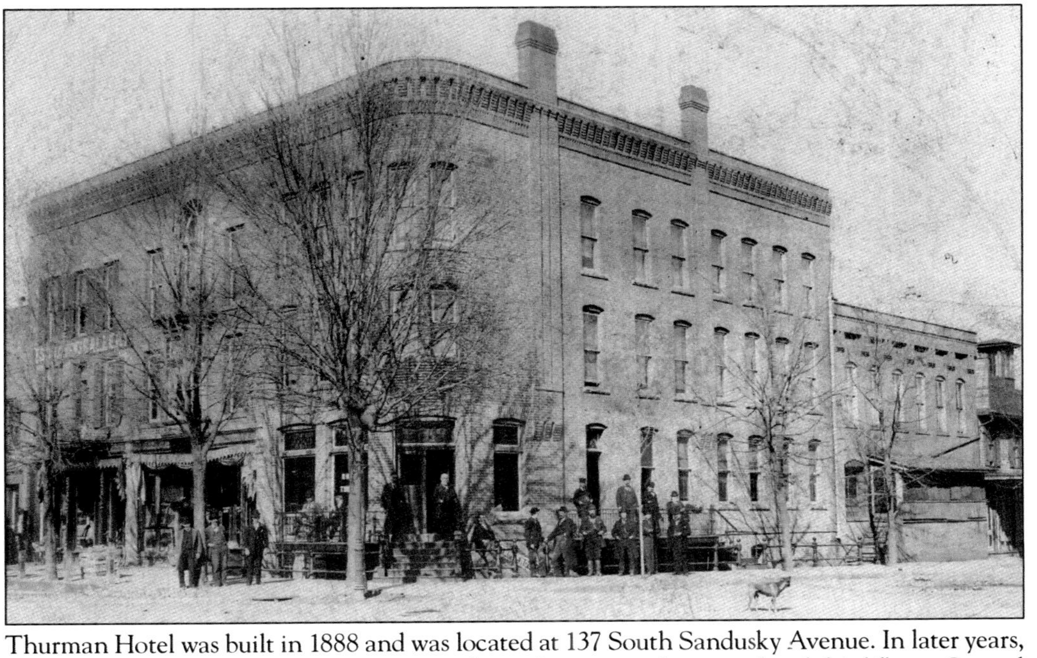

Thurman Hotel was built in 1888 and was located at 137 South Sandusky Avenue. In later years, the hotel was divided up into apartments and rental rooms on the second and third floors. Several businesses occupied the ground floor. In the street on the right of the hotel, a dog stands alone and watches something that caught his eye.

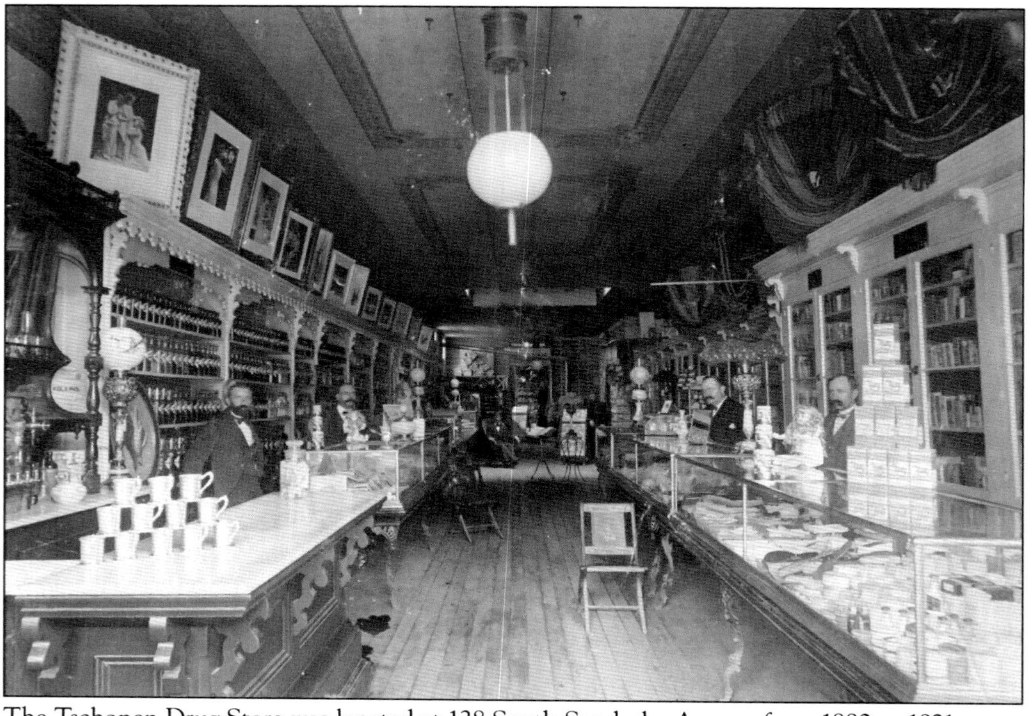

The Tschanen Drug Store was located at 128 South Sandusky Avenue from 1880 to 1921.

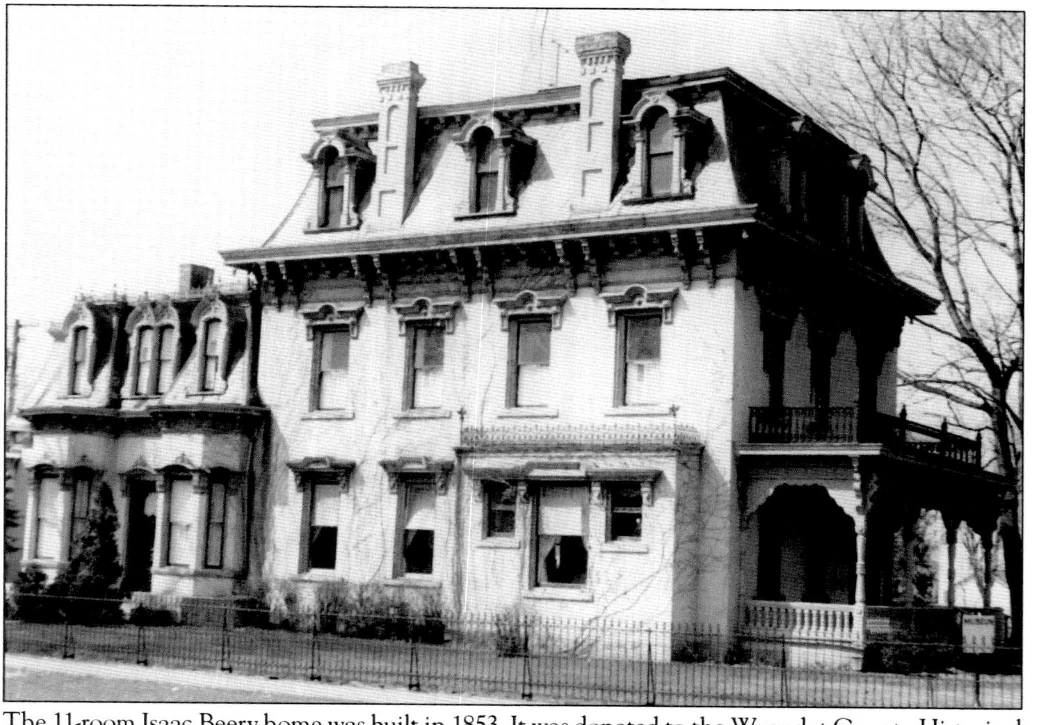

The 11-room Isaac Beery home was built in 1853. It was donated to the Wyandot County Historical Society in 1962 and now houses the Wyandot County Museum.

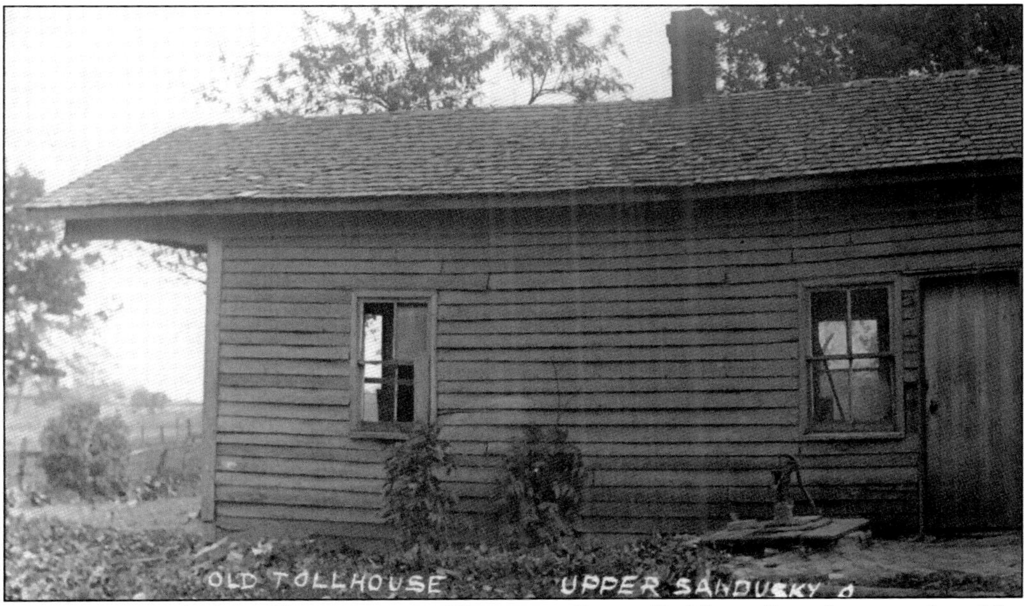

The Upper Sandusky tollhouse was on Ohio State Route 53. The toll road was preferred by travelers because its wooden planks made traveling easier. Travelers who did not pay the fee had to stay off the planks and ride in the dirt and mud. Plank roads were used frequently until brick and asphalt roads replaced them.

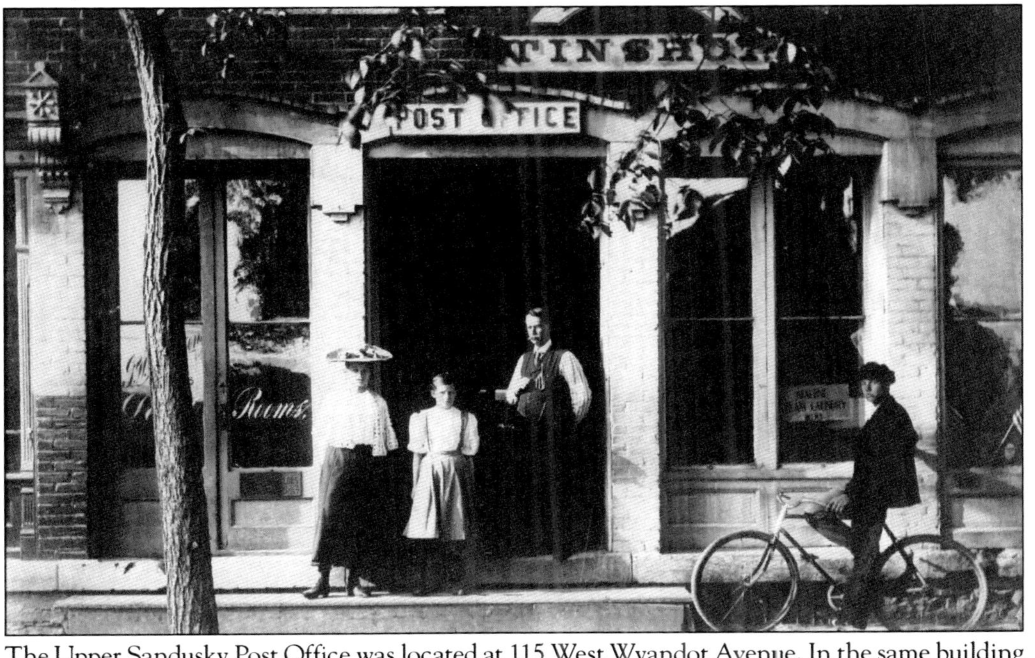

The Upper Sandusky Post Office was located at 115 West Wyandot Avenue. In the same building was I. L. Rock Tin Shop from 1848 to 1868. A small sign on the door at the left reads "Dental Parlors up stairs." To the left of the boy on his bicycle is a sign that reads "Malone Steam Laundry office." It was very common to have several businesses in one building sharing space. When a fire consumed a building in that period, it usually affected more than one business.

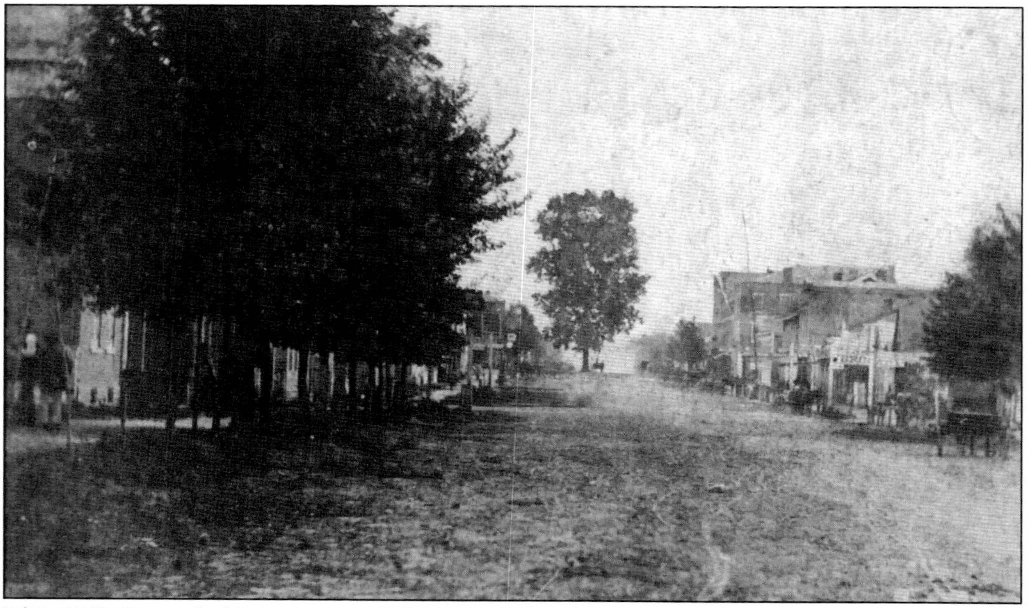

This 1861 Carte de Visite is one of the earliest known photographs of Main Street in Upper Sandusky. The tree in the middle of the street was planted during the War of 1812 by Gen. William H. Harrison's men to cover the grave of a prominent officer. General Harrison built Fort Ferree in Upper Sandusky to use as his headquarters during the war. The tree was taken down in 1873. (Photograph from the collection of Tom and Marnie Hill.)

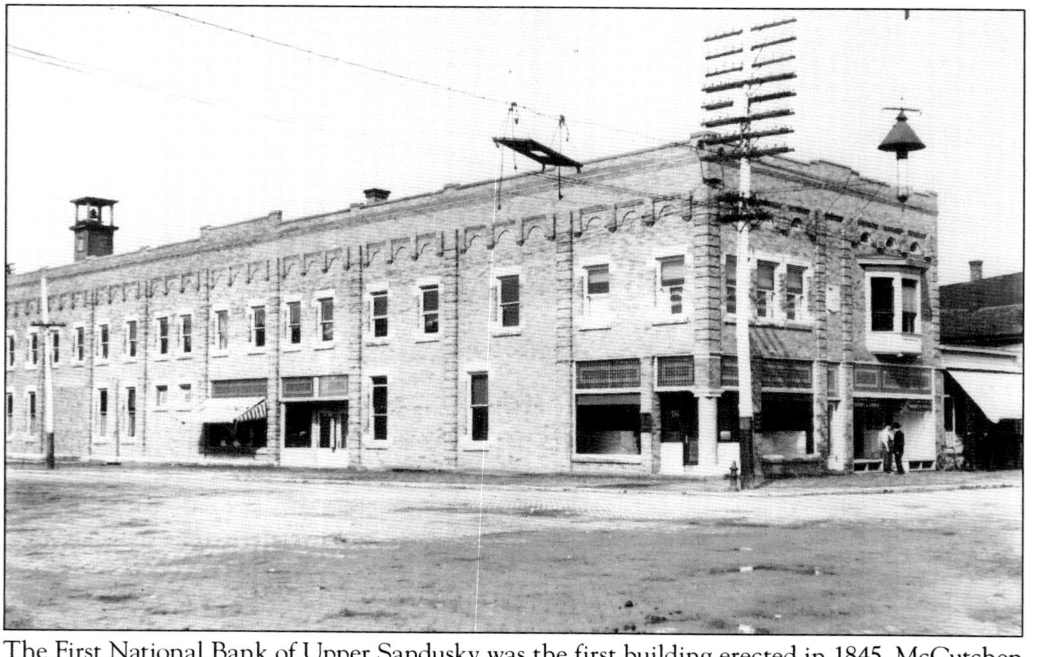

The First National Bank of Upper Sandusky was the first building erected in 1845. McCutchen Grocery was the first business in the building. A new building was put up in 1906 and Citizens Savings Bank conducted business there from 1907 to 1946. First Citizens National Bank moved into the location in 1946 and is still there today.

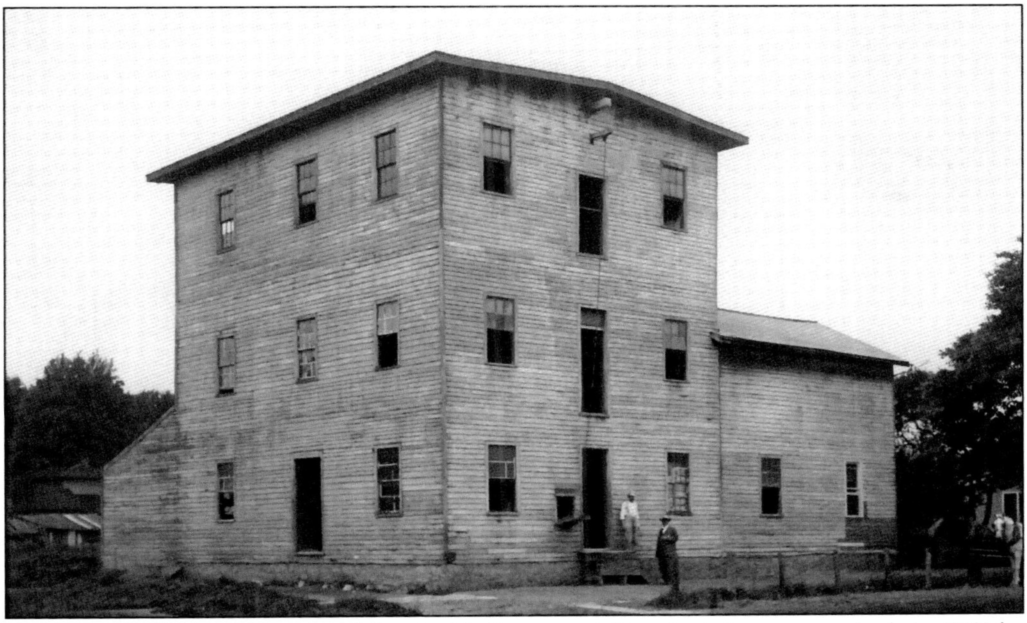

Kerr's Flour Mill at the corner of South 7th Street and Crawford Avenue was built in 1859 by Roberts and Graff. James and Robert Kerr bought it in 1876. It was destroyed by fire around 1926. At that time it was owned by S. N. Clark.

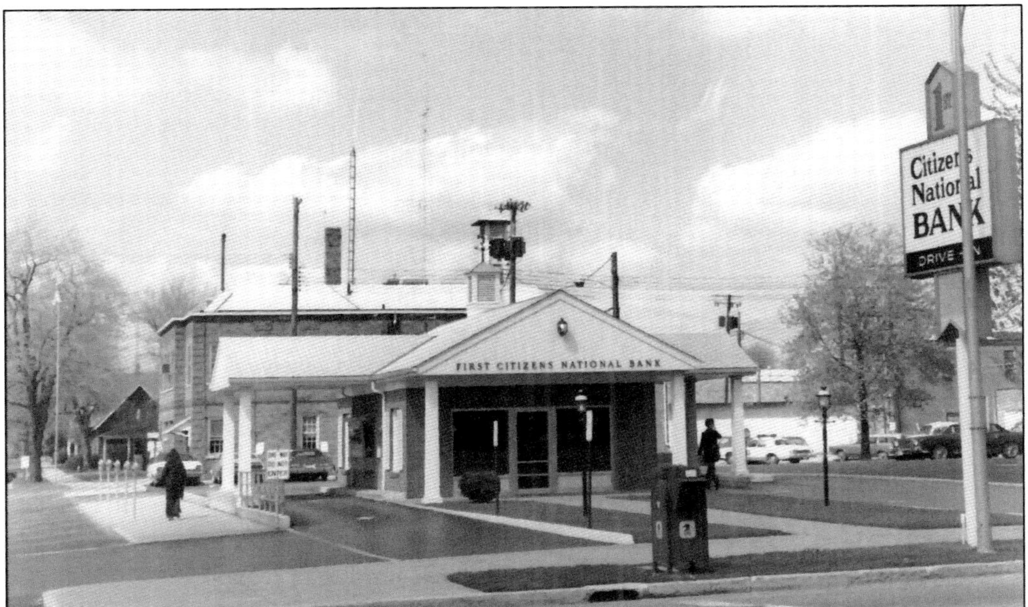

The First Citizens National Bank, 7th Street branch, was built in 1966 and remains in use today. (Photograph courtesy of John and Mary Jane Constien.)

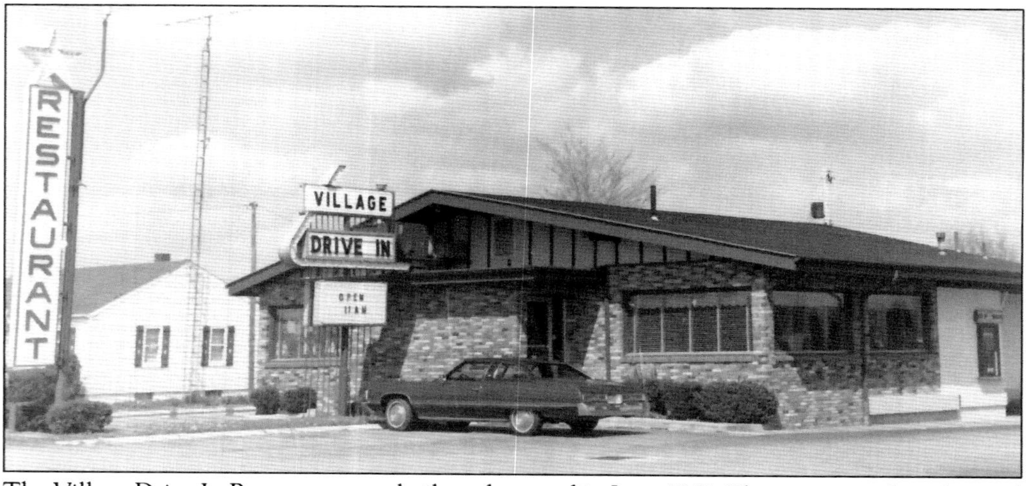

The Village Drive In Restaurant was built and opened in June 1961. The restaurant has changed ownership just three times since then. The first owners were Phil Cavanaugh and his wife. In 1990, Tom Hill (no relation to the author) bought the restaurant and sold it to the present partnership of Rex and Becky Vanhorn with Dan and Anna Patchett in June 1998. The restaurant is still in operation. (Photograph courtesy of John and Mary Jane Constien.)

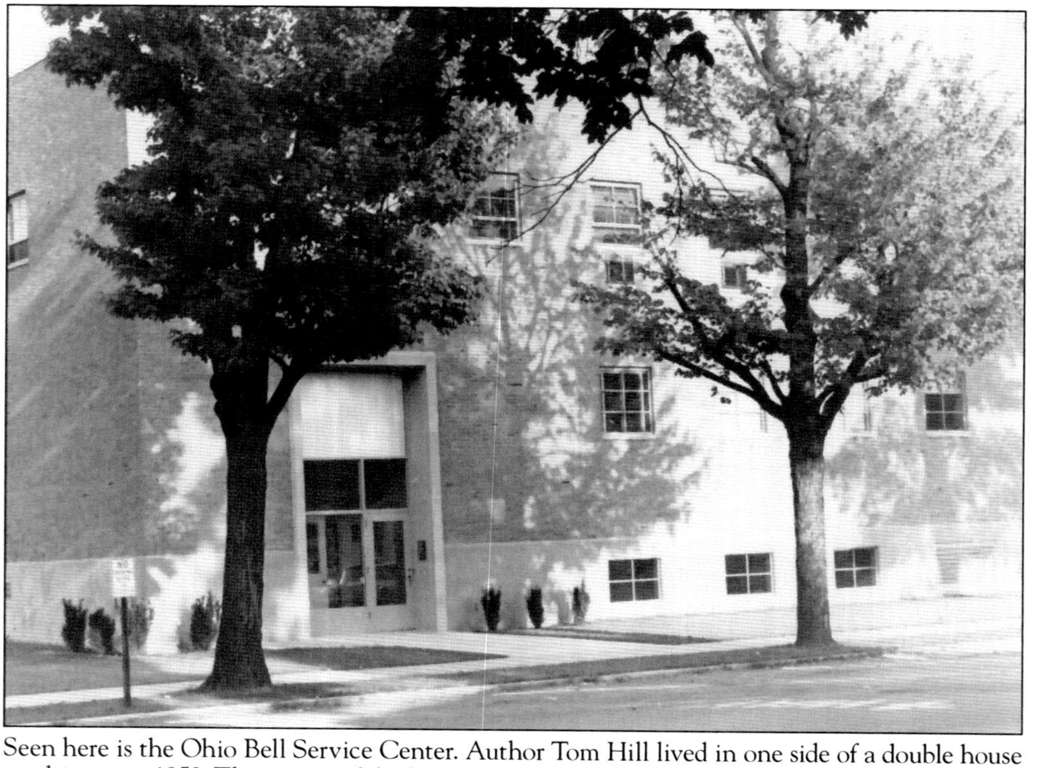

Seen here is the Ohio Bell Service Center. Author Tom Hill lived in one side of a double house on this site in 1959. The corner of the house was on top of quicksand and had sunk down several inches, making the house lean. When Bell Telephone Company put their building on the site, they had to drive a good amount of piling to support the weight of the building. (Photograph courtesy of John and Mary Jane Constien.)

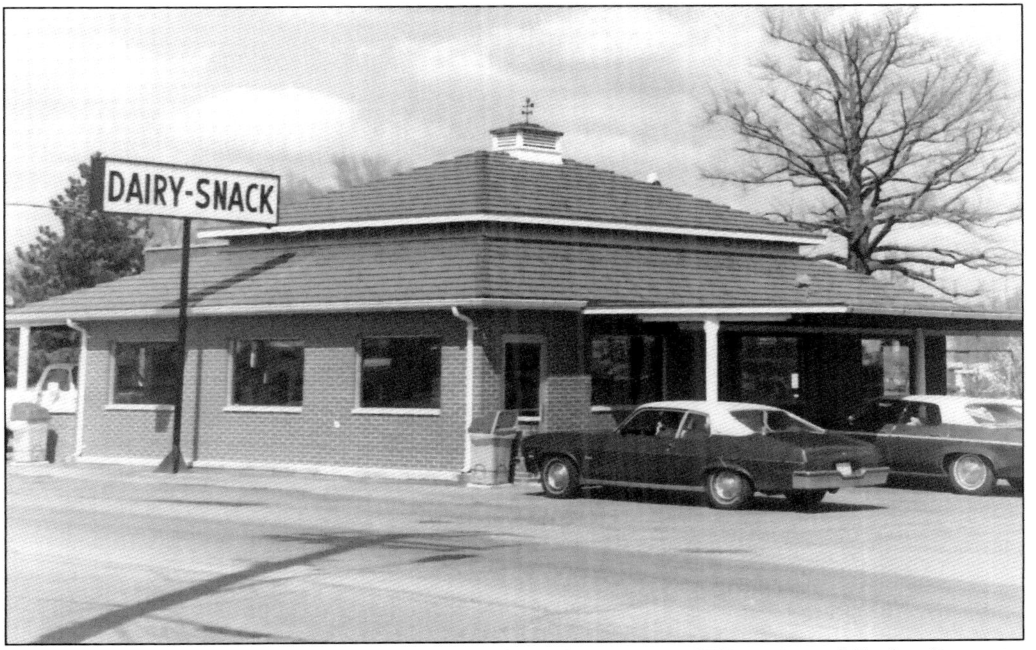

Tom and Olive Miller opened the Dairy Snack at the corner of Warpole and Finley Street in 1958. They introduced the "Kurly Que French Fry," which was very popular not only with locals but also travelers from out of state. In the mid 1970s their daughter Sara Lou and her husband Don Brown purchased the eatery from them. It has since had several owners and is still serving customers today. (Photograph courtesy of John and Mary Jane Constien.)

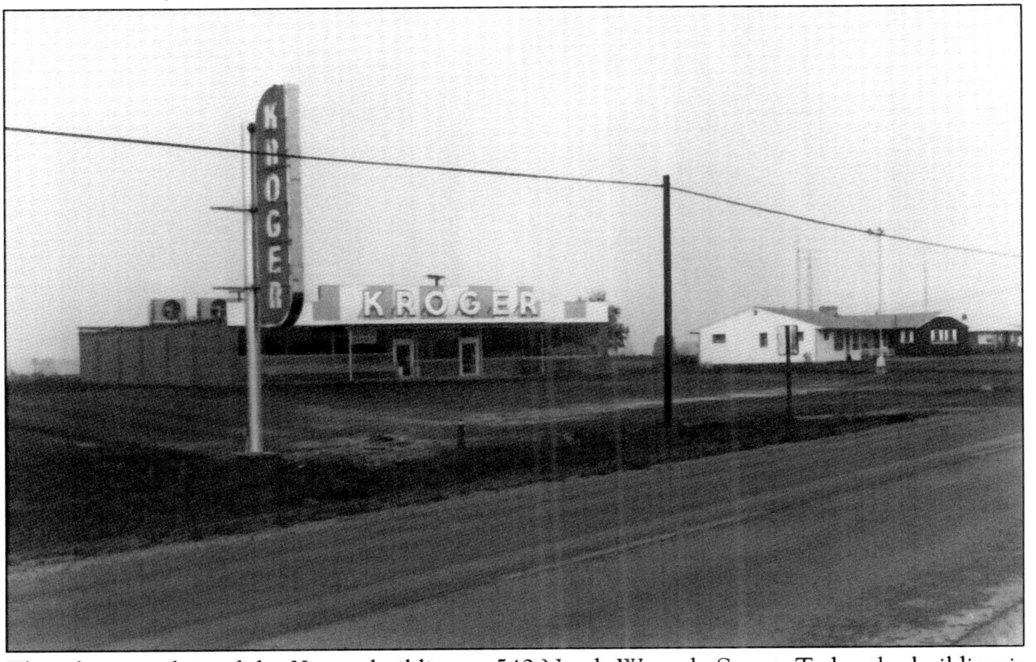

This photograph is of the Kroger building at 540 North Warpole Street. Today the building is occupied by the Dollar Store. (Photograph courtesy of John and Mary Jane Constien.)

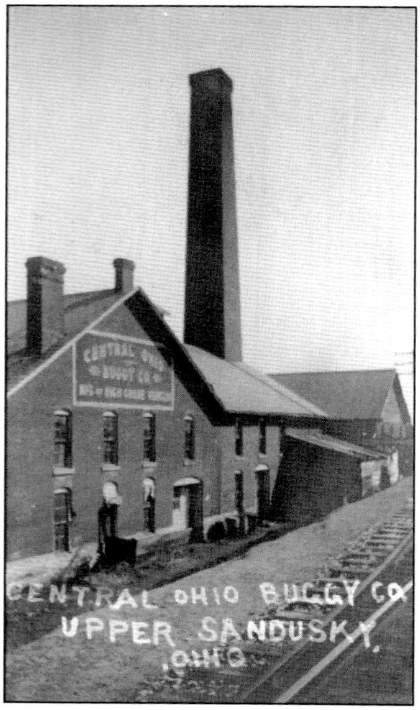

Pictured here is the Central Ohio Buggy Company in the early 1900s. (Photograph from the collection of Tom and Marnie Hill.)

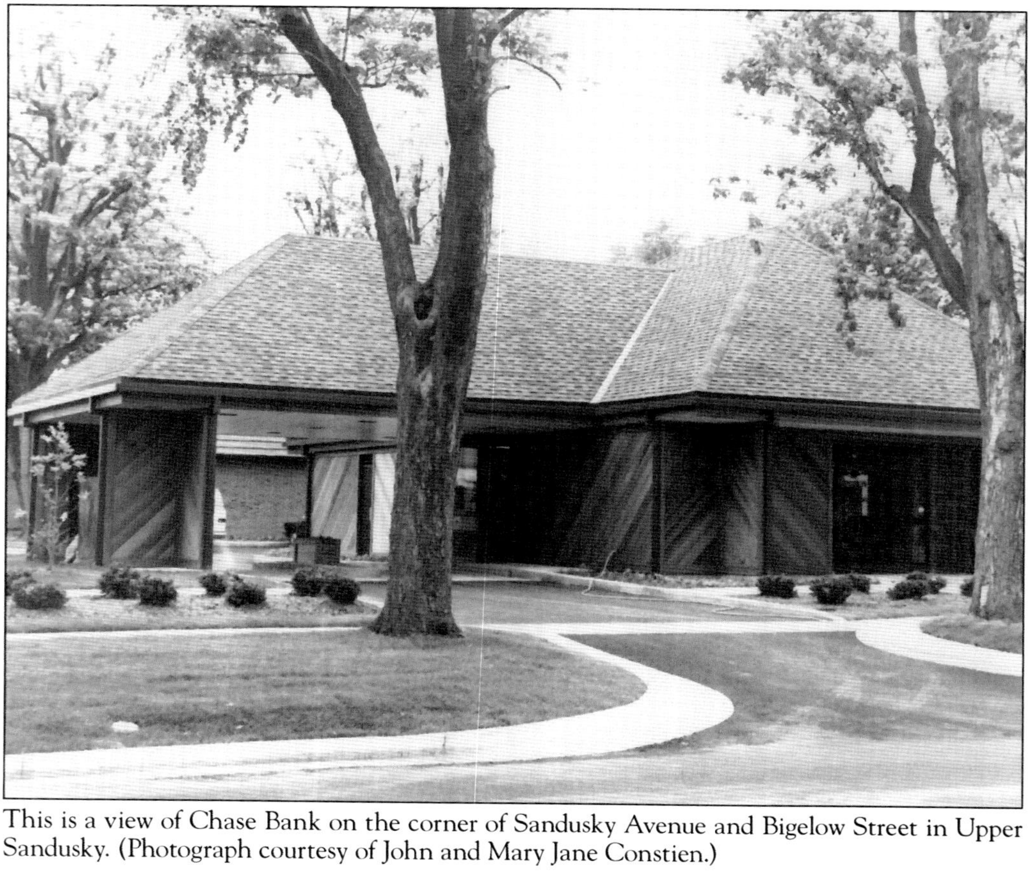

This is a view of Chase Bank on the corner of Sandusky Avenue and Bigelow Street in Upper Sandusky. (Photograph courtesy of John and Mary Jane Constien.)

Four

EDUCATION AND FAITH

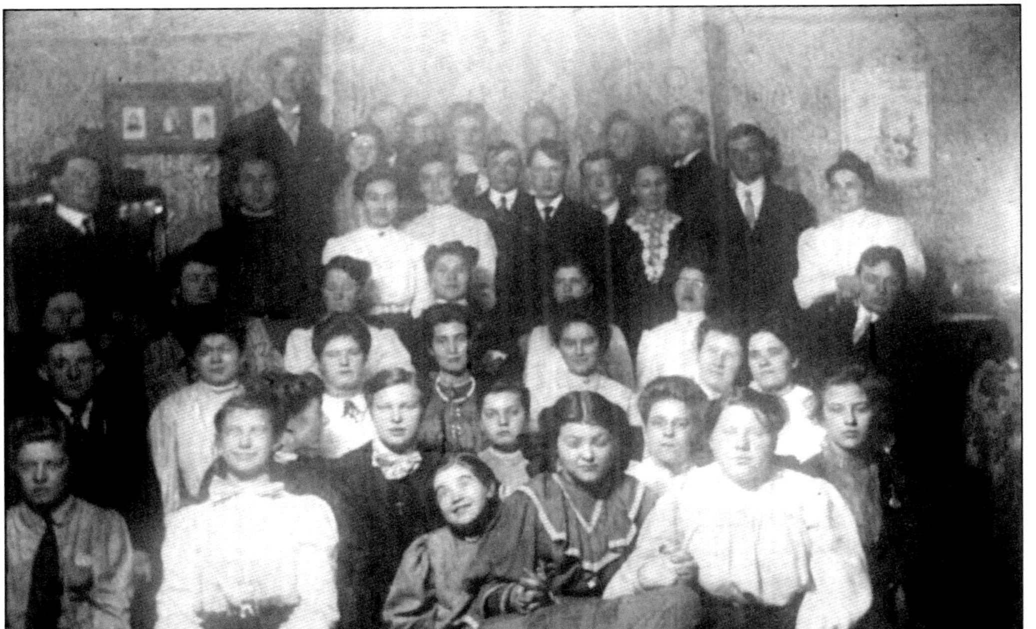

This is a photograph of members of the Christian Indian Society. Not much is known about this organization. Although Upper Sandusky did have a Redman's Lodge, it is unknown if the society was affiliated with the lodge.

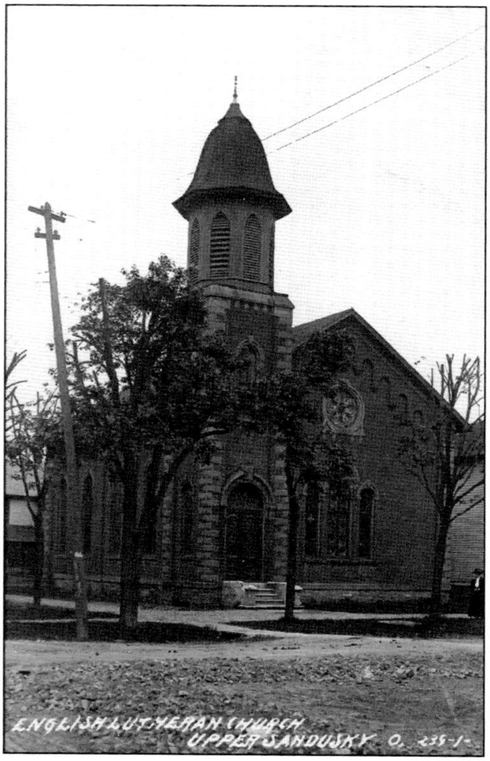

The first English Lutheran Church in Upper Sandusky was organized by Rev. Jacob Schaner. Meetings were held at the house of George Wolford on February 5, 1849. Earlier meetings had been held in the Indian Council house. The first brick structure of the church was built in 1859. In 1879, a new building was started on the corner of North 8th Street and West Wyandot Avenue. This photograph shows the second structure. It was completed in 1880 at a cost of $5,000.

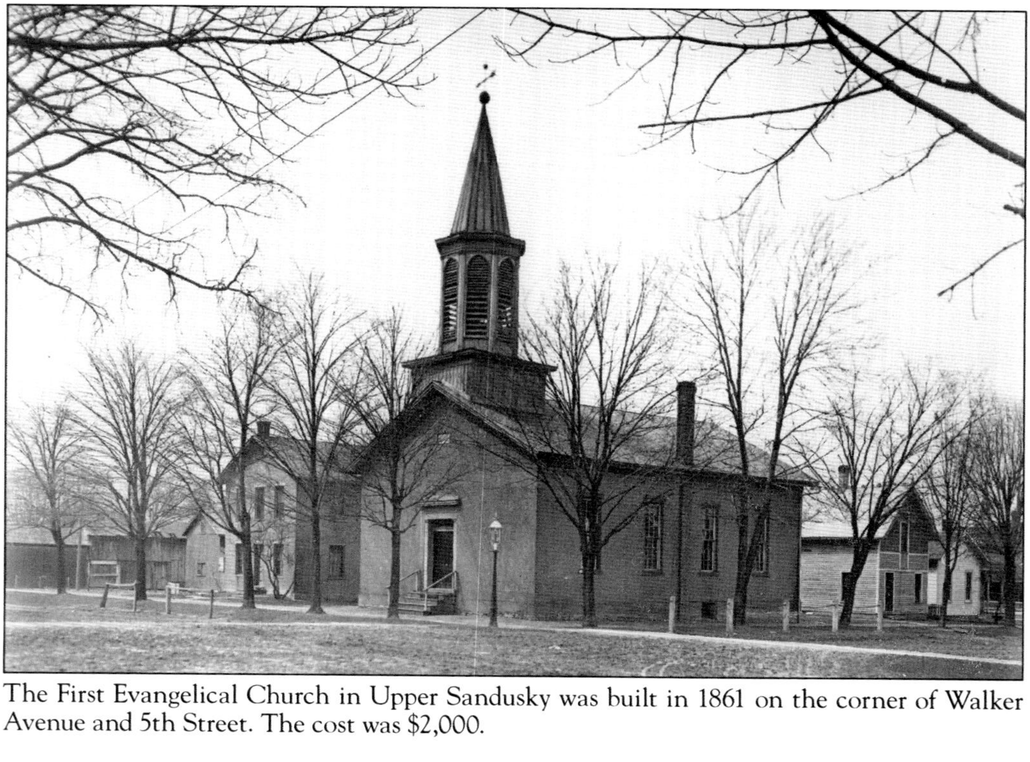

The First Evangelical Church in Upper Sandusky was built in 1861 on the corner of Walker Avenue and 5th Street. The cost was $2,000.

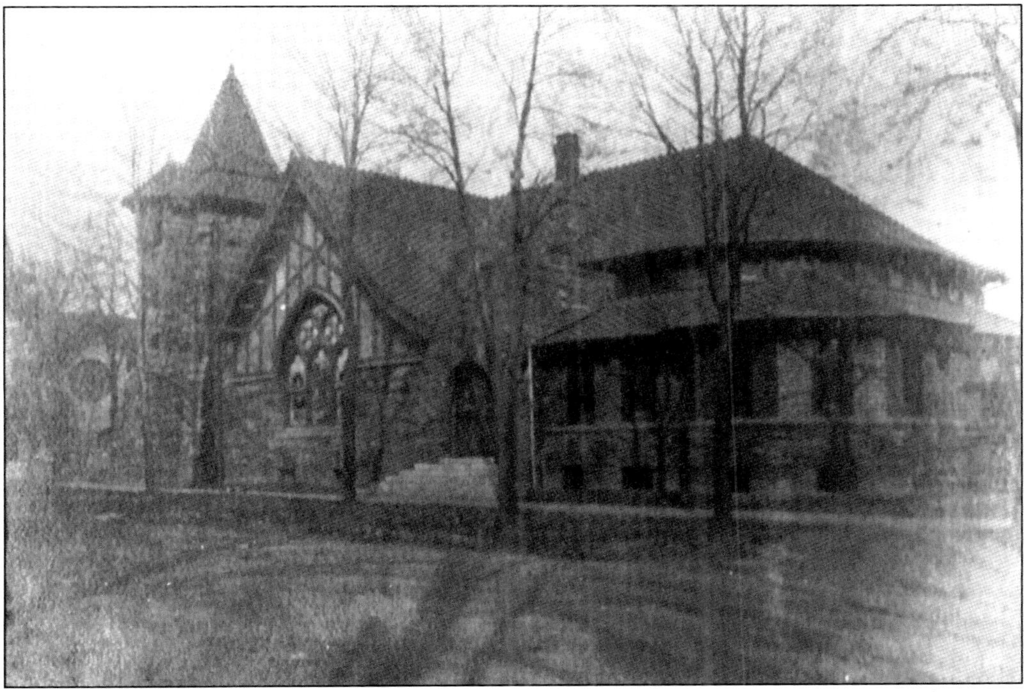

Construction on the First Presbyterian Church started in 1899. The church was dedicated on June 24, 1900. It still stands on the corner of West Johnson Avenue and South 7th Street.

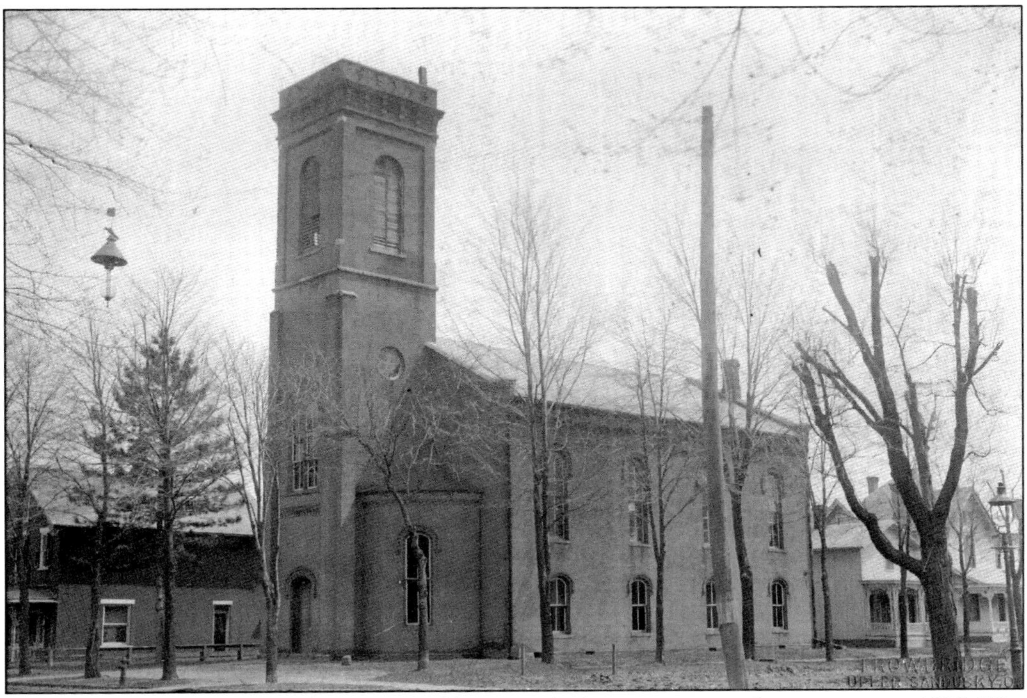

The Old Presbyterian Church is pictured here just before it was torn down in spring 1899. The walls of the church started to spread in 1898, and the building was declared unsafe.

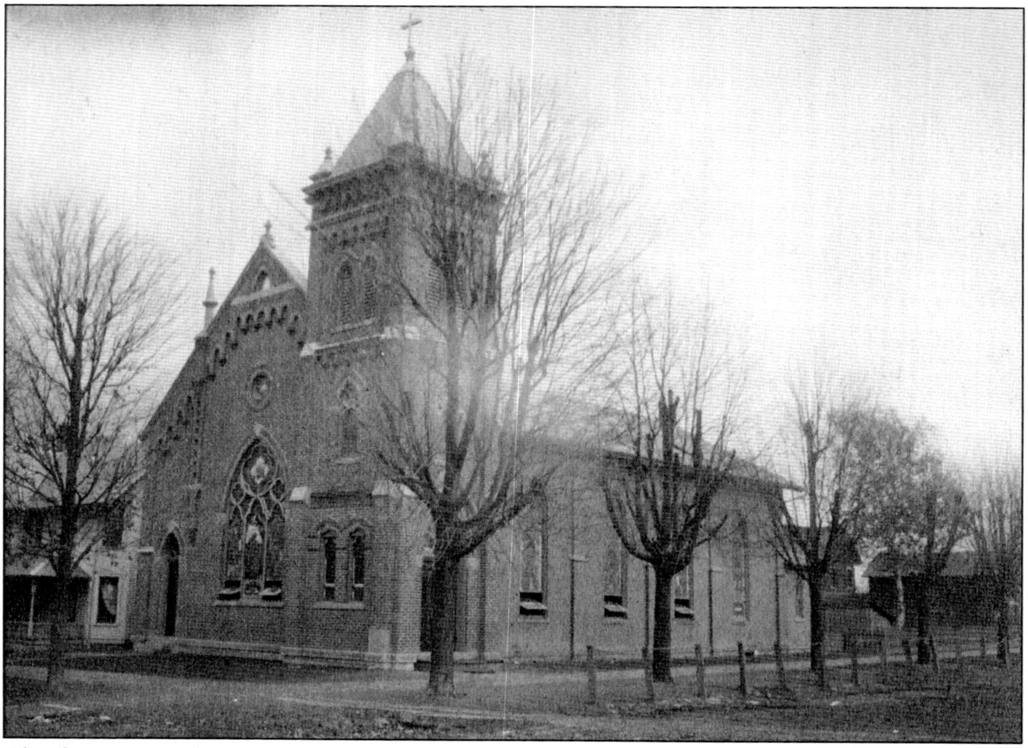

The first St. Paul Lutheran Church was built around 1867 on the corner of Bigelow Street and Sandusky Avenue. It was used by the congregation until 1927. Later, it became the V. A. Menningen Sunoco gas station. The building is still standing today, although its appearance has been significantly changed.

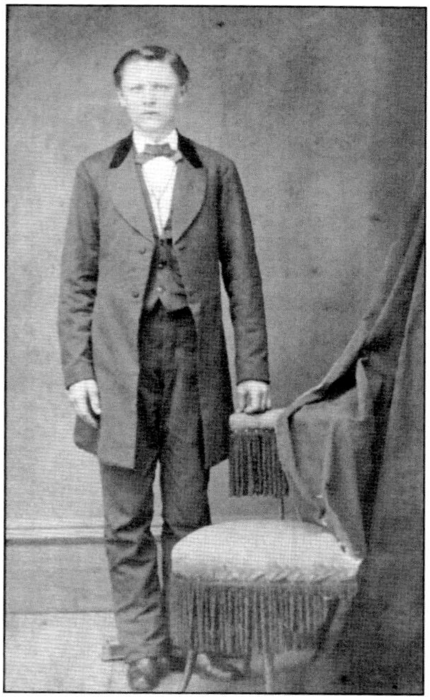

This photograph of the Reverend Fredrick C. Stecher was taken between 1870 and 1884 by Daniel Rider.

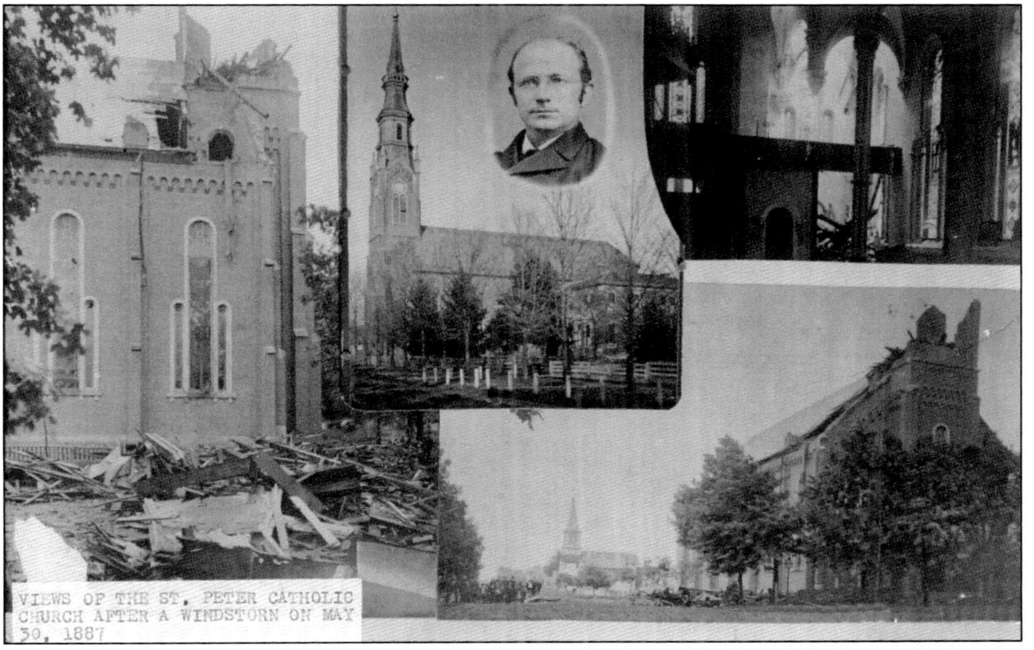

This is a collage of St. Peters Church. The photographs show the church before and after the May 30, 1887, windstorm. The 200-foot-tall steeple is in ruins at the base of the church and across Finley Street. The church was built in 1857.

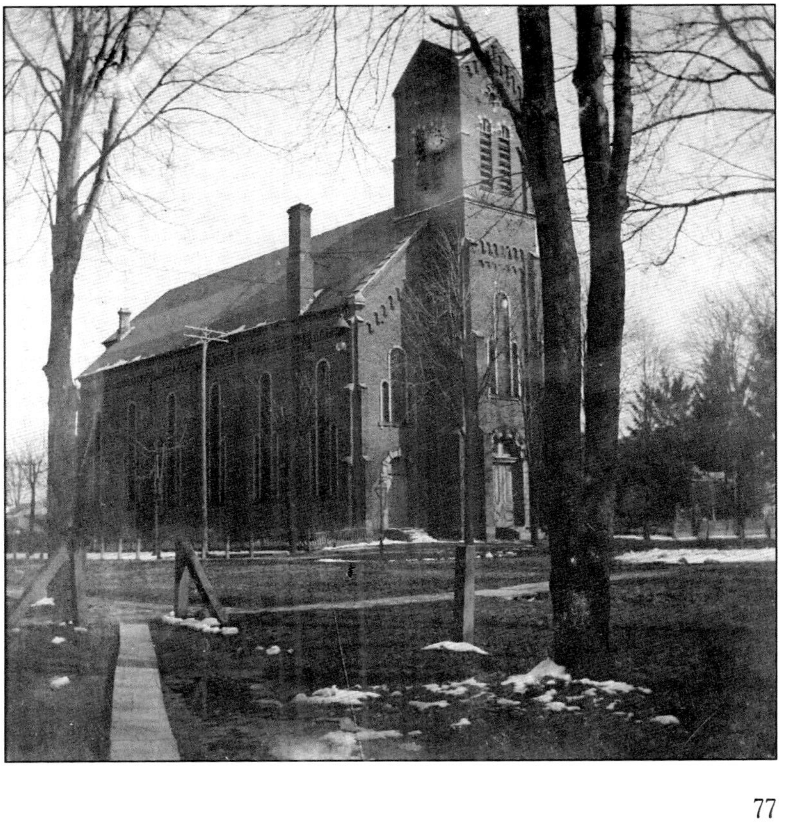

This image of St. Peters Church shows the base of the old steeple that was kept after the 1887 storm. Except for some minor changes, the church and the streets around it look much the same today.

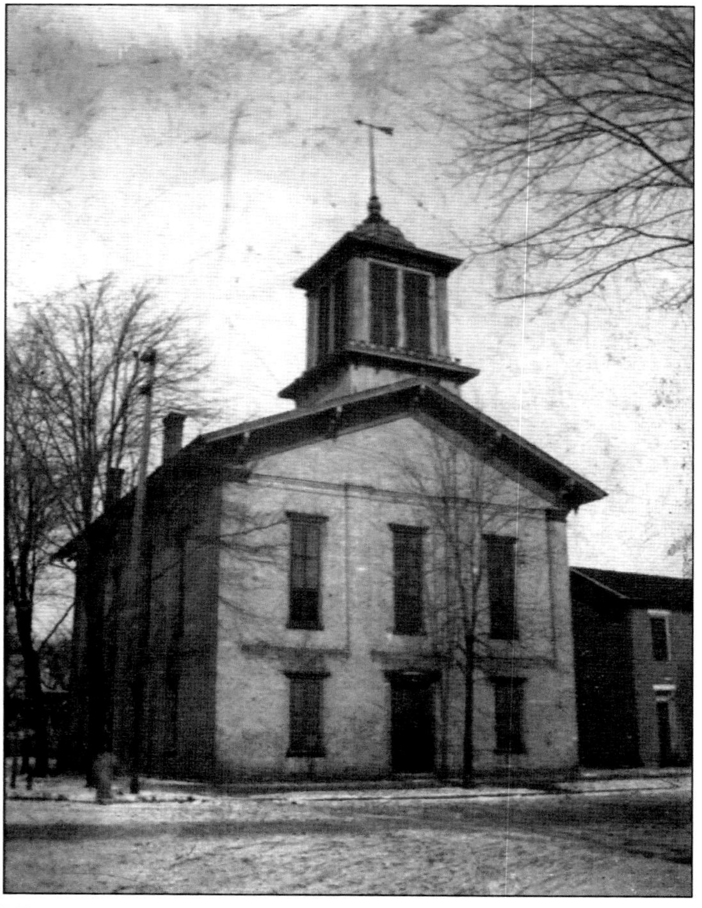

There has been a Methodist church on the corner of South 7th and West Johnson Streets since 1845. The photograph here depicts the second church and parsonage built in 1856. In 1898 it was torn down to make room for the new structure, which was built the following year.

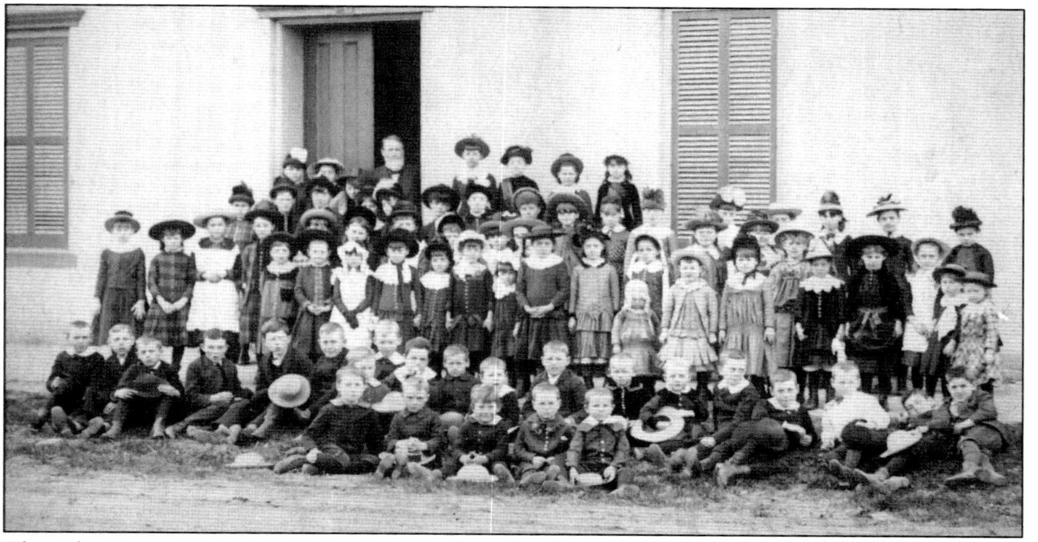

The John Stewart United Methodist Sunday school class of 1885 is seen in this picture. Notice the person standing in the doorway of the building.

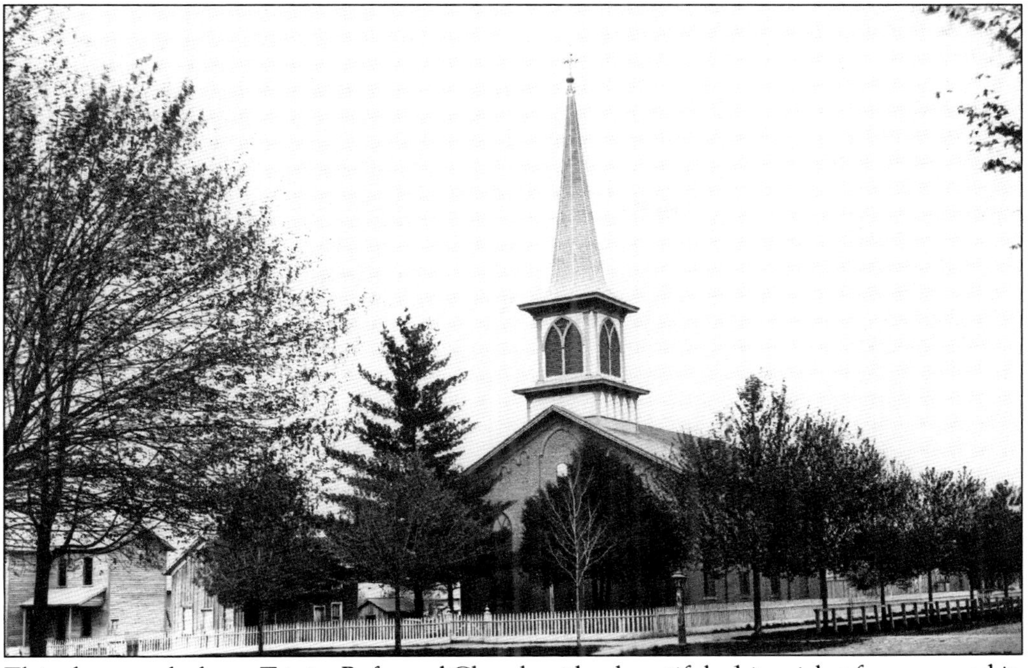

This photograph shows Trinity Reformed Church with a beautiful white picket fence around it. Notice the wooden frame homes to the left of the church.

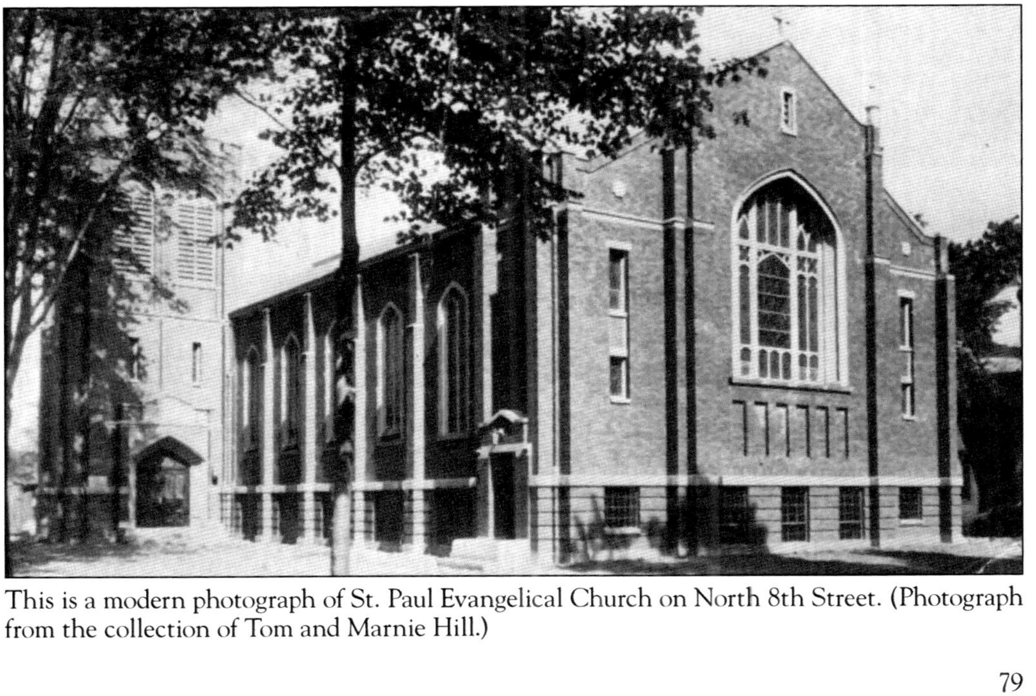

This is a modern photograph of St. Paul Evangelical Church on North 8th Street. (Photograph from the collection of Tom and Marnie Hill.)

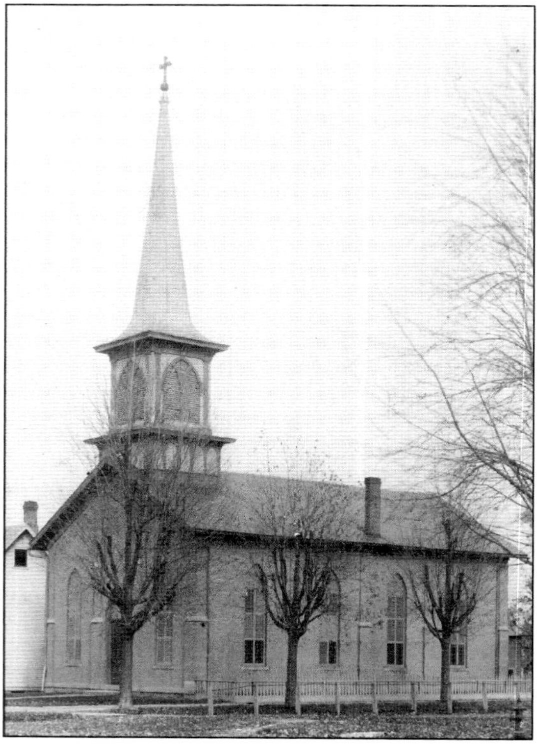

Starting in 1866, several church denominations used the corner of 5th and Finley Streets, including English, Lutheran, German, Trinity, and United Church of God. The Reformed Church was at this location during the 1920s and 1930s.

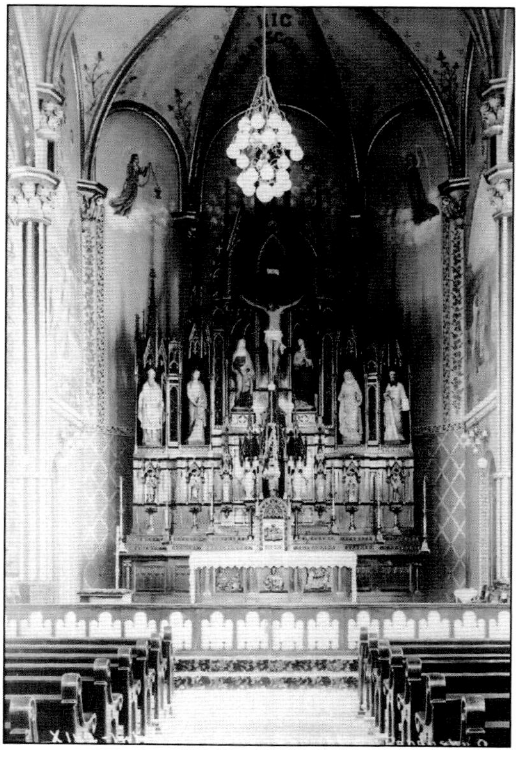

Pictured here is the sanctuary and high altar of St. Peter's Church. Although changes have taken place over the years, the church still has the ornate ceilings and statues of earlier times.

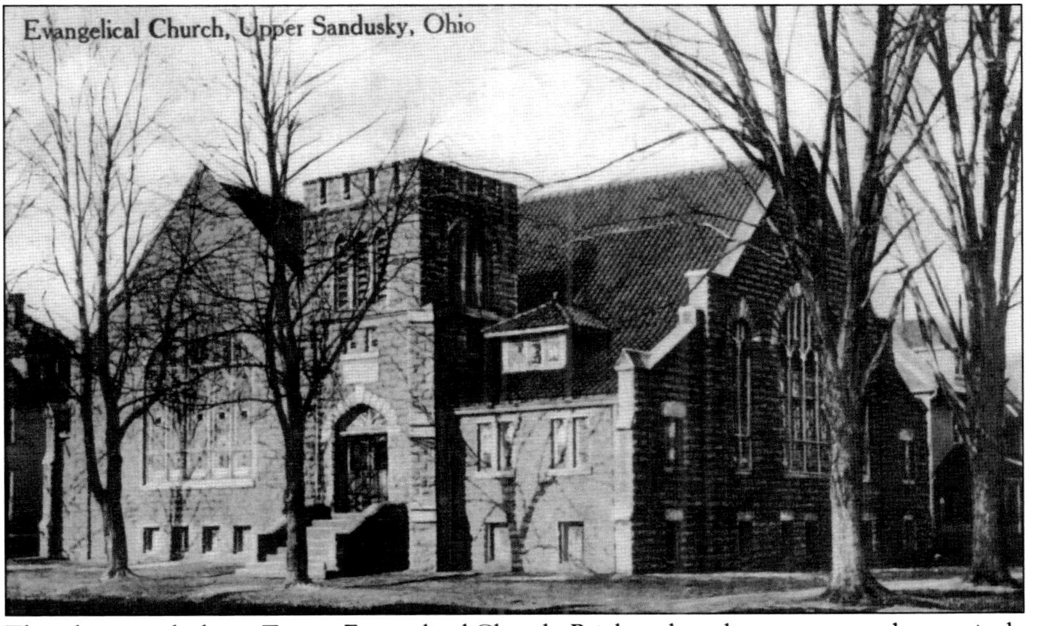

This photograph shows Trinity Evangelical Church. Brick and sandstone were used extensively by early builders in the area. That, combined with beautiful stained glass windows, makes them some of the best looking structures in town. (Photograph from the collection of Tom and Marnie Hill.)

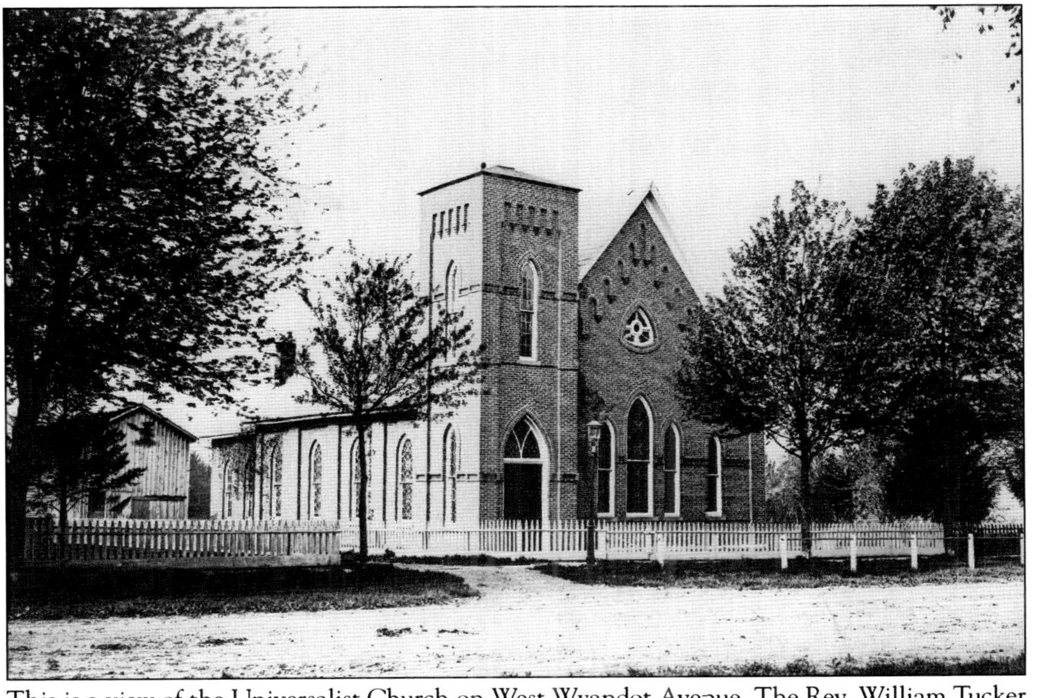

This is a view of the Universalist Church on West Wyandot Avenue. The Rev. William Tucker was the minister at the time.

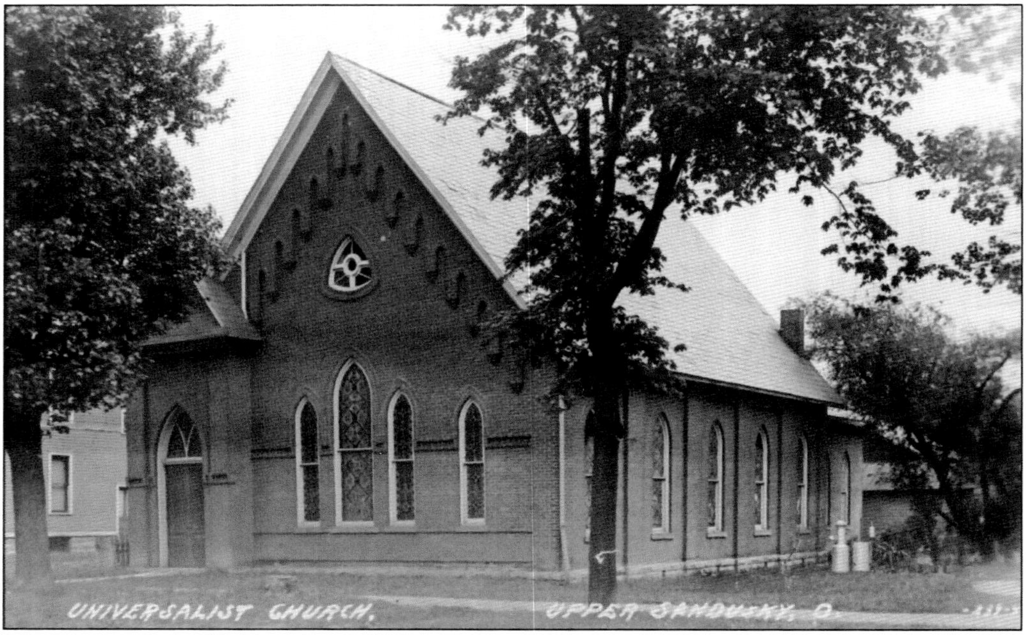

The Universalist Church is located on West Wyandot Avenue. (Photograph from the collection of Tom and Marnie Hill.)

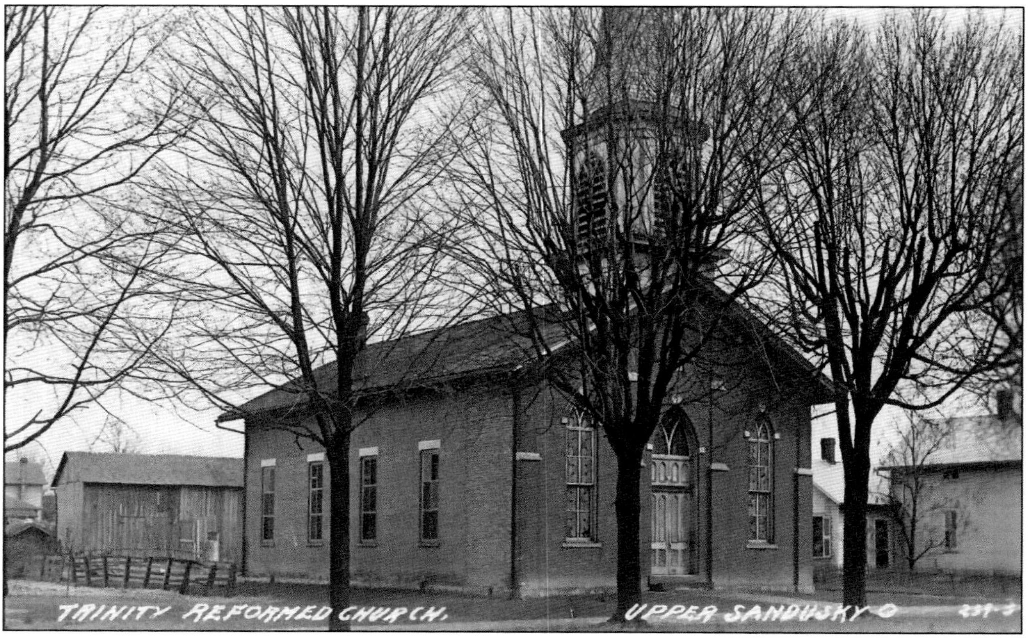

The Trinity Reformed Church was in close proximity to several homes.

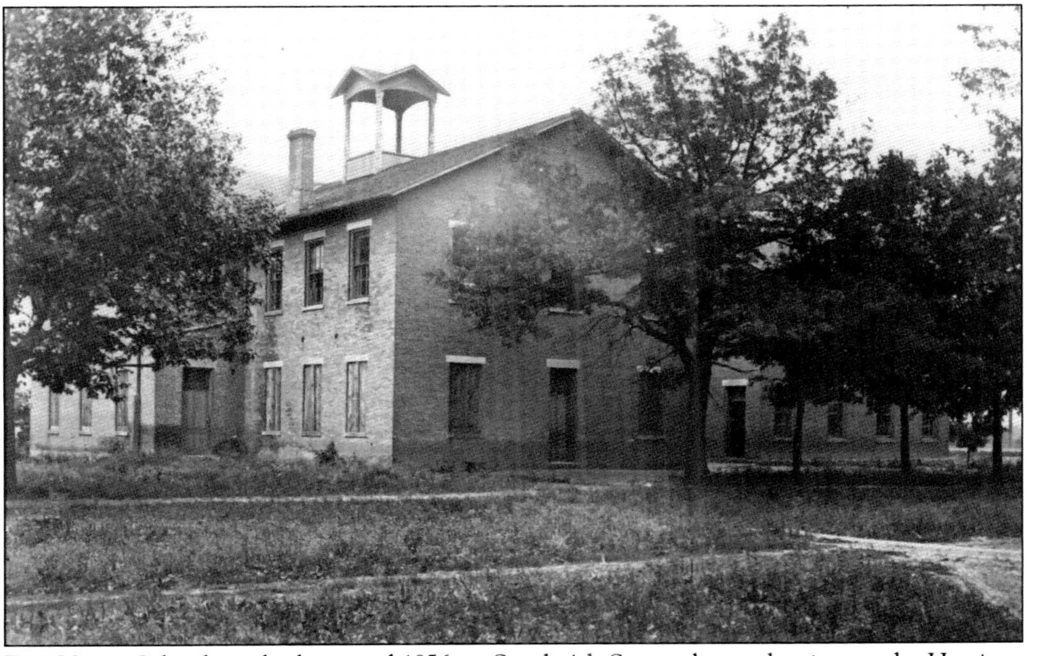

First Union School was built around 1856 on South 4th Street above what is now the Harrison Smith Park. The larger building on the left was constructed sometime in the 1860s.

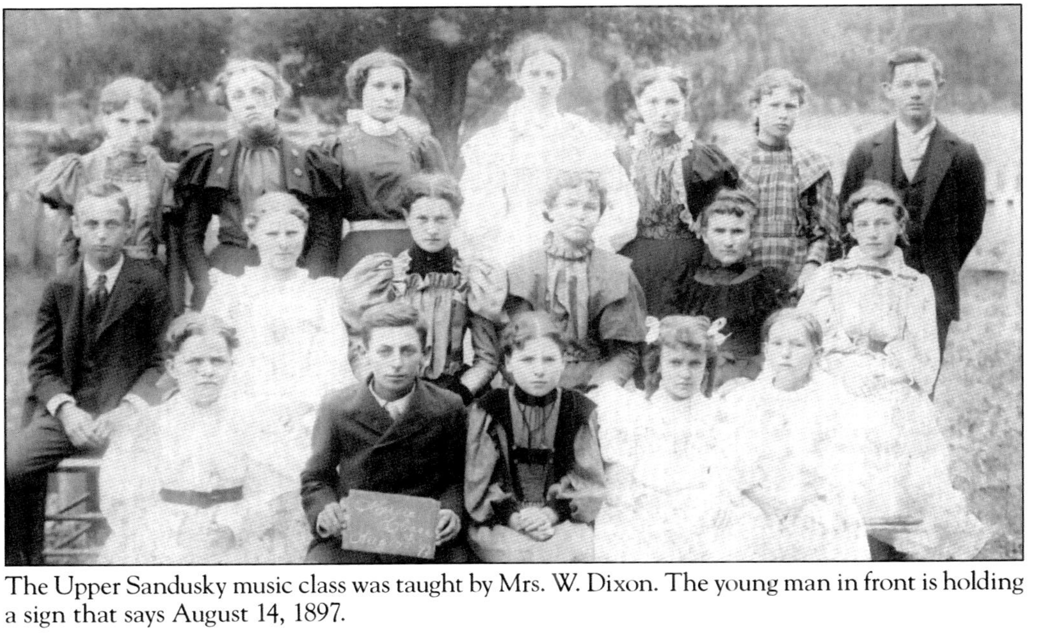

The Upper Sandusky music class was taught by Mrs. W. Dixon. The young man in front is holding a sign that says August 14, 1897.

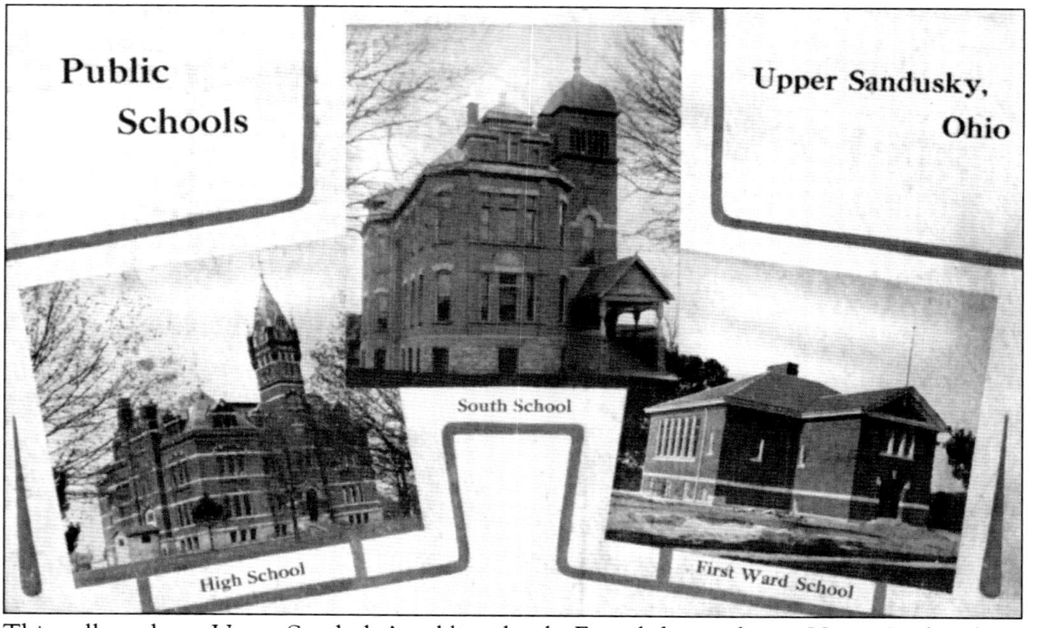

This collage shows Upper Sandusky's public schools. From left to right are Union High School (built in 1882), South School (built in 1896), and First Ward School (built in 1910). First Ward School is now called East School.

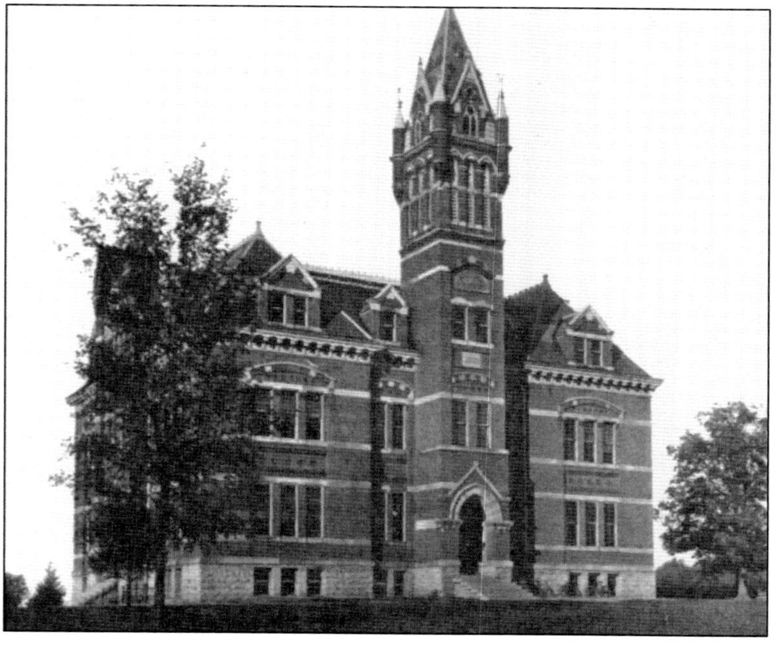

The Old High School was built in 1882 at a cost of $34,304.75. It had three floors. The tower and roof were removed around 1935. The building was razed in 1973. (Photograph from the collection of Tom and Marnie Hill.)

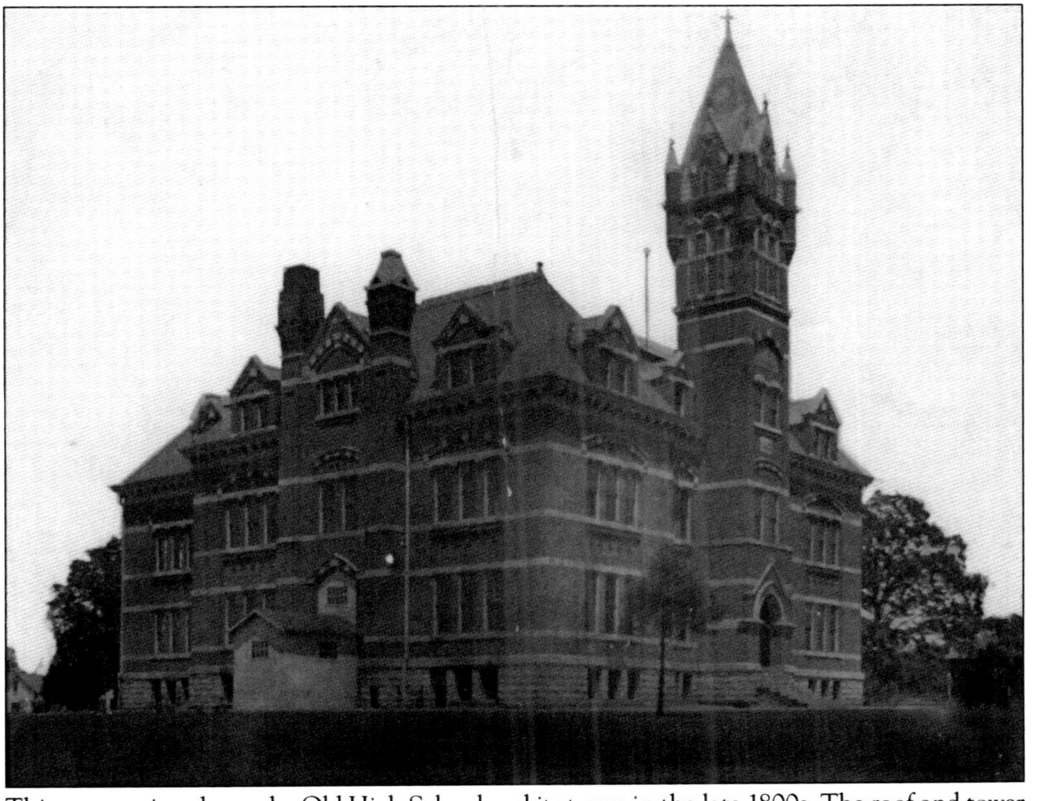

This corner view shows the Old High School and its tower in the late 1800s. The roof and tower of the building were lined with ornate trim.

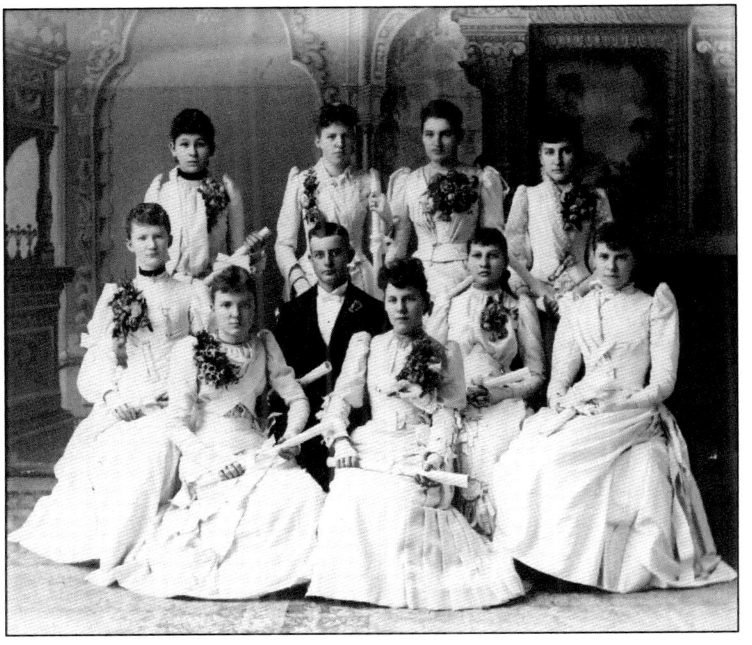

The graduating class of 1890 is shown holding their diplomas. Nine ladies and one gentleman were in the class: Zora (Adams) Frank, Clara Brauns, Ella (Clinger) Hackton, Minnie Hale, Zella (Mease) Woodcock, Fannie (O'Brien) Fleck, Mattie Paessler, George Sting, Carrie (Stockton) Byron, and Emma Thompson.

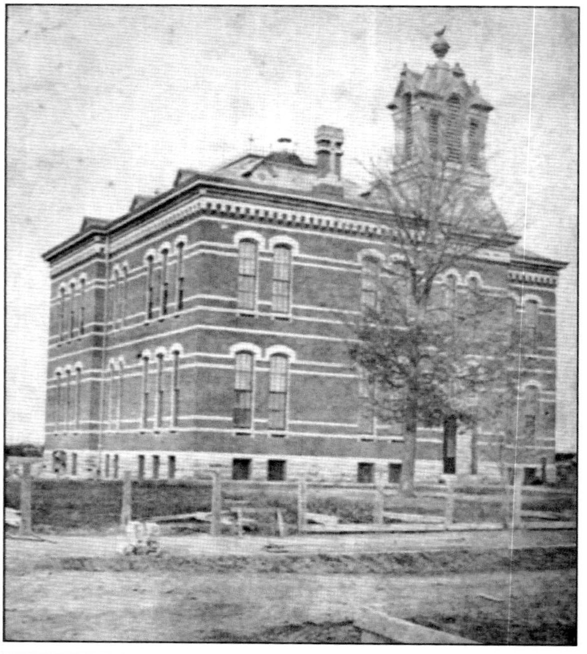

An early side view shows the Union School in Upper Sandusky in the 1800s.

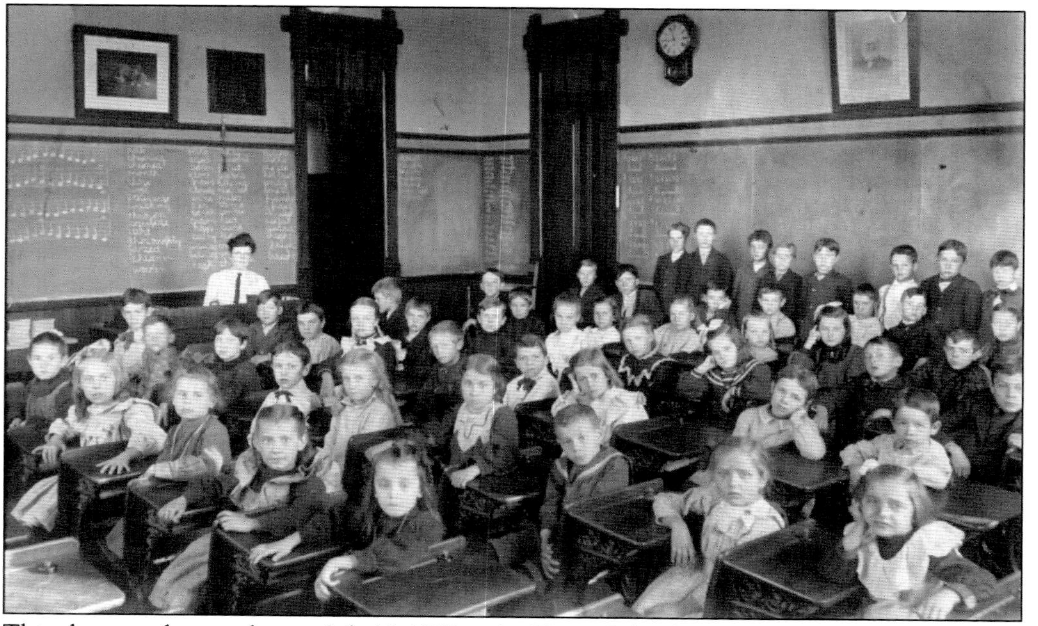

This photograph was taken on July 10, 1917, at the Union School in Upper Sandusky. The teacher was Shirley Hare. In the first row, from left to right, are Hazel Houser, Genedine Smalley, Helen Beinbreck, Maggie Cartnell, Alma Stevens; (second row) three unidentified, George Tschnaman (sp), Venus Staggs, Sarah Von Blon, Robert Pagnard, unidentified, Martha Altenberger; (third row) unidentified, Curtis Snoffer, Mayme Myers, unidentified, Herbert Bush, Helen Smalley, unidentified, Harold Scheufler; (fourth row) five unidentified, Helen Wall, Fredrick Marston, Carl Seebach; (fifth row) two unidentified, Esther Lowry, unidentified, Geneva Biniau (sp), Martha Kirschner, and Robert Pagnard. The rest are unidentified.

This is an early photograph of South School built on the corner of Henderson and South Eight street in 1895. On September 13, 1892 land was purchased from Randolph Stevenson and on December 5, 1895 a lot was purchased from John Sheely. The two story building was put up soon after for children living on the south end of Upper Sandusky.

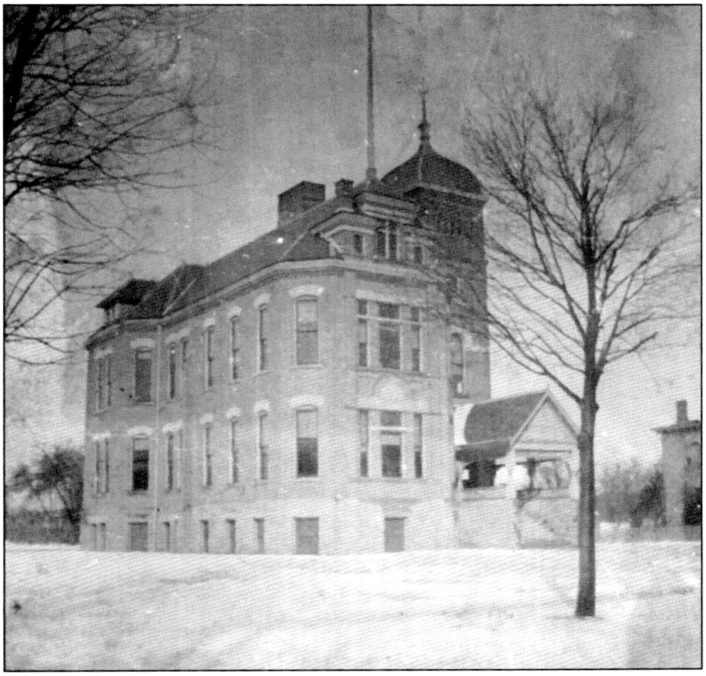

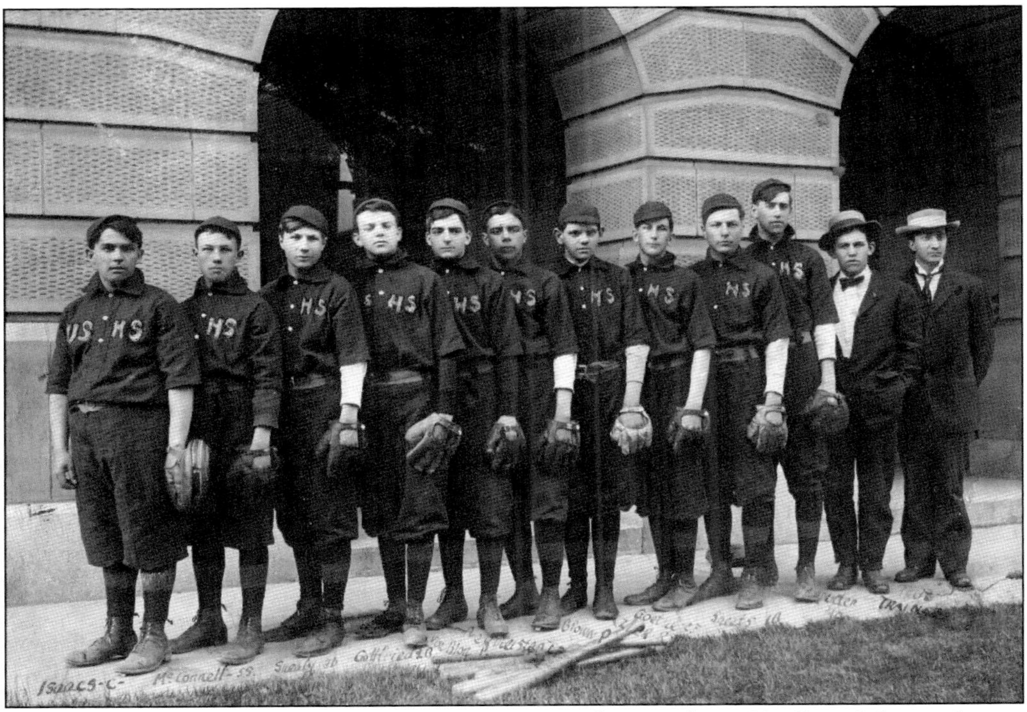

The Upper Sandusky High School baseball team poses here in the 1900s. From left to right are: Isaacs, catcher; McConnell, short stop; Shealy, third base; Gottfried, second base; Von Blon, pitcher; Neumeister, left field; Brown, pitcher; Zier, right field; Goethe, center field; Sheets, first base; Carpenter, manager; and True, trainer.

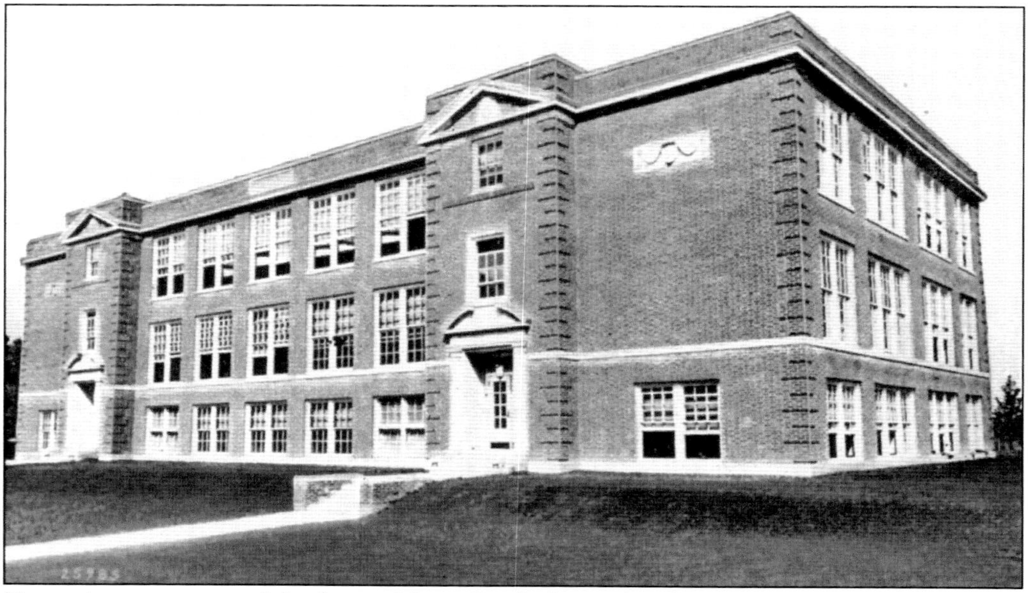

Shown here is a view of the former Upper Sandusky High School at 290 West Walker Street. The building currently houses Union Middle School. (Photograph from the collection of Tom and Marnie Hill.)

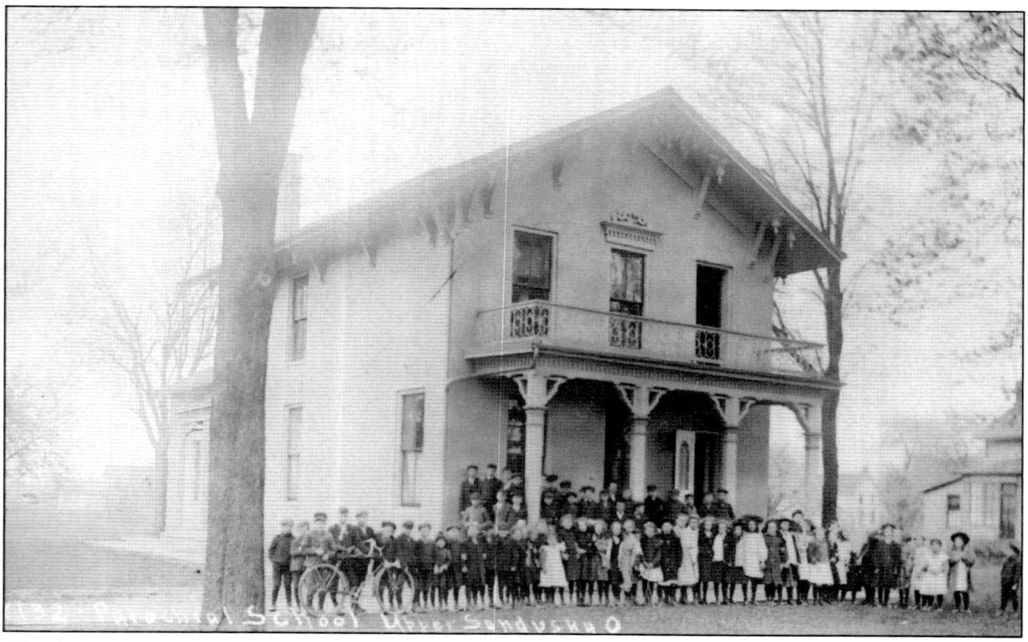

The first St. Peter's School, pictured here, was in operation from 1898 to 1927. It was located at 314 North 8th Street in Upper Sandusky. (Photograph from the collection of Tom and Marnie Hill.)

Five

A Portrait in Time

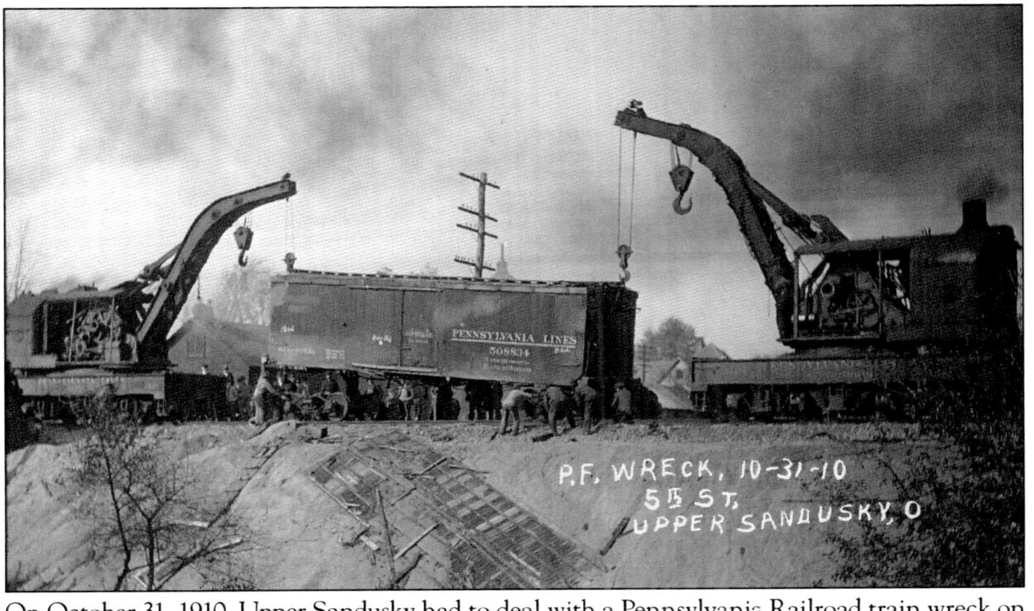

On October 31, 1910, Upper Sandusky had to deal with a Pennsylvania Railroad train wreck on 5th Street. In this photograph, the workers are sitting a boxcar back on its wheels. To the right of the power pole, Lady Liberty can be seen atop the courthouse in the background. (Photograph from the collection of Tom and Marnie Hill.)

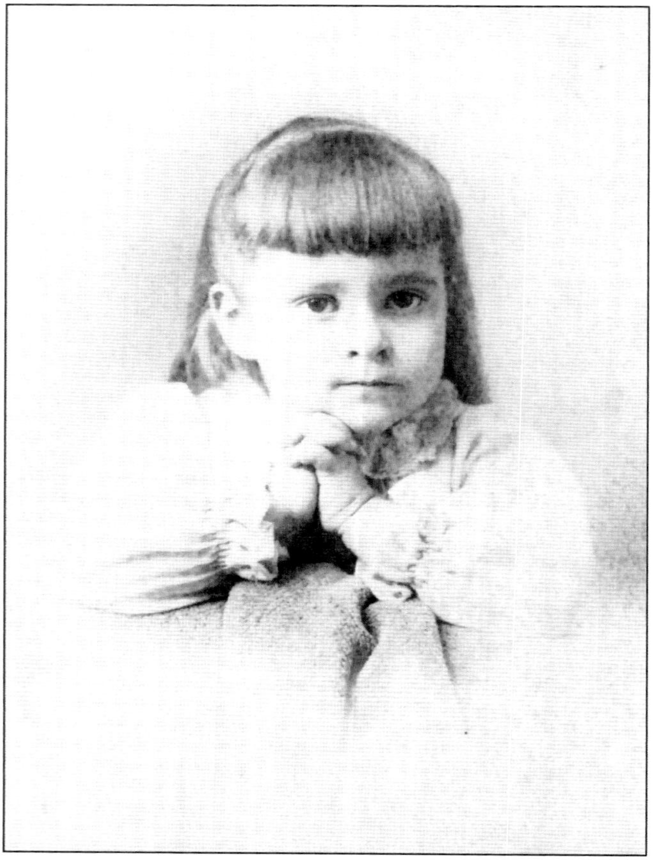

C. F. Tschanen took this photograph of a little girl between 1896 and 1899.

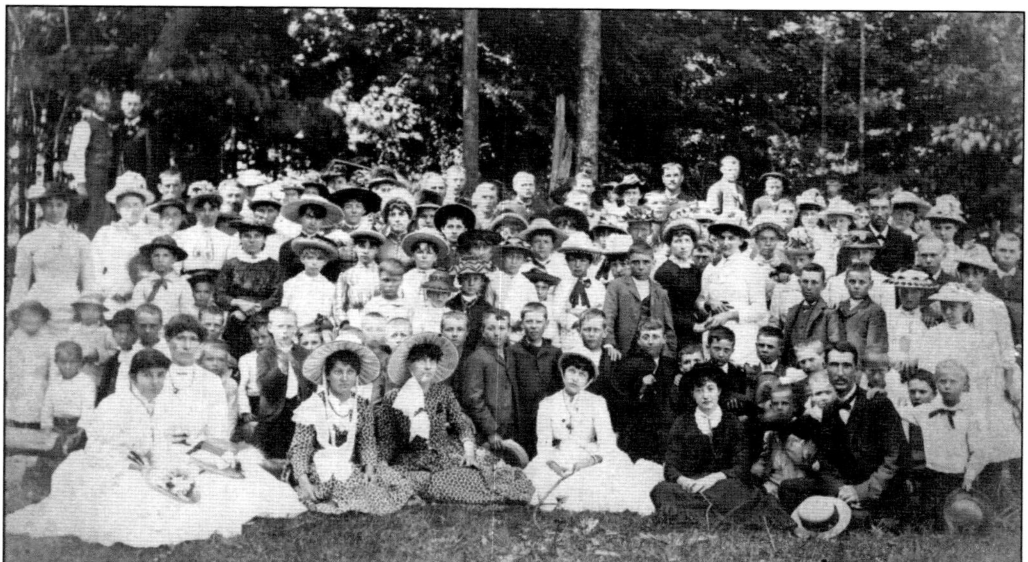

Seen here is a social gathering. The photograph was taken by J. D. Cress and Company in 1889. (Photograph from the collection of Tom and Marnie Hill.)

Cyrus Sears was commissioned first lieutenant October 12, 1861 with the 11th Ohio Independent. He was promoted to captain of the 49th United States Colored Troops, then promoted to lieutenant colonel of the same. He was discharged at Vicksburg, Mississippi, on March 26, 1866. He received the Medal of Honor for gallantry at the Battle of Iuka. Sears is shown wearing his Medal of Honor in this photograph from December 31, 1892.

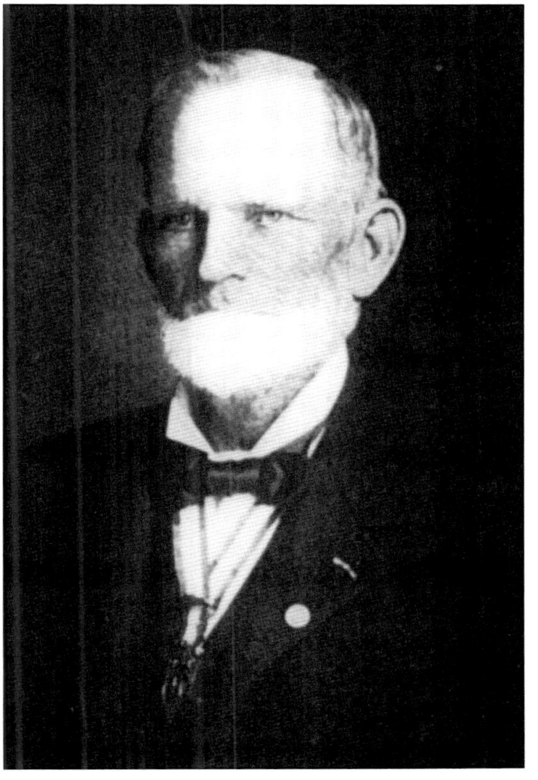

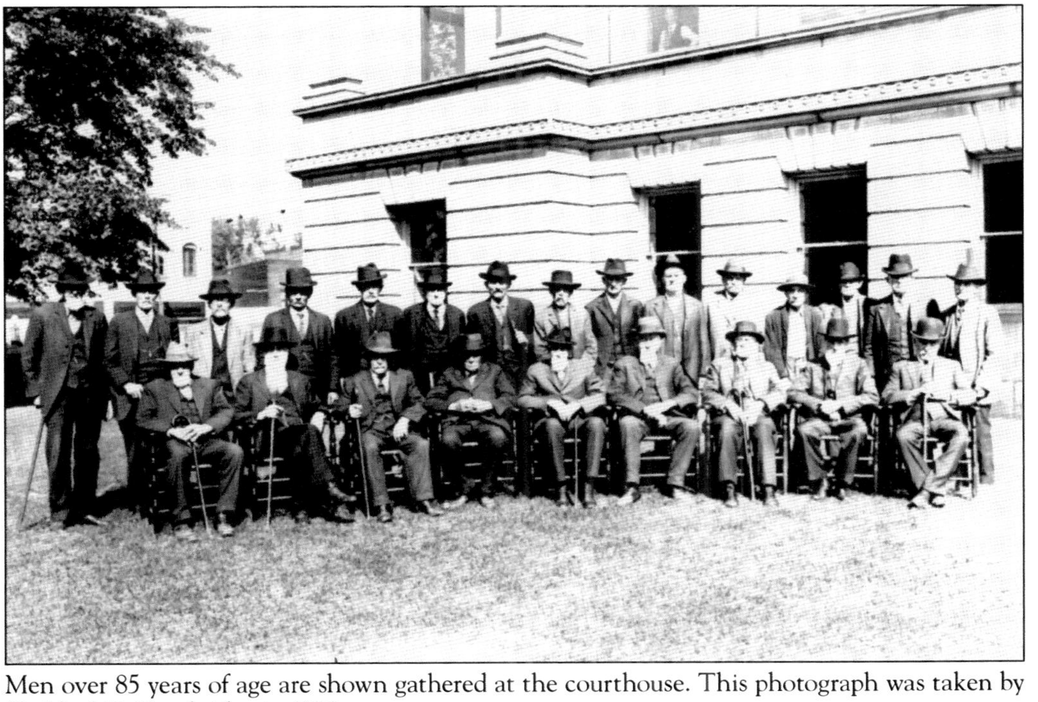

Men over 85 years of age are shown gathered at the courthouse. This photograph was taken by Guilford D. Trowbridge in 1918.

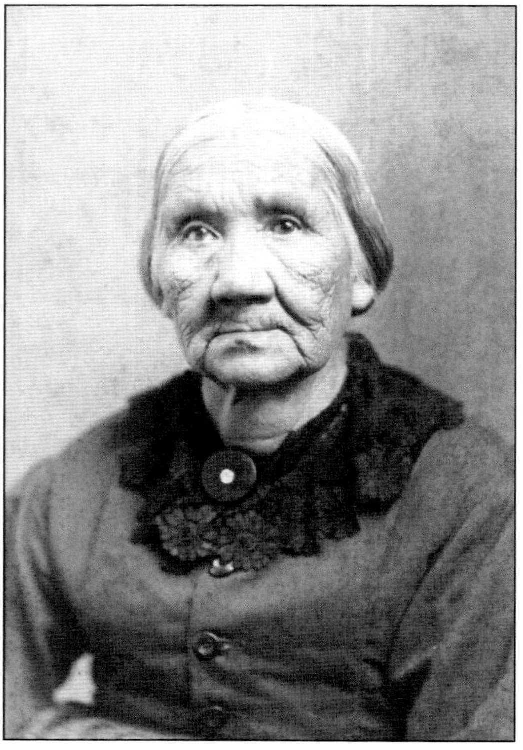

This photograph of Margaret Grey Eyes (Mother Solomon) was taken between 1885 and 1889. (Photograph from the collection of Tom and Marnie Hill.)

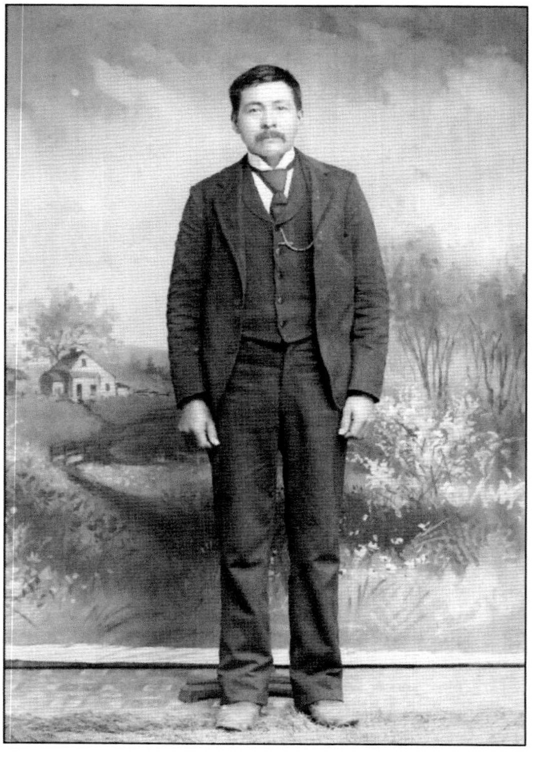

Jimmy Guyamme, Mother Solomon's nephew, brought her back from the reservation to Upper Sandusky to live. The photograph was taken by Orestes B. Turner between 1894 and 1895 in Findlay, Ohio. (Photograph from the collection of Tom and Marnie Hill.)

This composite photograph of Upper Sandusky residents was taken by C. F. Tschanen between 1896 and 1899.

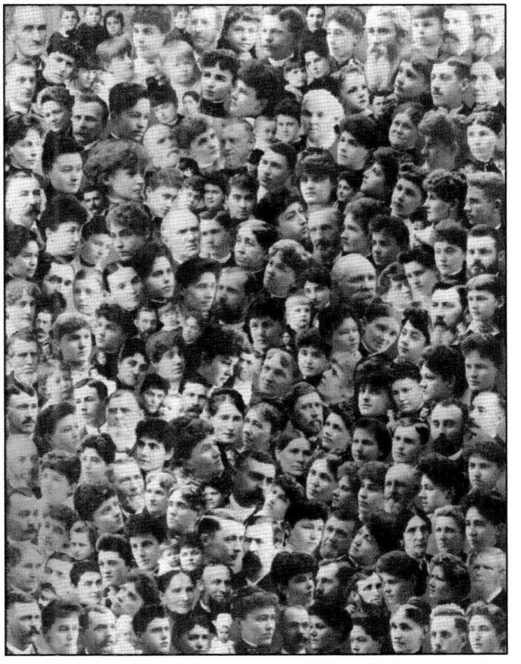

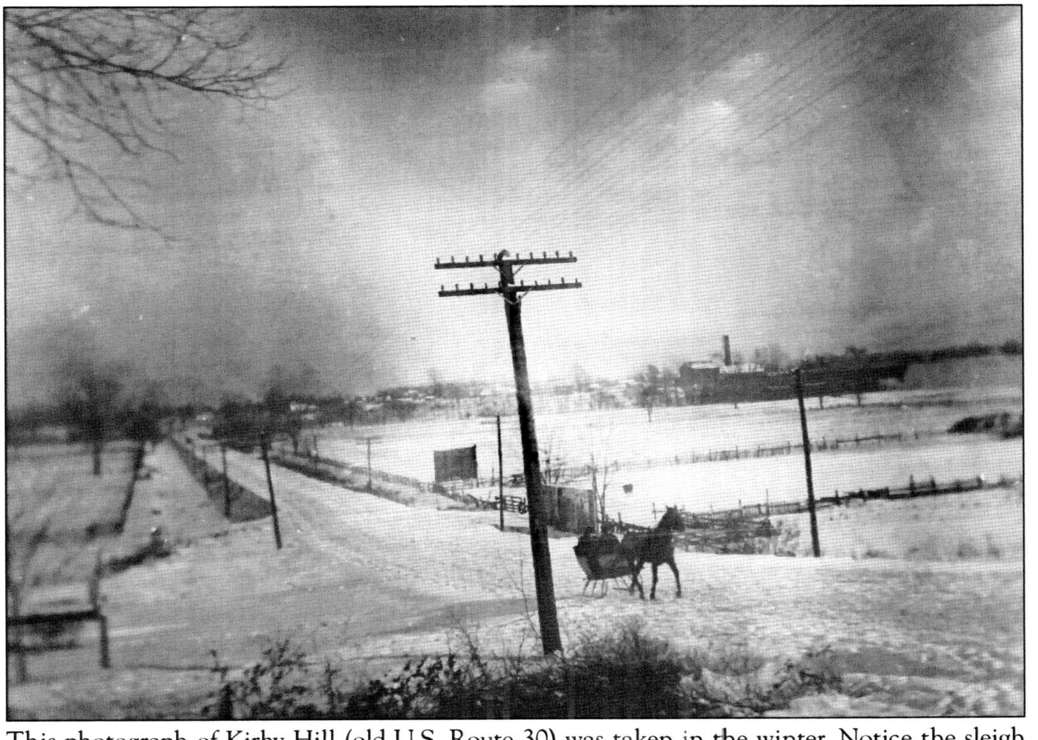

This photograph of Kirby Hill (old U.S. Route 30) was taken in the winter. Notice the sleigh with its two occupants bundled up for the chilly air. Just above the sleigh there is a cow standing in the field that would become Harrison Smith Park. The chimney of the Straw Board Factory can be seen in the background.

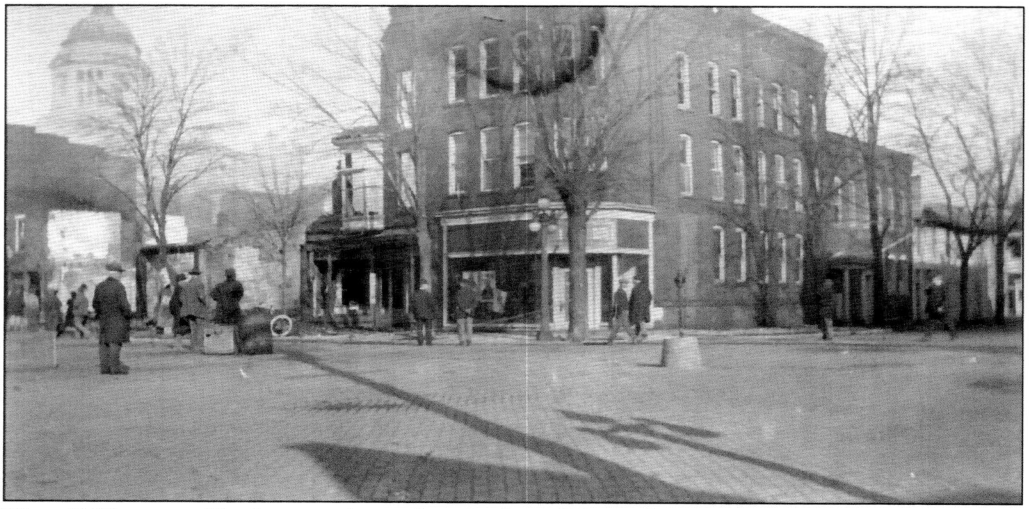

The old Thurman Block is seen here after the fire of November 12, 1918. The fire started in the back of the Bon Ton Restaurant operated by Wilfred P. Osborn. Fire departments form Carey, Marion, and Bucyrus, Ohio, were called to assist the Upper Sandusky Fire Department in battling the blaze. Losses were estimated at $300,000.

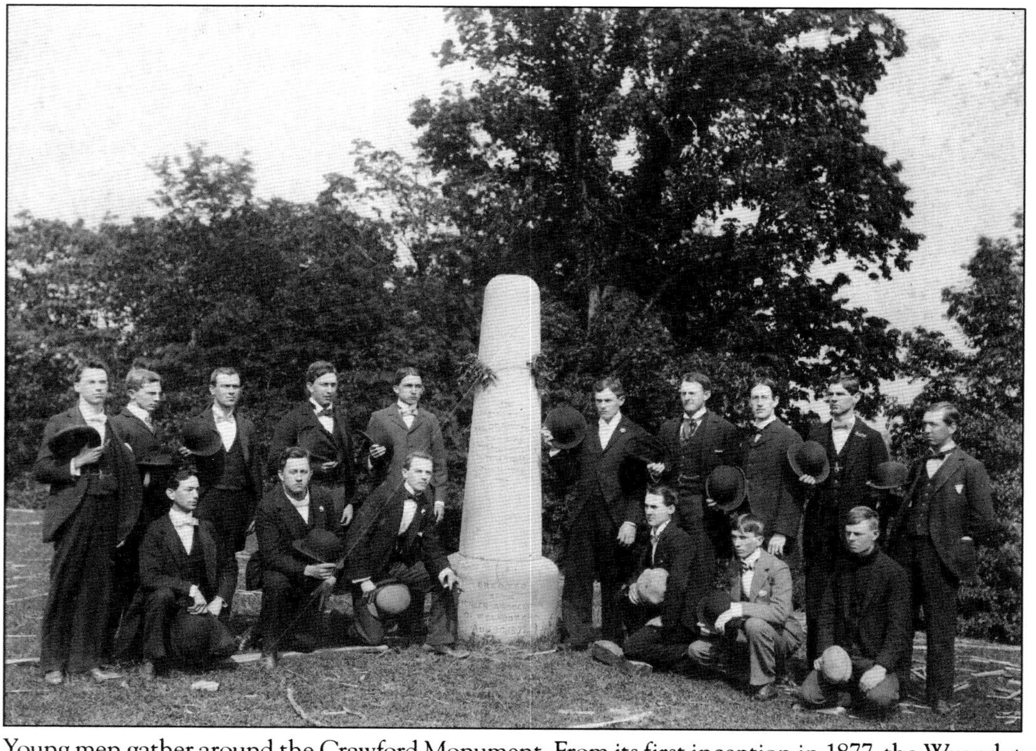

Young men gather around the Crawford Monument. From its first inception in 1877, the Wyandot Pioneer Association held an annual pioneer picnic at the site. The last picnic was held on June 13, 1935. Pictured are (first row) Fred Kramer, George Pool, Charles Bowman, Fred Kenan, Noah Harman, Ralph Beidler; (second row) Fred Tracht, Charles Glaser, Frank Gear, Harley Pool, Carl Ruopp, A. J. Ulrich, Avery Peters, Ben Hedges, Guy Selegman, and Percy Hale.

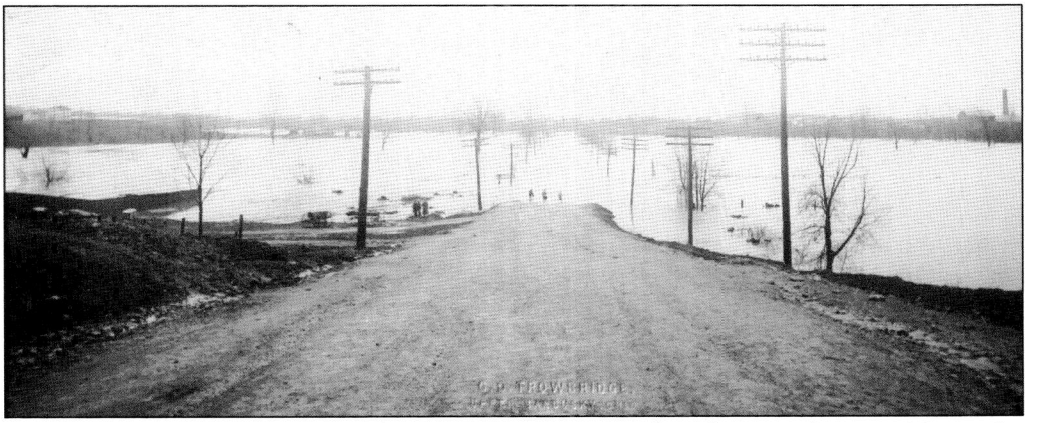

During the flood of 1913 the area that is now Harrison Smith Park was underwater. Notice the Straw Board Factory at the upper right. On the left side of the road are some wagons and just left of the wagons is the top of a building. The flood devastated not only Upper Sandusky but most of Ohio as well. (Photograph from the collection of Tom and Marnie Hill.)

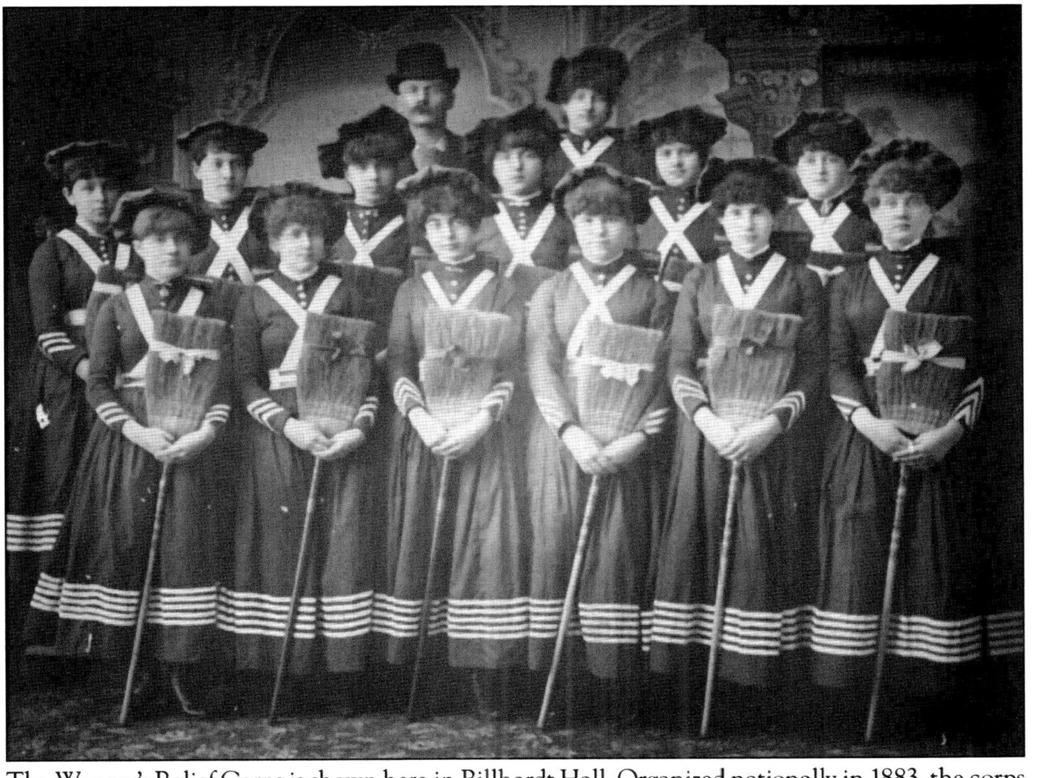

The Women's Relief Corps is shown here in Billhardt Hall. Organized nationally in 1883, the corps was one of three women's organizations created to serve the country's veterans. They decorated veterans' graves, cared for disabled veterans, and took care of the needs of widows and orphans of the Civil War. They were an auxiliary of the Grand Army of the Republic. Those identified in this photograph include Albert, an unidentified commander, Nettie Hitchcock, Hattie Stevenson, Mamie Stevenson, Lizzie Hale, Hattie Tschanen, ? McKelvy, Ida Pontius, Lucy Savage, Maggie Welch, Rachel Agerter, Ida Kramer, Etta Sims, and Fannie Hartsough.

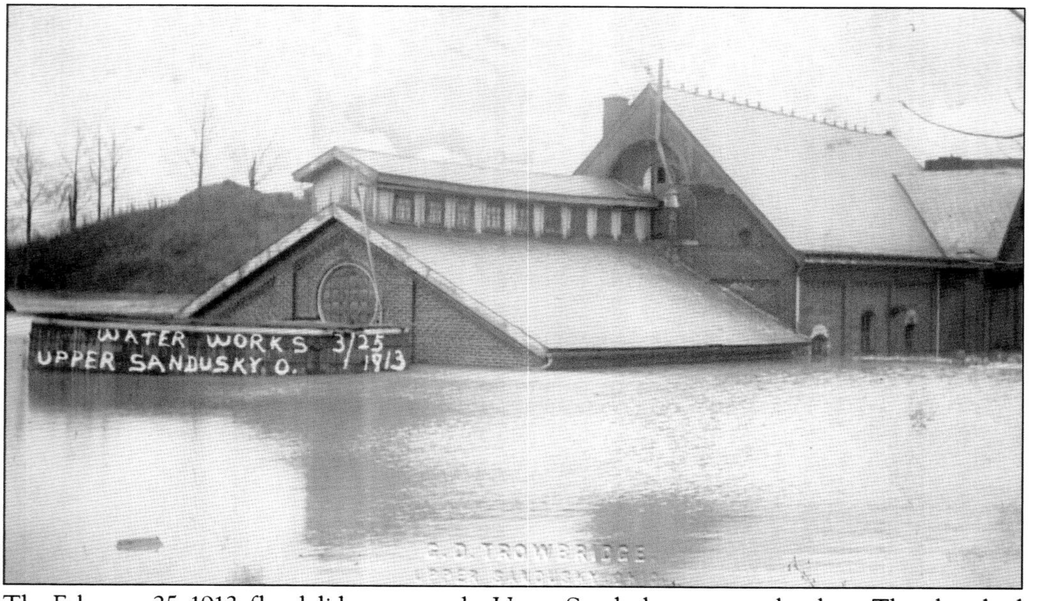

The February 25, 1913, flood did not spare the Upper Sandusky water works plant. The plant had extensive damage after the water receded. Any building close to the Sandusky River suffered the same fate. (Photograph from the collection of Tom and Marnie Hill.)

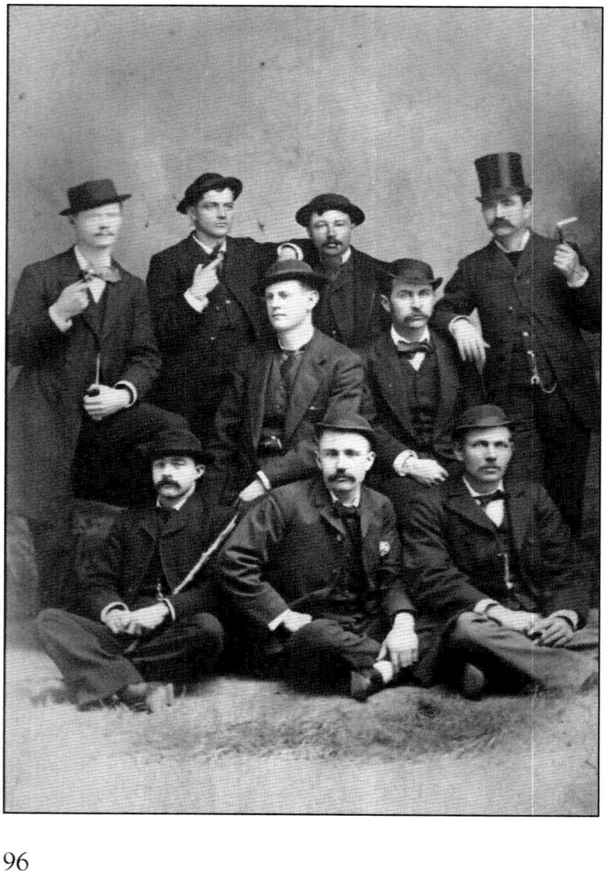

Dr. Jordan, a dentist who was practicing in Upper Sandusky, is standing in the third row wearing a top hat. The photographer had a studio in Upper Sandusky from 1868 to 1884.

This F. L. and A. Merrill Carte de Visite was taken between 1861 and 1864. It was most likely an advertisement showing what the photographer could do with his camera. (Photograph from the collection of Tom and Marnie Hill.)

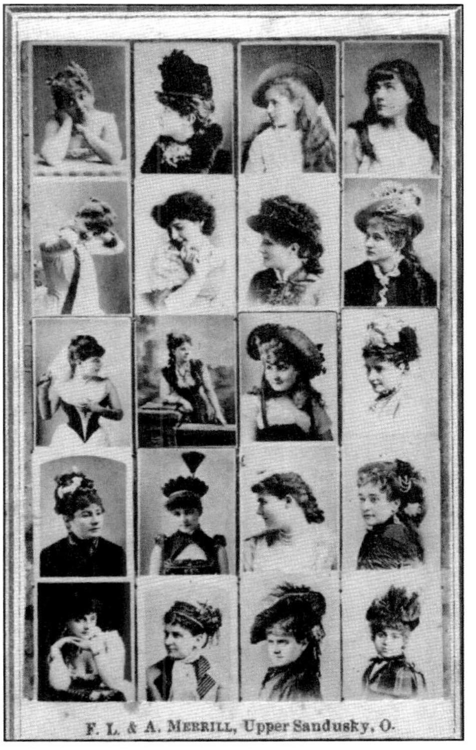

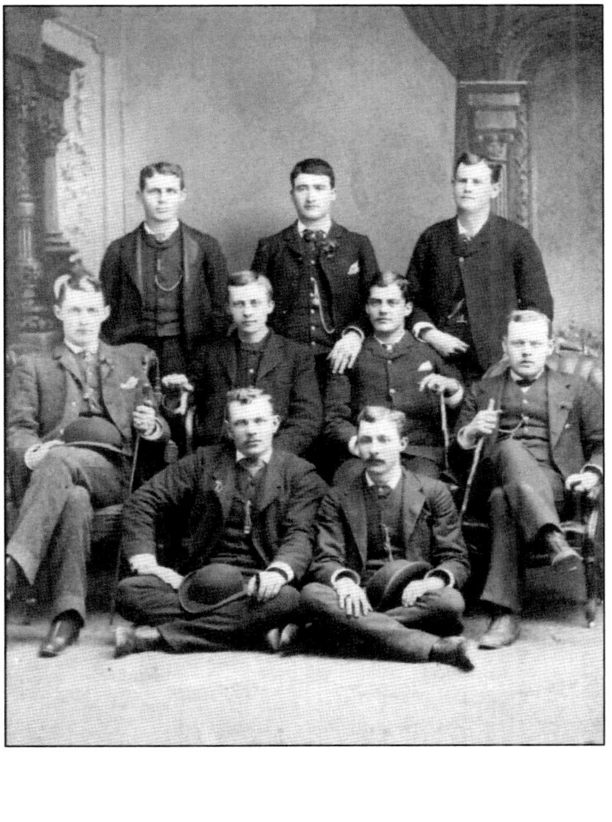

This Daniel Rider photograph of young Upper Sandusky men was taken between 1880 and 1884.

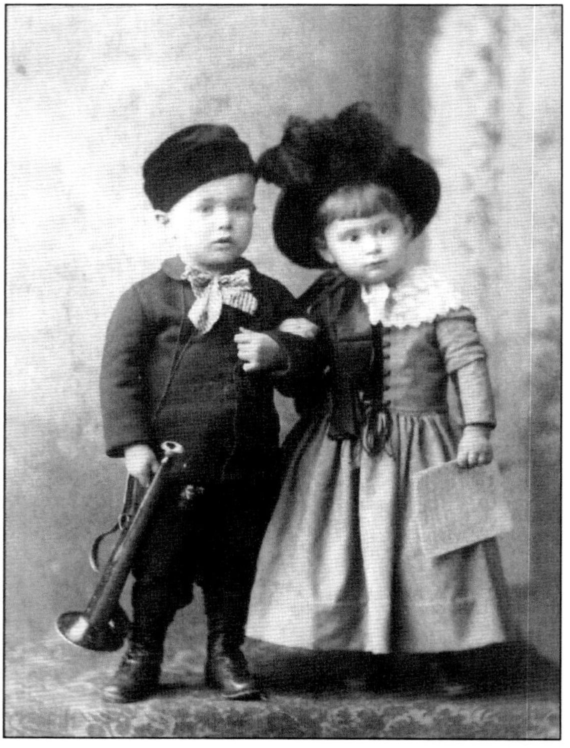

This J. McCahon photograph of a couple of Upper Sandusky children was taken between 1881 and 1889. The little boy is holding a horn while the little girl holds some sheet music.

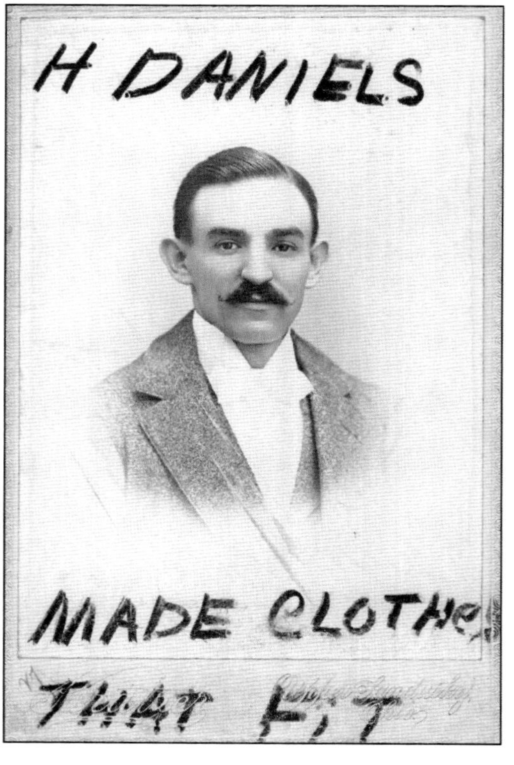

This photograph of H. Daniels was taken between 1896 and 1897. Daniels was in the clothing business from 1878 until 1909. His business was located at 102 South Sandusky Avenue.

C. F. Tschanen took this photograph of Nicholas Grundtisch between 1896 and 1899. Grundtisch was a town marshal for Upper Sandusky in the 1900s.

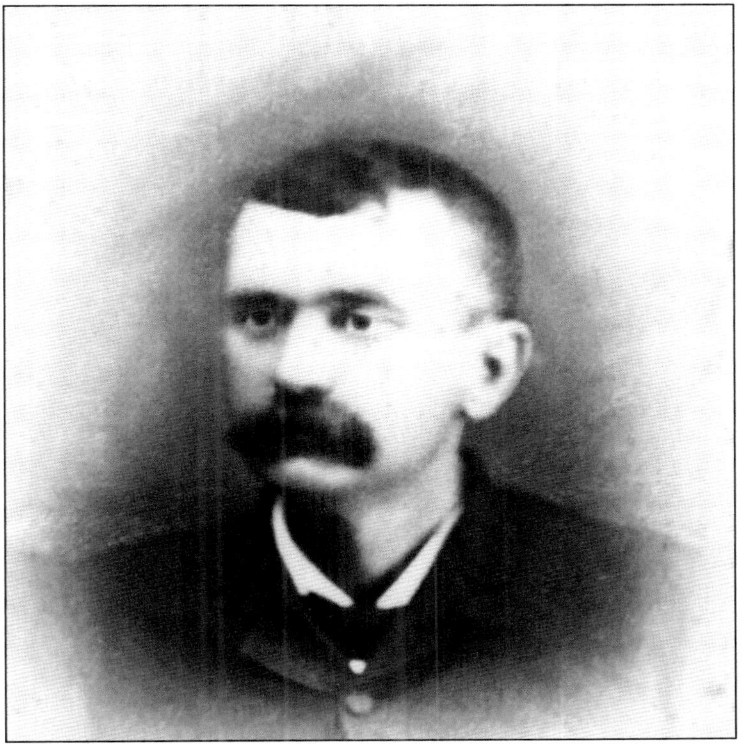

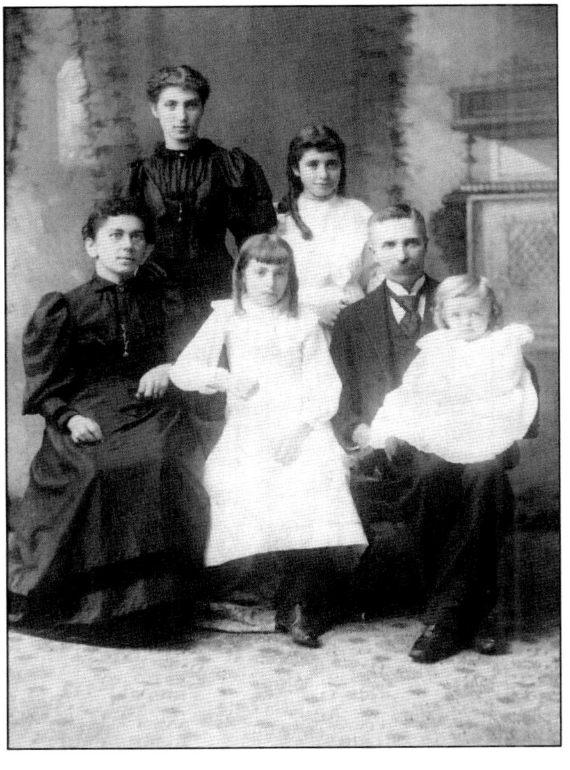

C. F. Tschanen also took this photograph of Louis Kinley and family between 1896 and 1899.

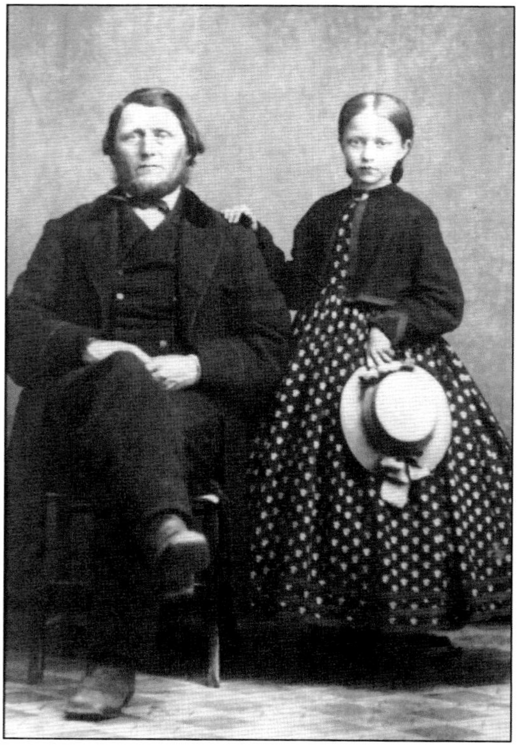

This early Carte de Visite of a gentleman and young girl was taken by Merrell and Brother in Upper Sandusky between 1861 and 1866.

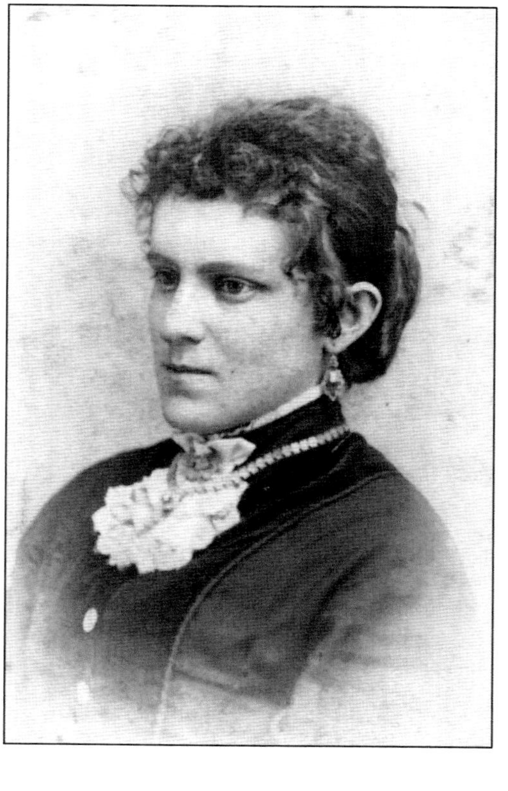

Daniel Rider took this photograph of a Mrs. Stecher between 1868 and 1870.

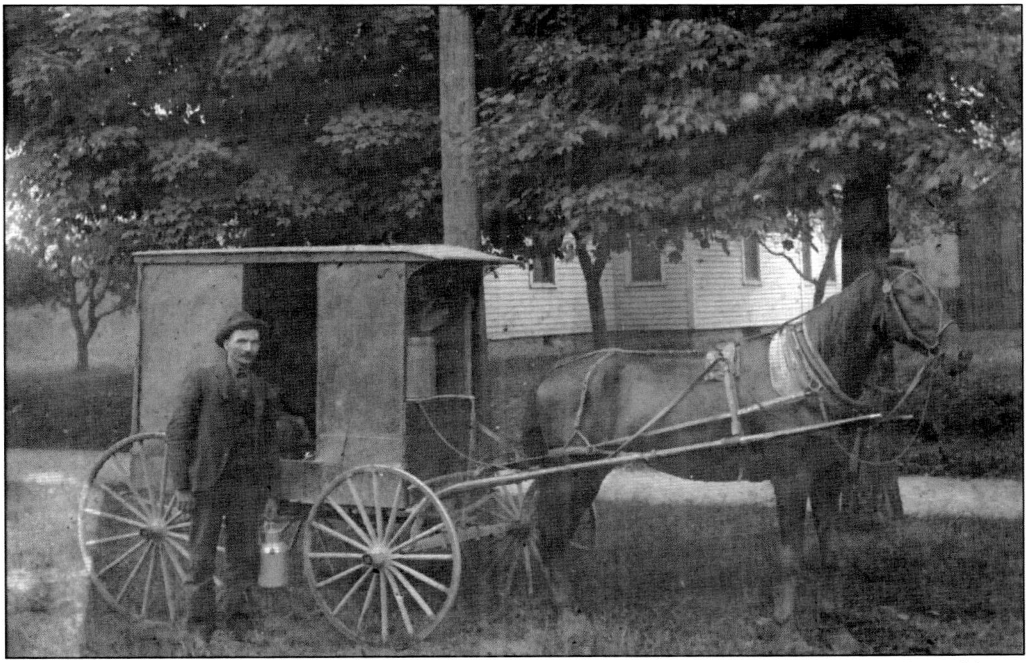

Jacob Hehr stands in front of his milk wagon in 1883. In Jacob's left hand is the milk pail he is getting ready to deliver to a residence.

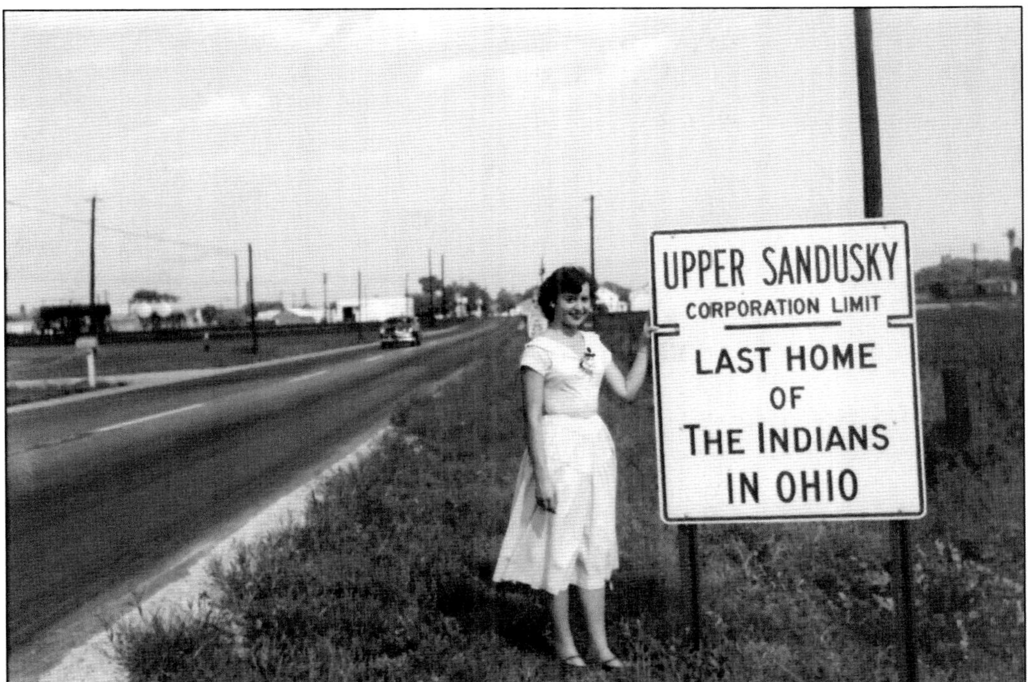

This young woman is standing on U.S. Route 30 just west of Upper Sandusky. Over her right shoulder is a white building that was the Fleetwing gas station.

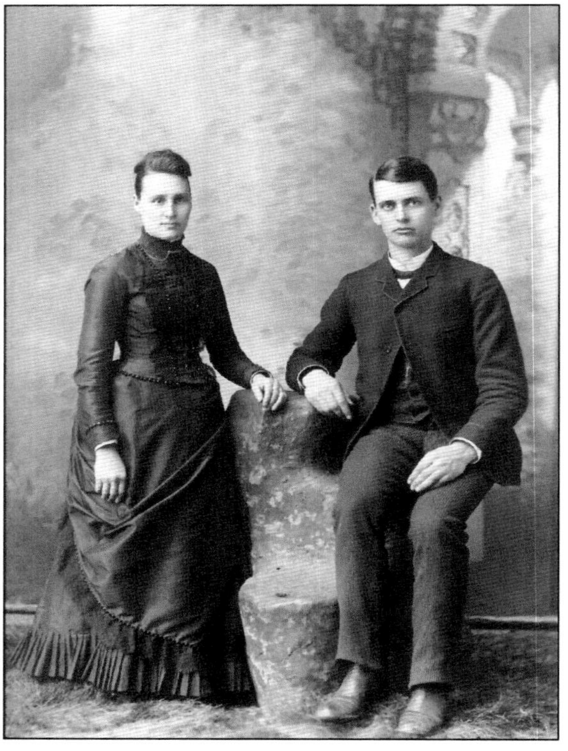

This photograph of a young couple was taken between 1887 and 1888 by J. McCahon.

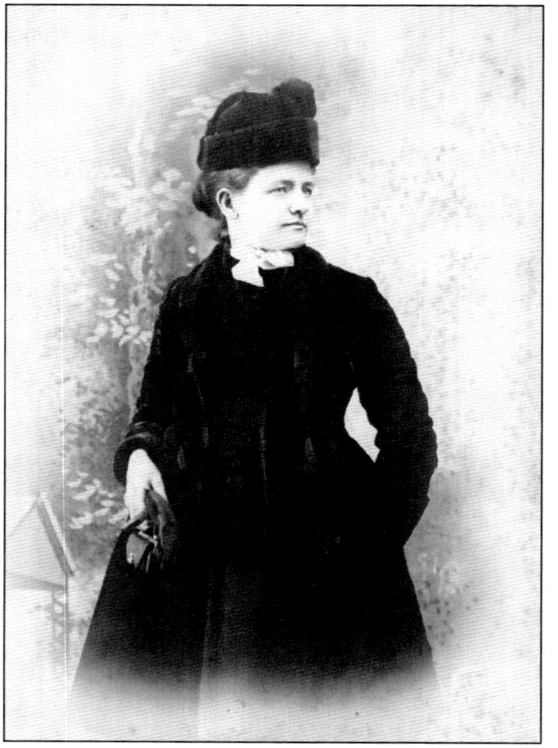

D. Brenner and Company Art Parlor took this photograph of an Upper Sandusky resident between 1896 and 1899.

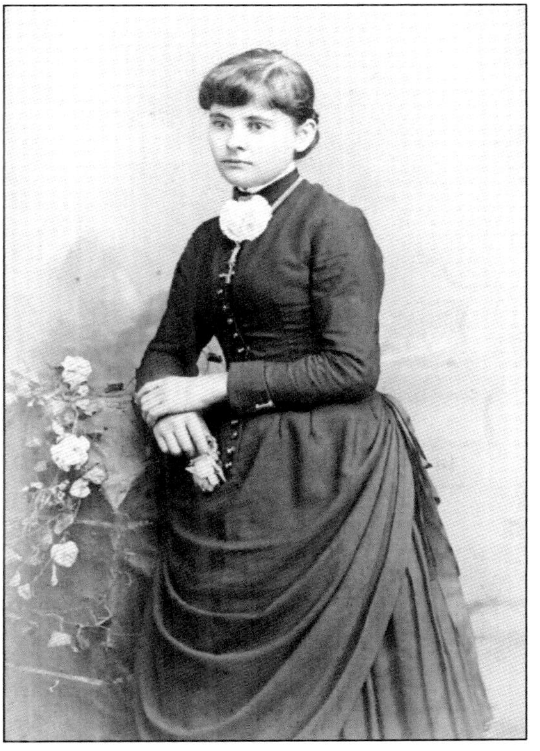

This Upper Sandusky woman's photograph was taken between 1885 and 1889 by James W. Wickenden.

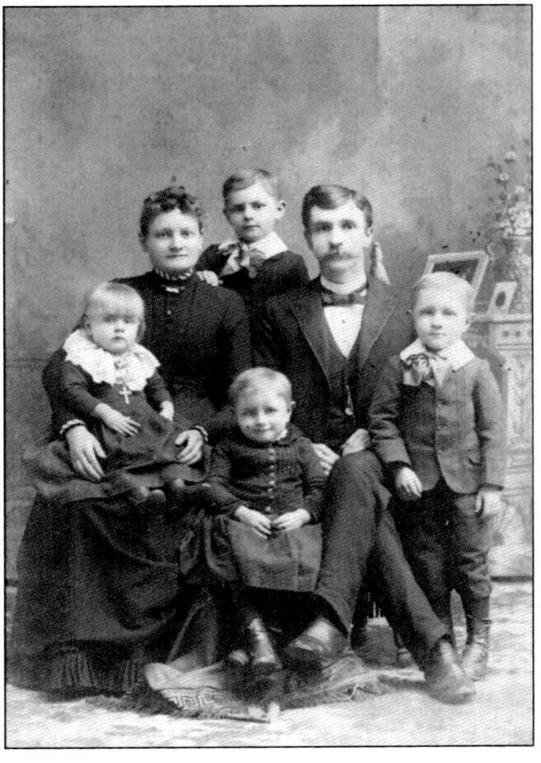

Stutz took this photograph of the John Kinley family. John is on the right and Caroline, his wife, is on the left. Their children were Harry, in the back; Villa, on the left; George, on the right; and J. Avery in the center.

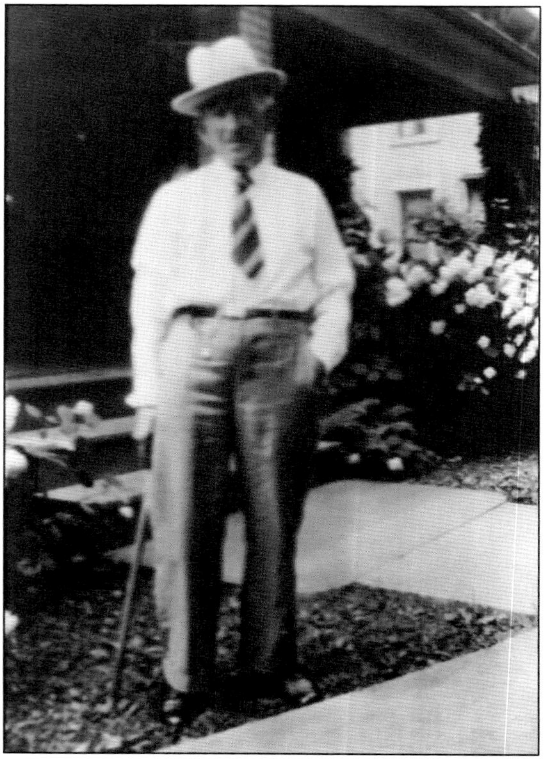

Frank H. Lang was born on June 26, 1856. As an adult, he was very involved in the Wyandot County Museum. He died on April, 24 1934.

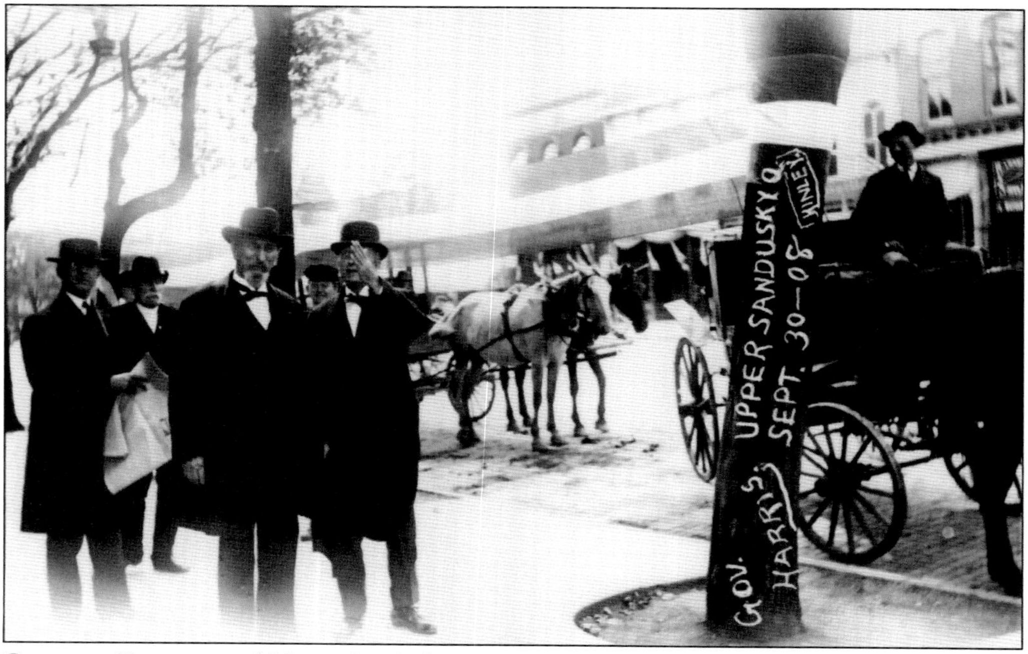

Governor Harris visited Upper Sandusky on September 30, 1908. This photograph was taken by Harry Kinley, a well known store owner and local historian. Harry was very dedicated to preserving the history of Upper Sandusky.

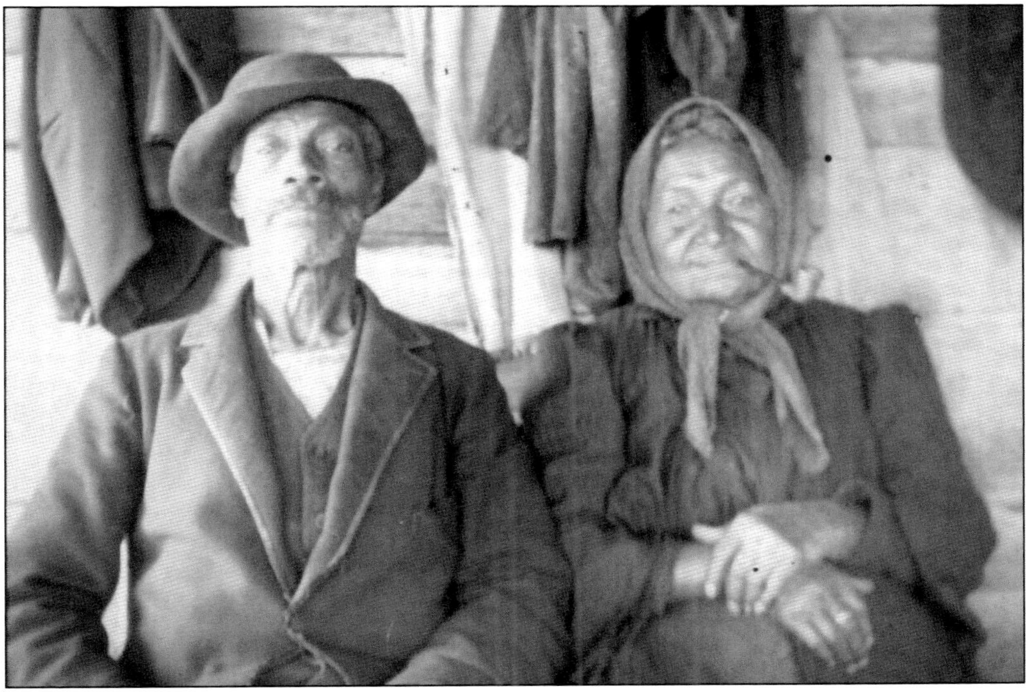

Written on the back of this photograph is "Mr. and Mrs. Peter Stansly, 108 Years Old, Last Negro couple to live in Upper Sandusky." The photograph is not dated.

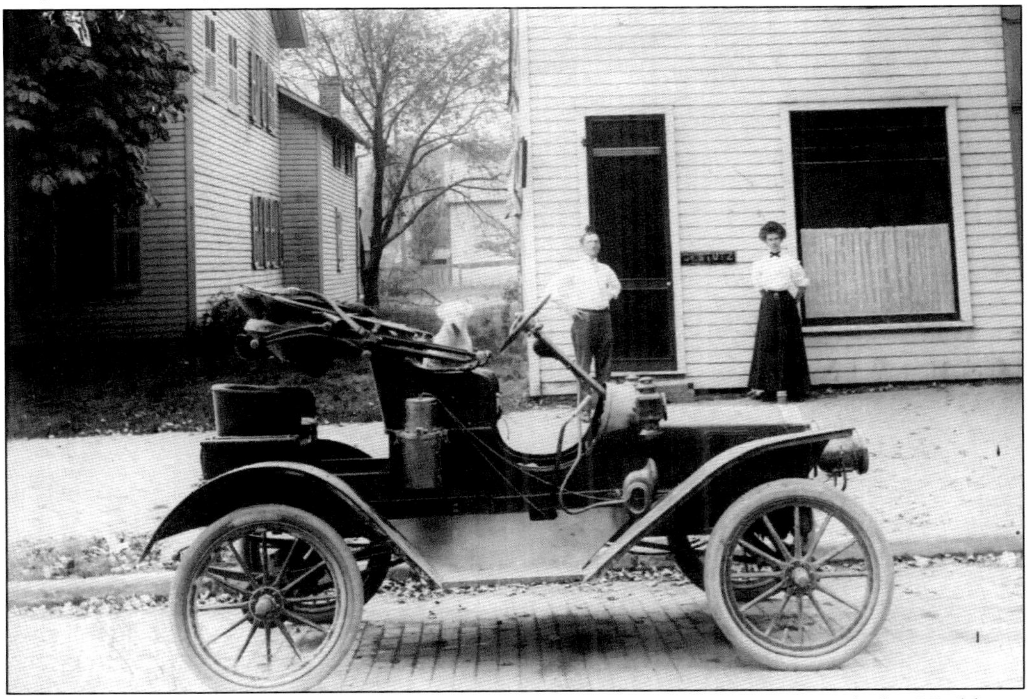

Doctor O. C. Stutz and his wife are standing in front of his office in Upper Sandusky. Visible on the house, to the right of the door, is his sign. A dog sits in the doctor's car.

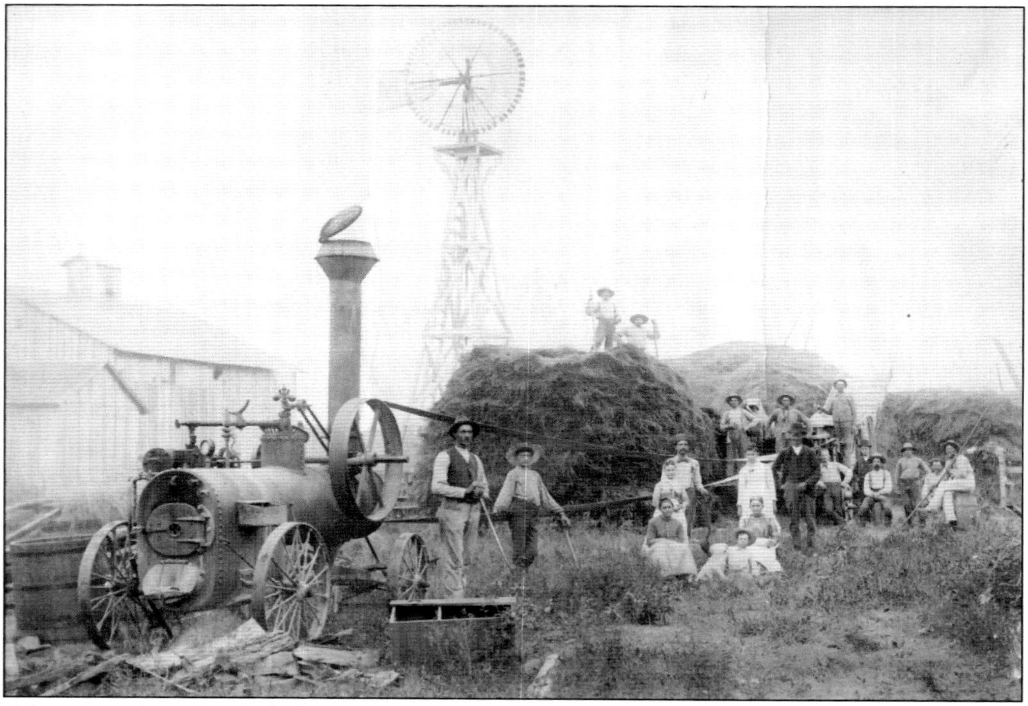

Often the whole family had a job to do when the threshing machine came to the farm. The women had to make sure everyone was fed while the men worked in the fields. Time was of the essence due to the scarcity of the thresher.

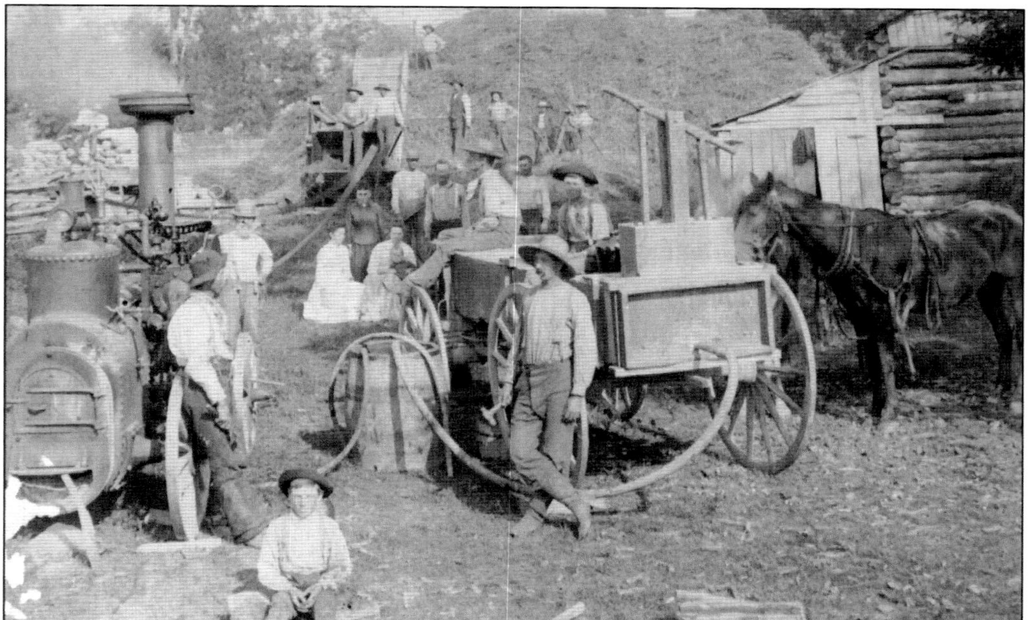

Here is a threshing machine in action during summer 1882. The threshing machines were often moved from farm to farm with the whole neighborhood involved.

Winter Halter was the ticket manager for the railroad station in Upper Sandusky.

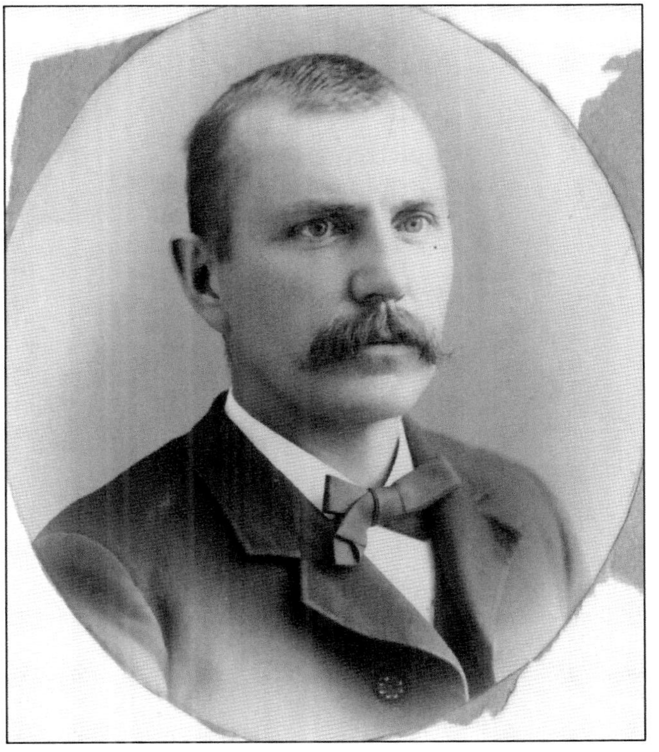

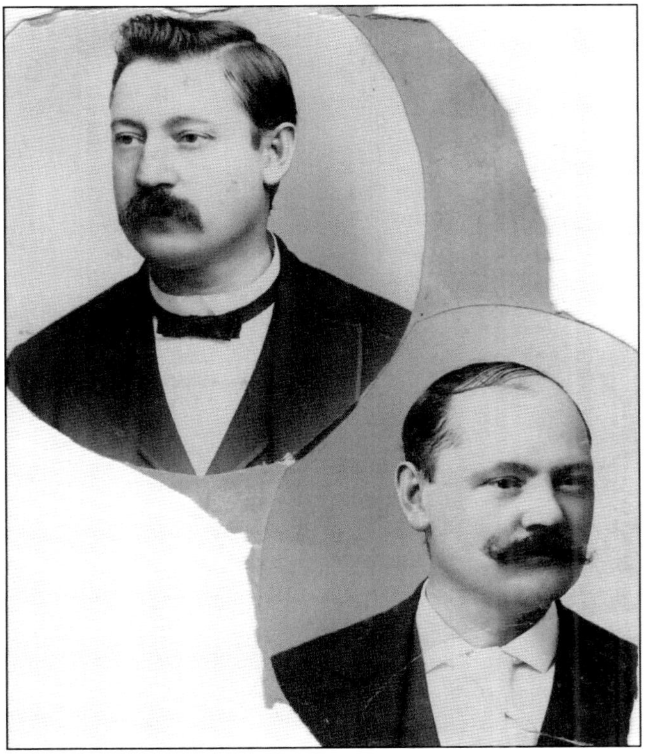

John Vogel (top) and Henry Vogel were the sons of Frank Vogel and kept the Vogel name in the clothing business for quite some time. This photograph of the brothers was taken around 1896.

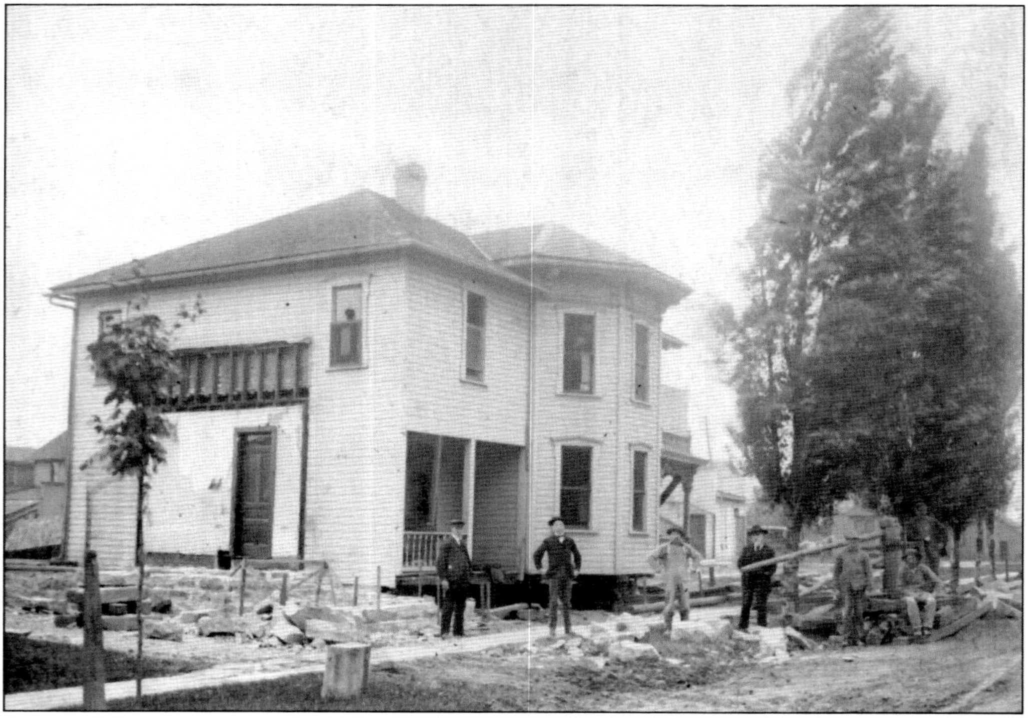

A remodeling project at the Saltsman House on West Wyandot Avenue is seen here. The Saltsman family was involved in a livery stable business on the corner of West Wyandot Avenue and North 7th Street.

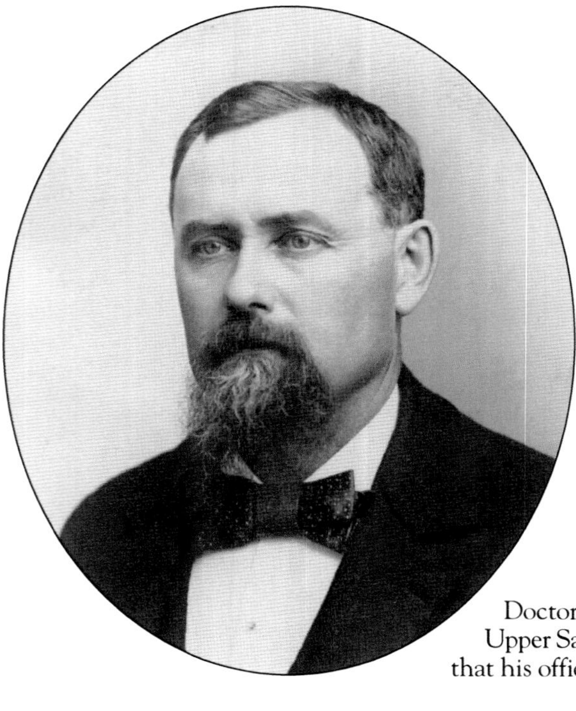

Doctor W. J. Matthews had a dentist practice in Upper Sandusky during 1927 and 1928. It is believed that his office was in the rear of his residence.

Six

Home Life and Happy Times

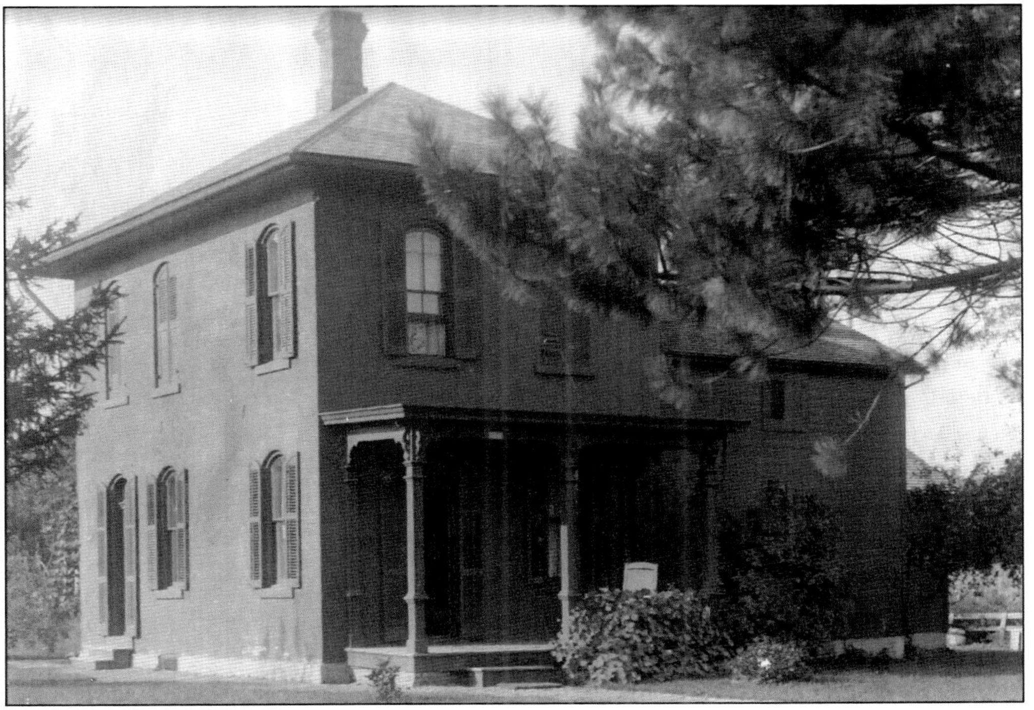

Pictured here is the home of Doctor W. J. Matthews on West Wyandot.

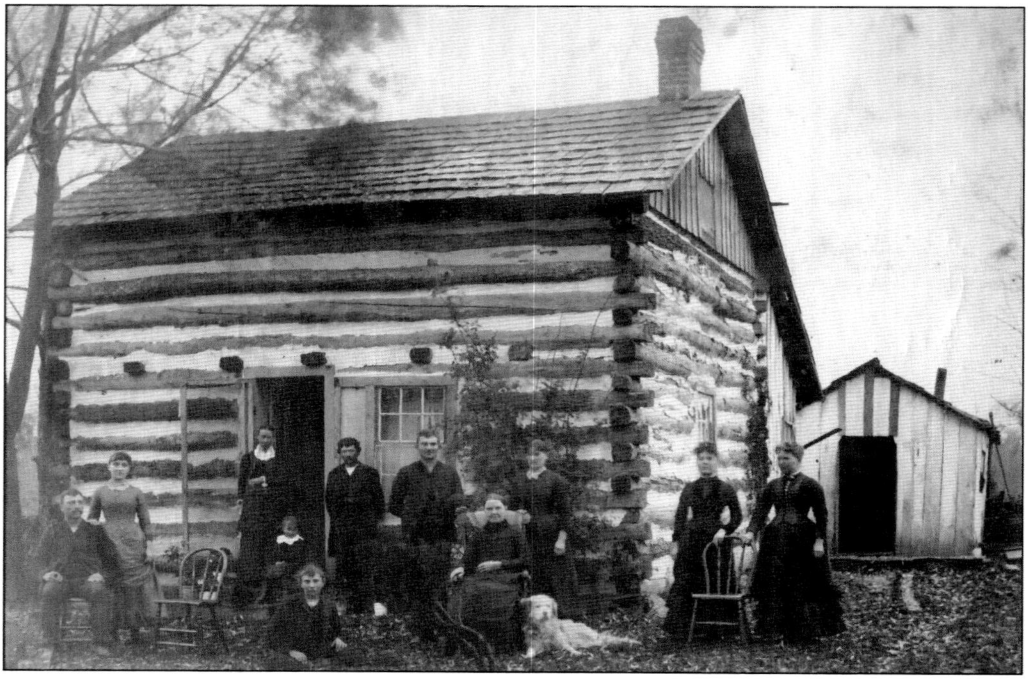

The Mrs. S. Disher farm is pictured here in 1885. A log cabin and shed are in the back. It was common to have more than one family living in the same cabin.

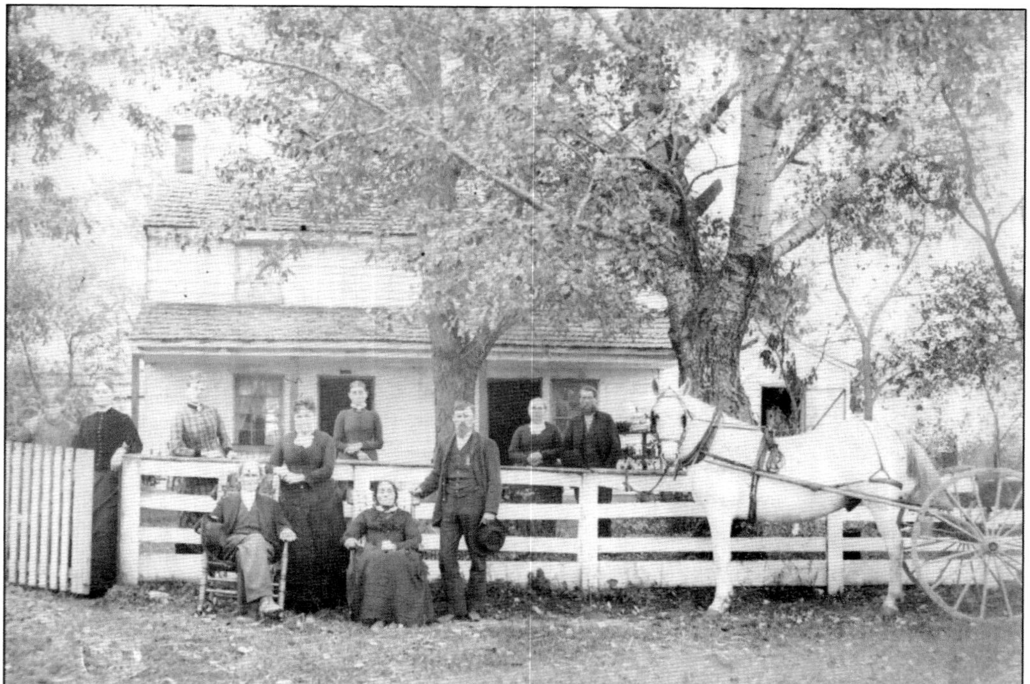

This is an 1885 view of the John Ragon Farm in Crane Township. The man on the far right wears a Grand Army of the Republic badge and ribbon on his jacket.

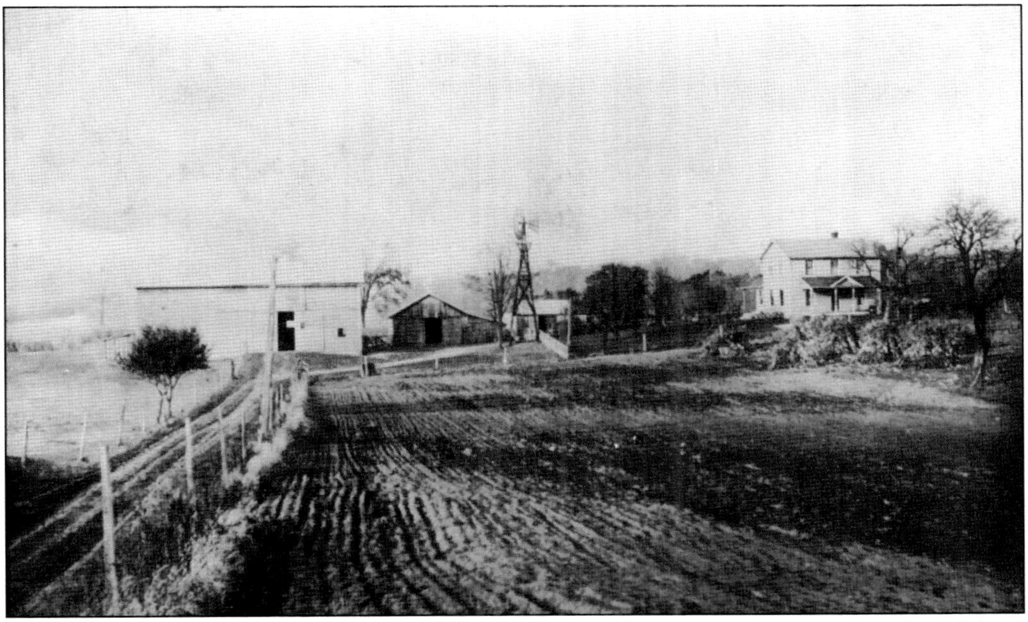

The Michael M. Schwebel farm, located on Hardscrabble Road in Crane Township, is seen here in 1915. (Photograph from the collection of Tom and Marnie Hill.)

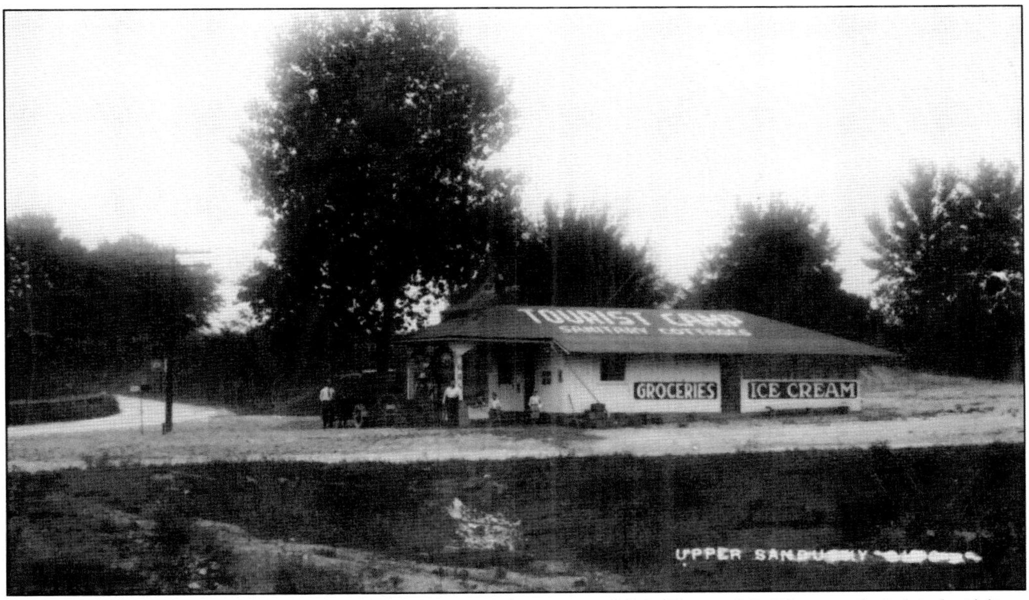

Travelers could always count on a place to stay when using U.S. Route 30. The roof of this building just outside of Upper Sandusky reads "Tourist Camp Sanitary Cottages." The establishment also had groceries for the hunger pain and gasoline for automobiles. (Photograph from the collection of Tom and Marnie Hill.)

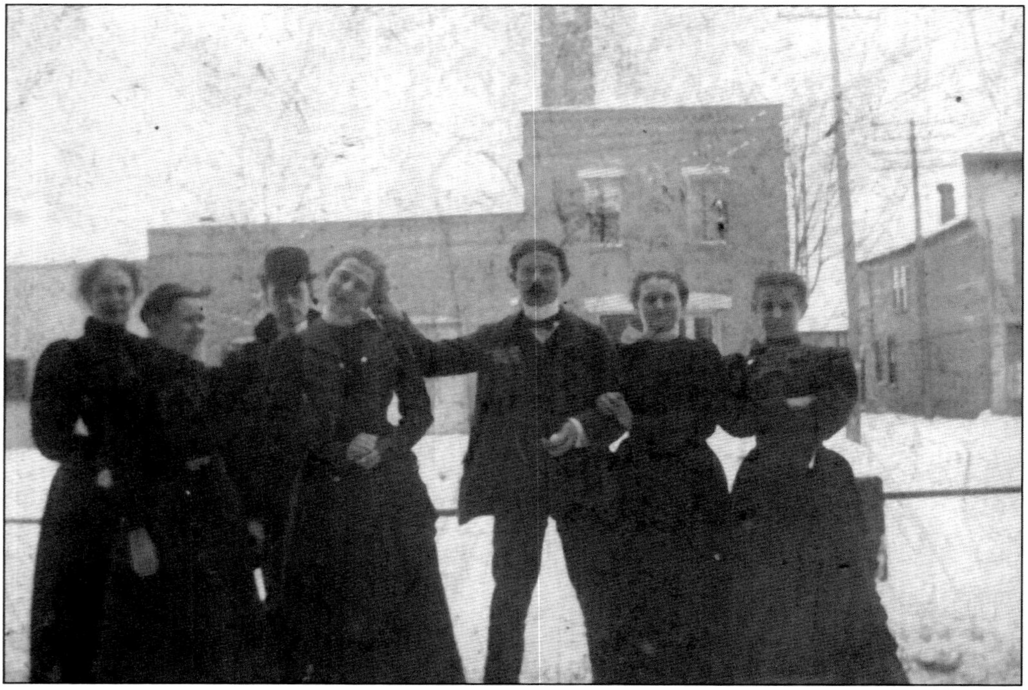

Upper Sandusky residents gather in front of Worellos Ice Cream parlor at 116 West Wyandot Avenue on December 7, 1891. The old city building is in the background.

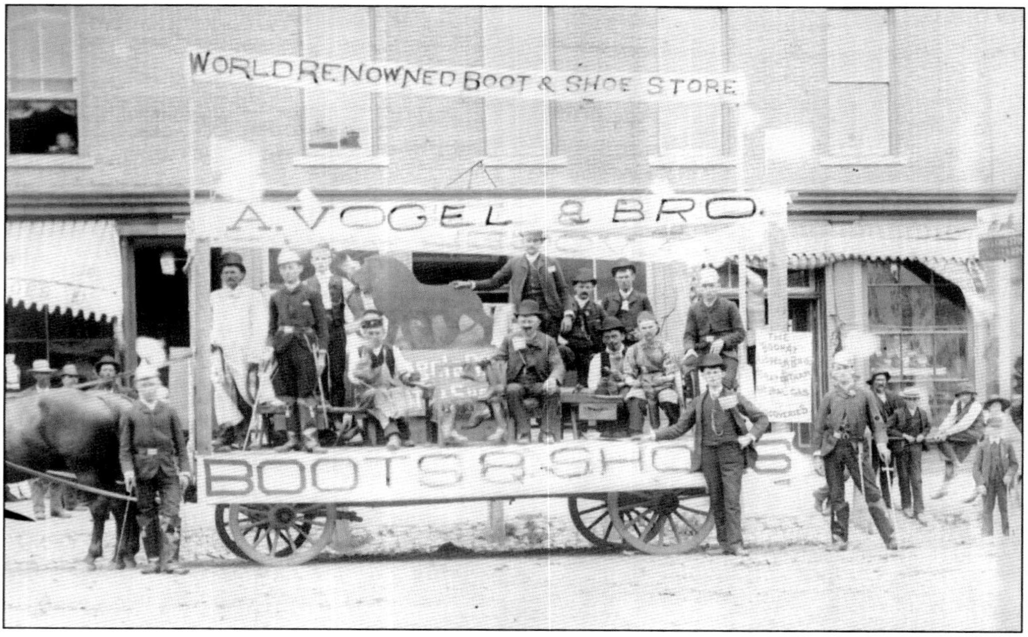

This photograph of the Upper Sandusky Parade featuring the Vogel and Brothers Shoe Store Float was taken by photographer J. D. Cress and Company on July 4, 1888. The sign on the back of the float reads "The Boon at Vogel and Brothers Greater than Natural Gas Discoveries." This was their first year in business.

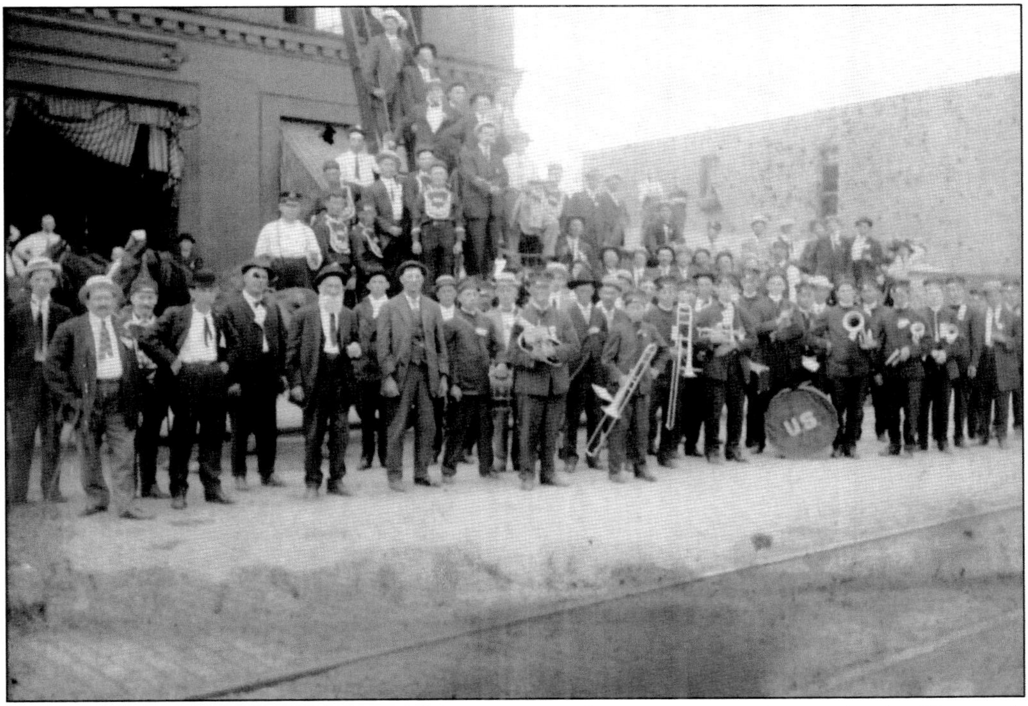

The Upper Sandusky band in Lima, Ohio, was on their way to participate in the Fireman's Convention. Firemen stand with ornate bibs on the front of their uniforms.

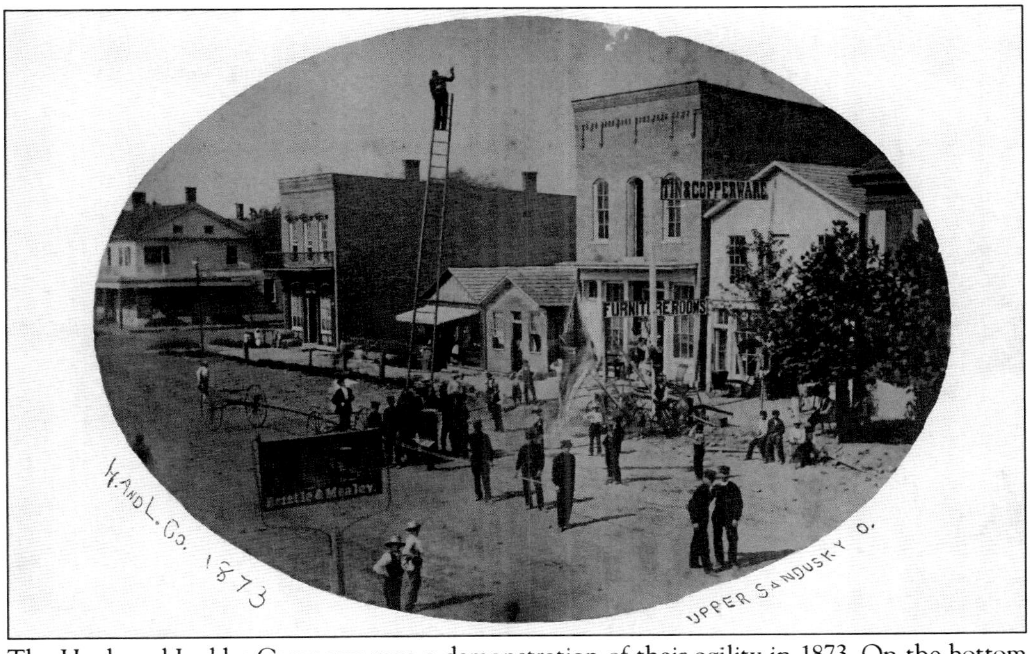

The Hook and Ladder Company gave a demonstration of their agility in 1873. On the bottom left, a sign reads "Beistle and Mealey." On the right, the sign on top of the white building reads "Tin and Copperware" and "Furniture Rooms."

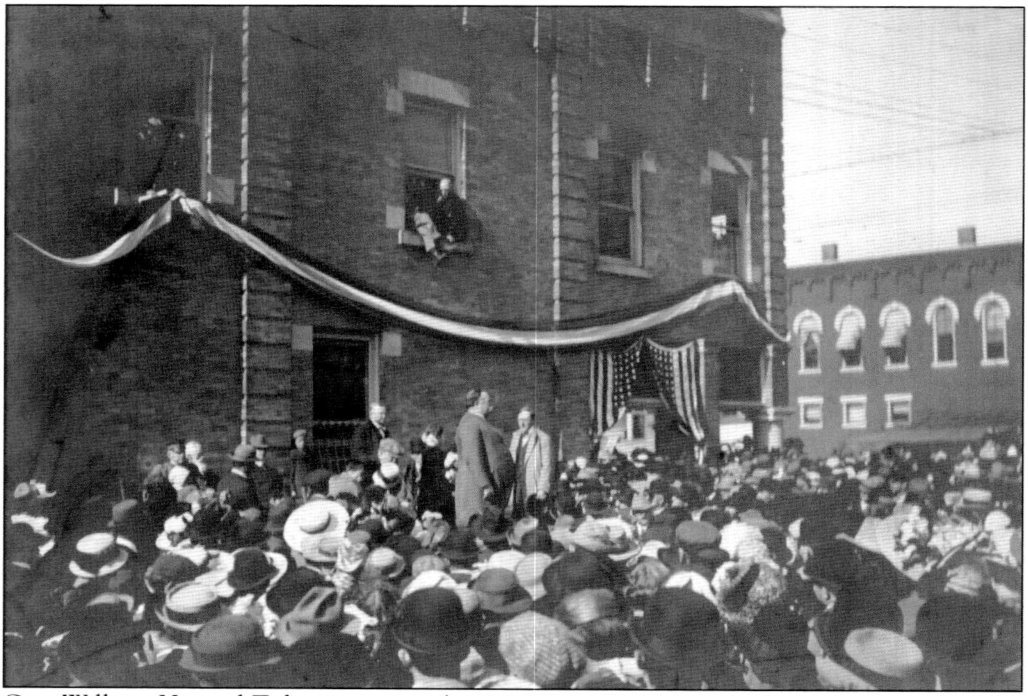

Gov. William Howard Taft gives a speech to spectators in Upper Sandusky around 1907. Taft became the 27th president of the United States and served from 1908 until 1912. Taft is standing in front of the Citizens Savings Bank, which is the First Citizens National Bank today. Note the spectators in the windows trying to get a better look at the festivities. (Photograph from the collection of Tom and Marnie Hill.)

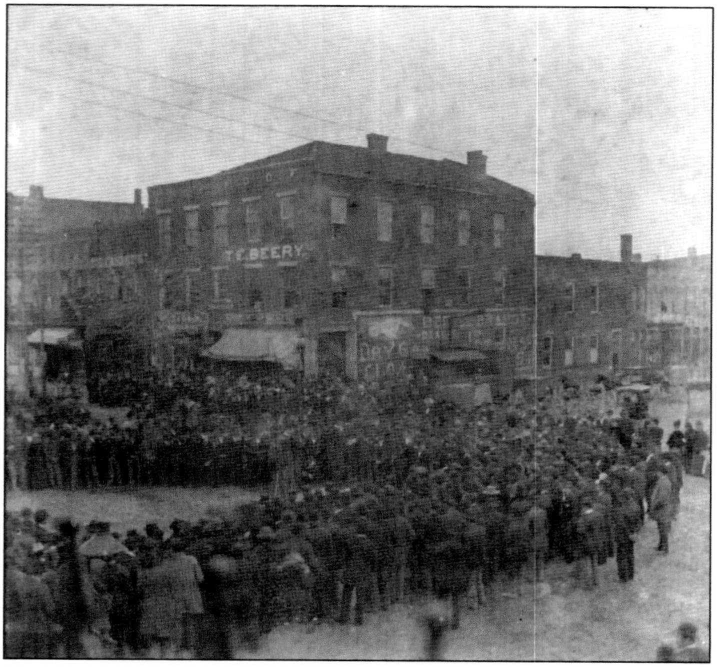

Spectators are gathered in front of the Beery Building in Upper Sandusky in the 1880s.

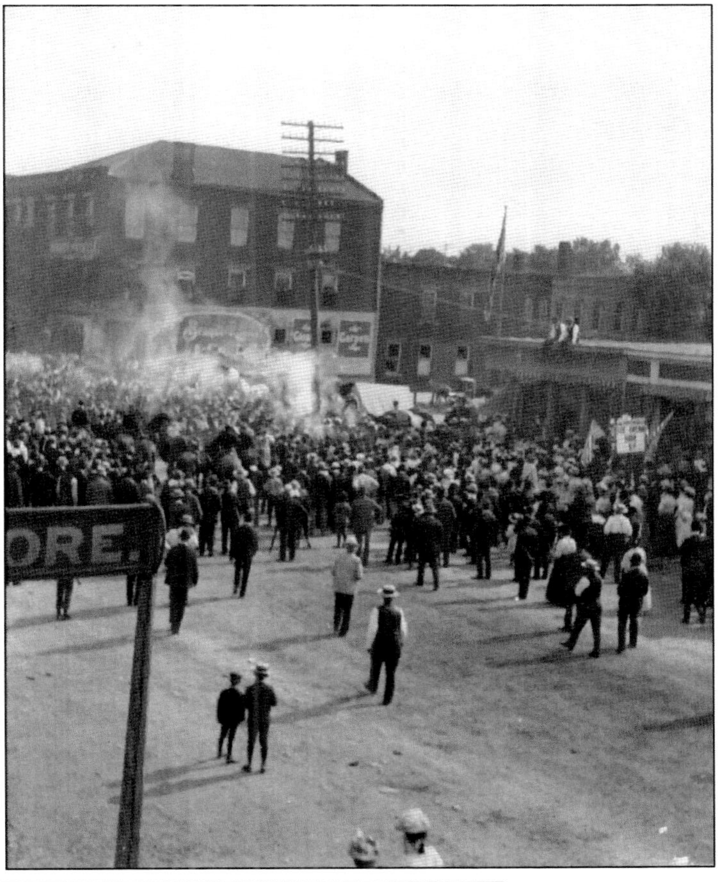

The Brandt Reille Block on Wyandot and Sandusky Avenues is pictured here in 1902. Sandusky Avenue was bricked in 1904. On the roof of the hardware building, men sit and watch the festivities. The sign to the right reads "Ice cream, soda 5¢."

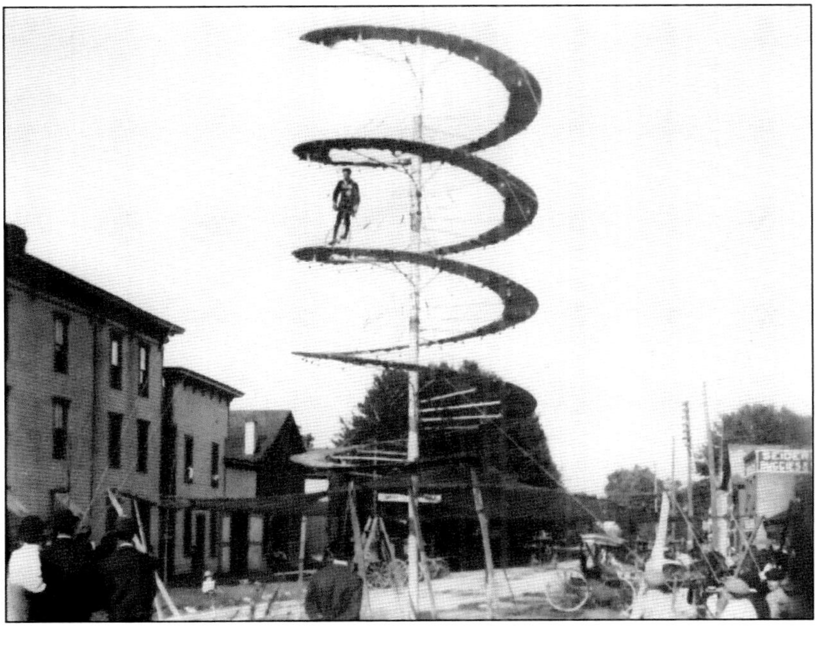

A carnival unicycle act performs for a crowd on East Wyandot Avenue by Seider and Son's Wagon and Storm Cabs Factory. Lights line the track all the way down to the ground. A net surrounds the structure in case of an accident.

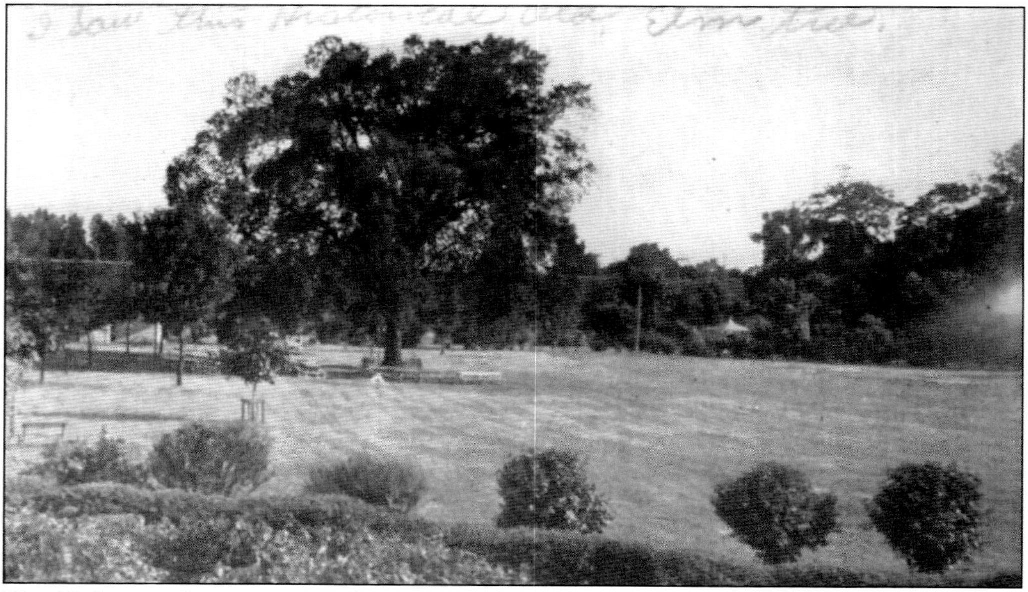

The Tschanen elm tree is seen here at Harrison Smith Park. After the tree was removed, a monument honoring the three men responsible for the park was erected on the spot where the tree formerly stood. (Photograph from the collection of Tom and Marnie Hill.)

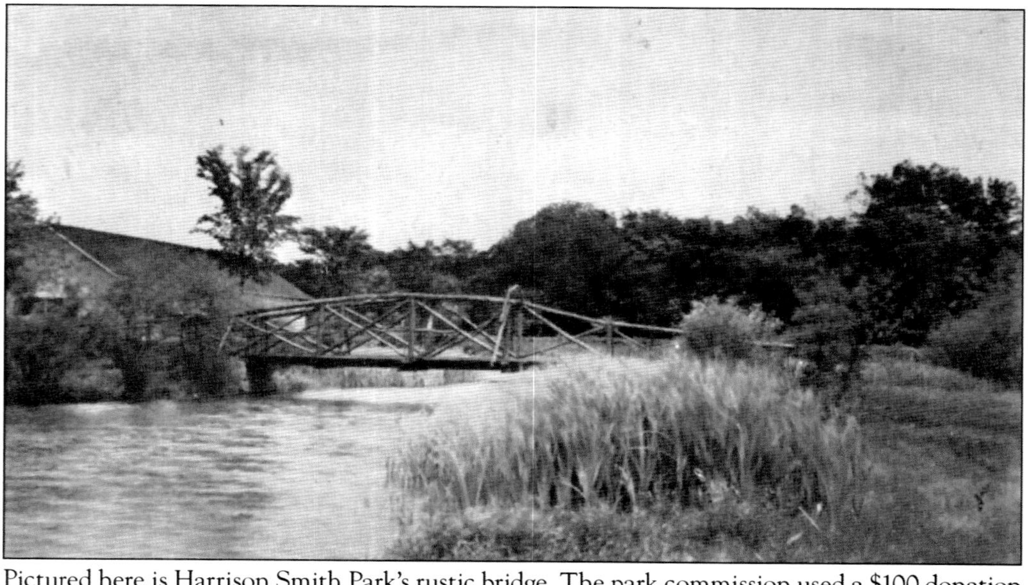

Pictured here is Harrison Smith Park's rustic bridge. The park commission used a $100 donation from the American Legion for the construction of the bridge, which connected the lagoon with the swimming pool. The bridge was built in the fall of 1923. The pavilion was built in the summer of 1923. (Photograph from the collection of Tom and Marnie Hill.)

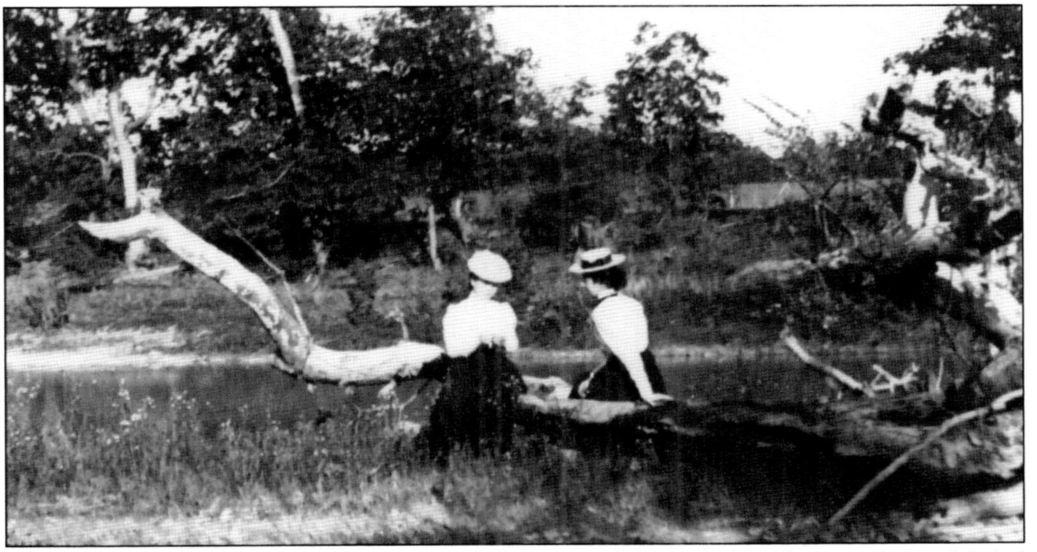

Young women sit on a sycamore tree in the 1800s or early 1900s. This photograph was labeled as Battle Island.

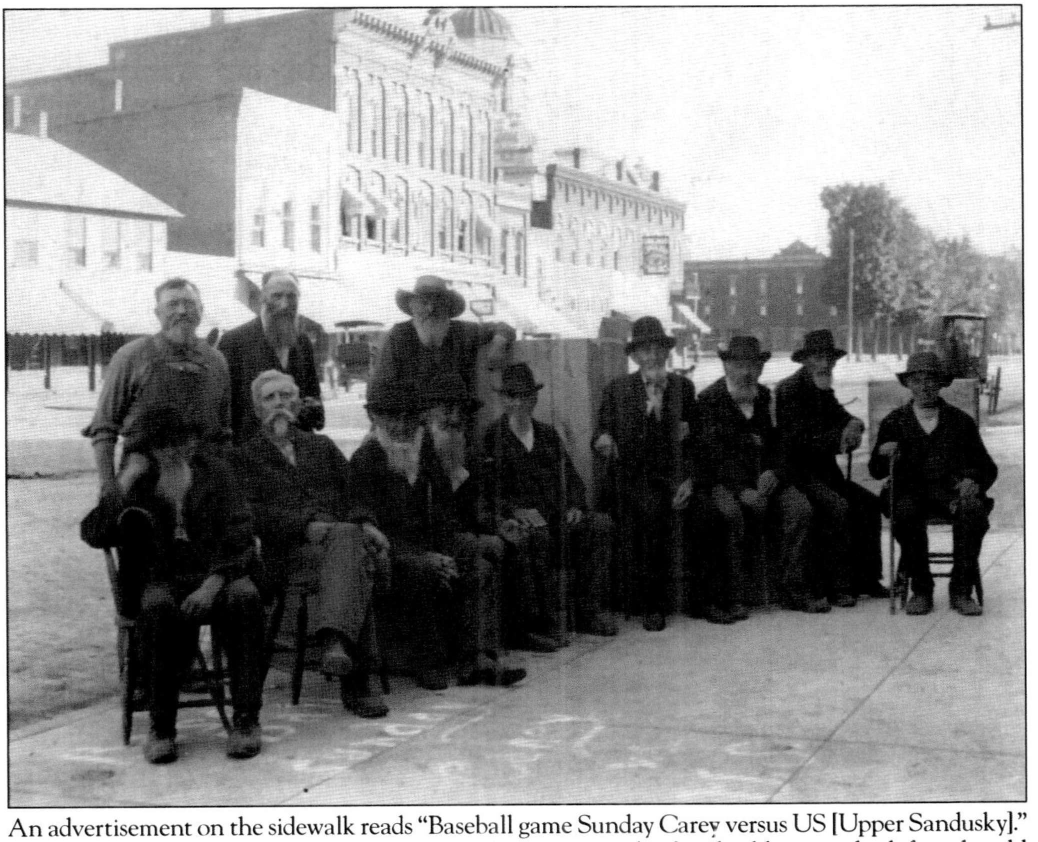

An advertisement on the sidewalk reads "Baseball game Sunday Carey versus US [Upper Sandusky]." This photograph was taken on North Sandusky Avenue. The first building on the left is the old Hinkleman Saloon, which today houses the Loose Family Furniture Store.

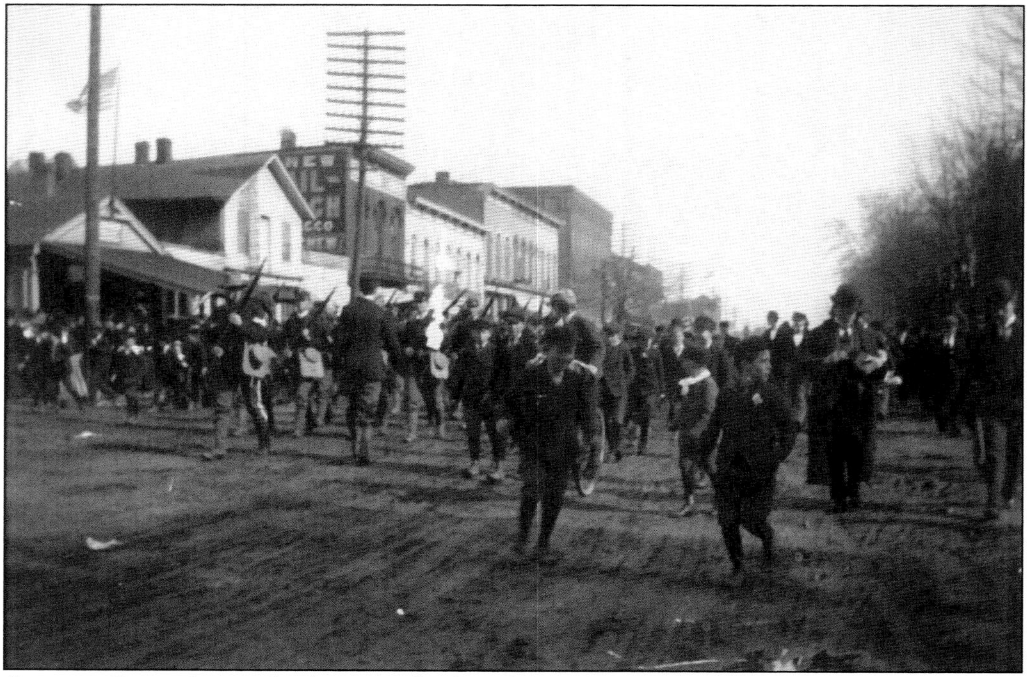

Company B marches to the depot on the day of their departure for the Spanish American War. The photograph, taken in 1898, shows buildings on the left at the Johnson Street corner.

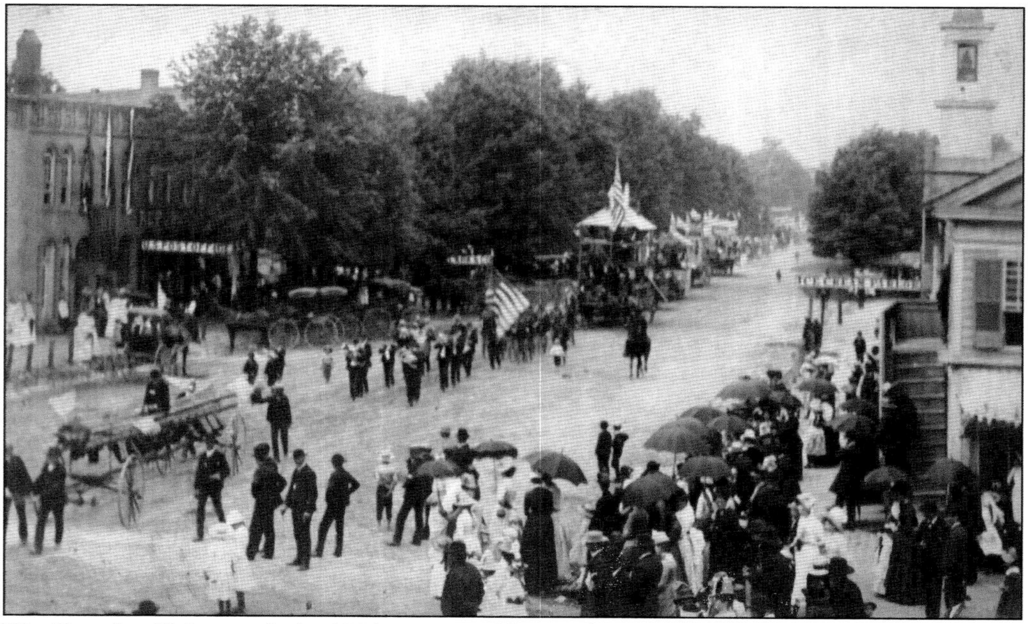

The Fourth of July parade for 1884 is pictured here. The Citizens Bank corner is on the right. The post office is on the left side of the street. On the same side, just a few doors down, is Clark and Company. On the opposite side of the street a sign reads "Ice Cream Parlor." Two men at the head of the parade pull a firemen's ladder wagon.

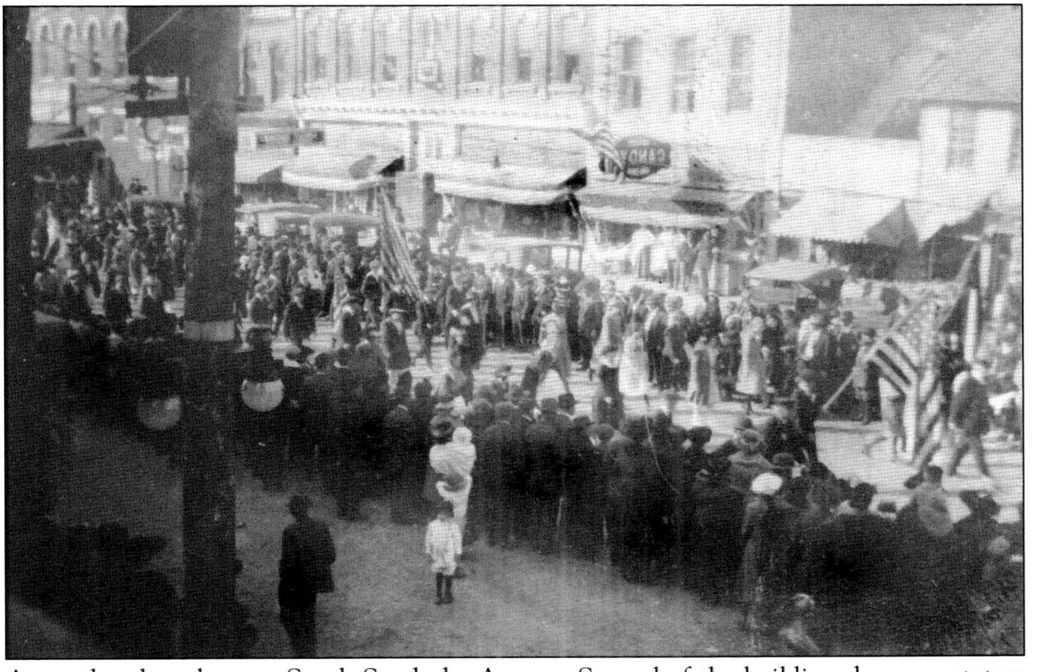

A parade takes place on South Sandusky Avenue. Several of the buildings have spectators watching from windows to get a good view of the activities. (Photograph from the collection of Tom and Marnie Hill.)

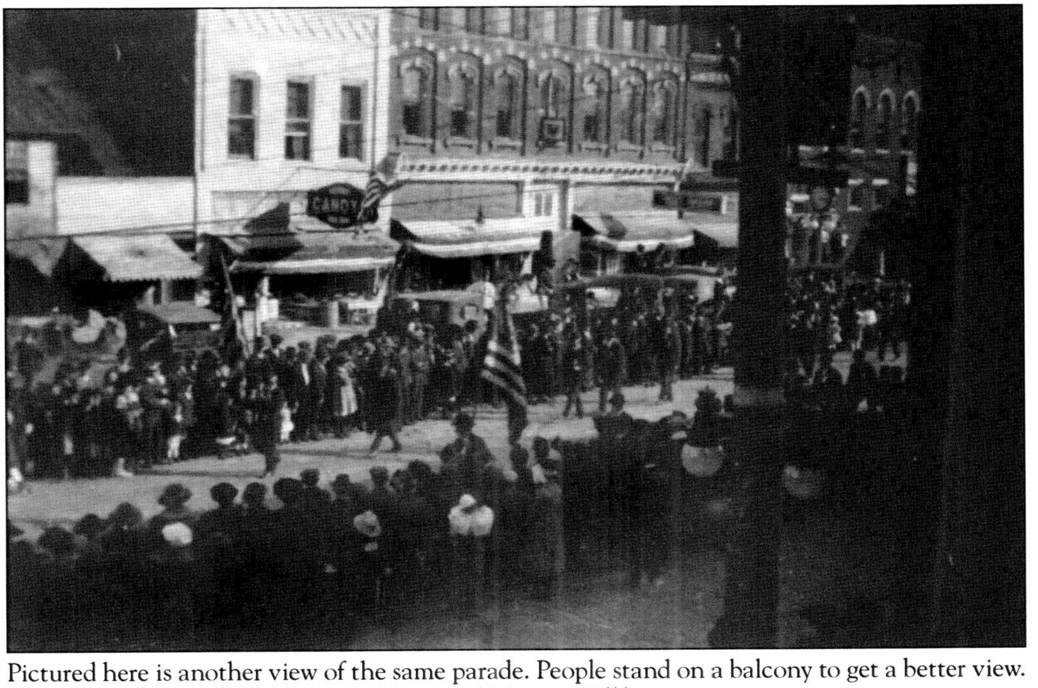

Pictured here is another view of the same parade. People stand on a balcony to get a better view. (Photograph from the collection of Tom and Marnie Hill.)

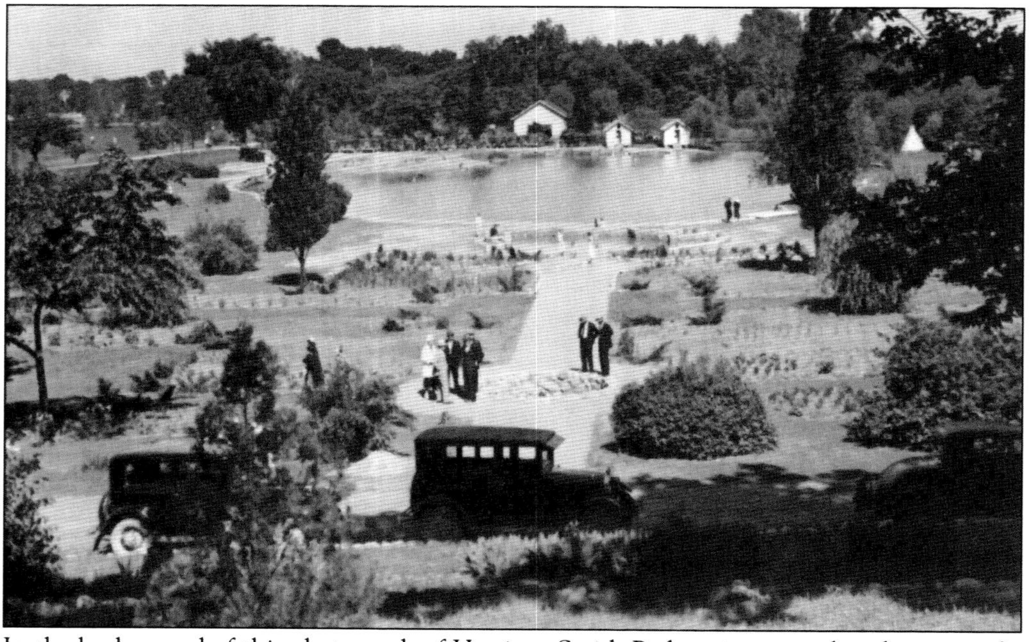

In the background of this photograph of Harrison Smith Park, swimmers take advantage of a summer day. A teepee stands between the trees to the far right. (Photograph from the collection of Tom and Marnie Hill.)

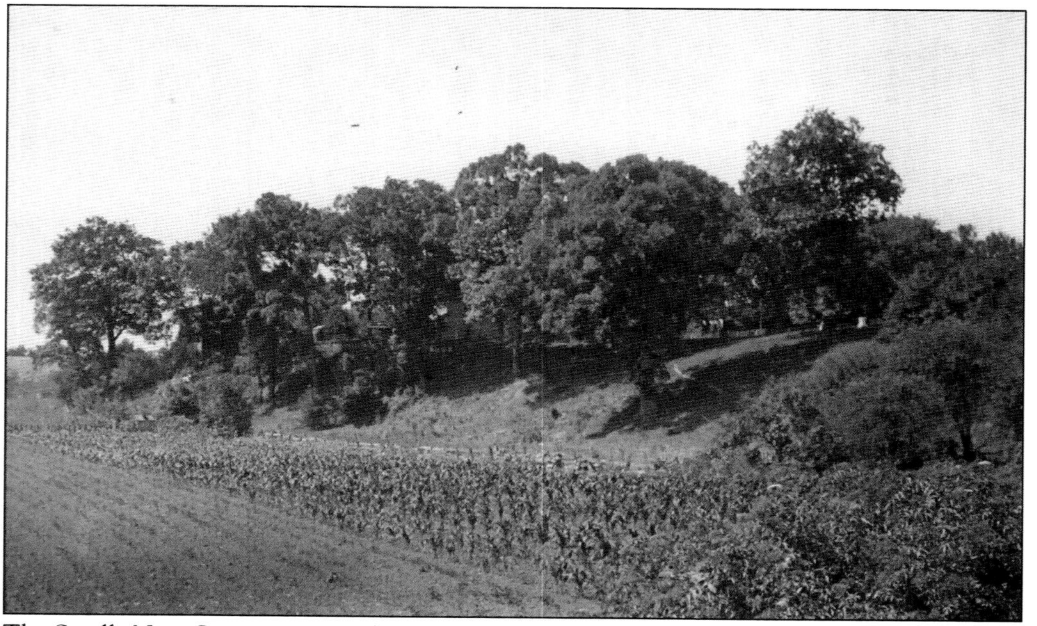

The Smally Naus Sanatorium can be seen in the background of this photograph of West Hill in Harrison Smith Park.

The Human Fly climbs one of the columns of the Wyandot County Courthouse. The back of his jacket reads "New Overland 4." The Human Fly was Henry "Dare-Devil" Roland. Roland was born in Germany on March 2, 1894, and grew up in Pennsylvania. Around 1915 he joined a circus as a juggler; it isn't known when he switched to climbing. Roland's wife Anna and daughter Helen would travel with him.

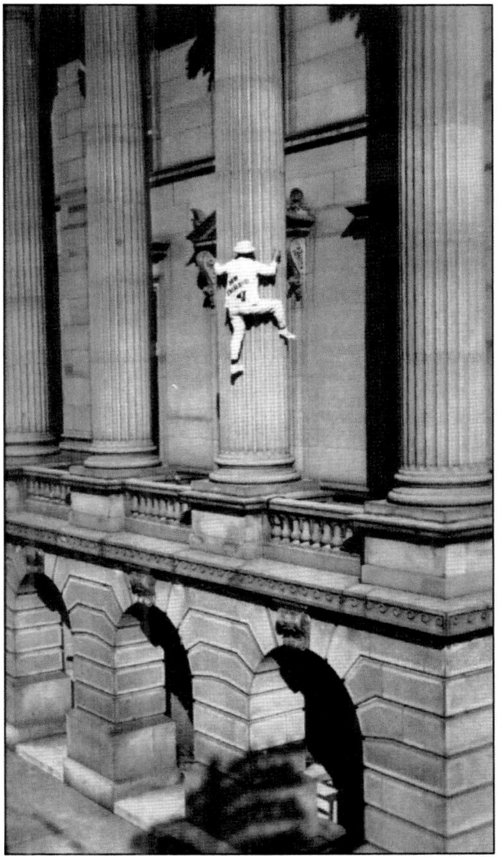

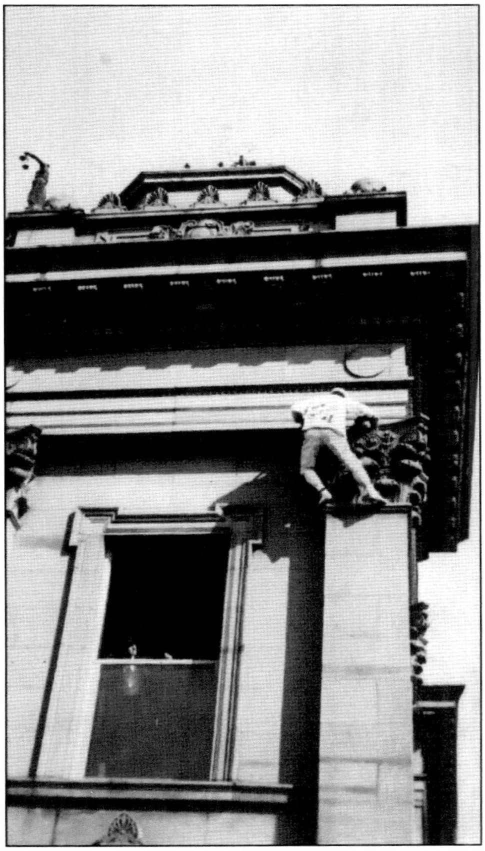

The Human Fly won international fame by balancing a chair on top of the 22-story Roosevelt Hotel in Seattle, Washington; his first mishap occurred when he fell 35 feet in Bloomfield, Iowa in 1924 and broke his hip. In 1925 he was in Lorain, Ohio to make another climb. On October 8, 1937, he fell 62 feet in Ottway, Tennessee and was rushed to the hospital in nearby Greeneville, Tennessee, where he was pronounced dead upon arrival. He was 43 years old.

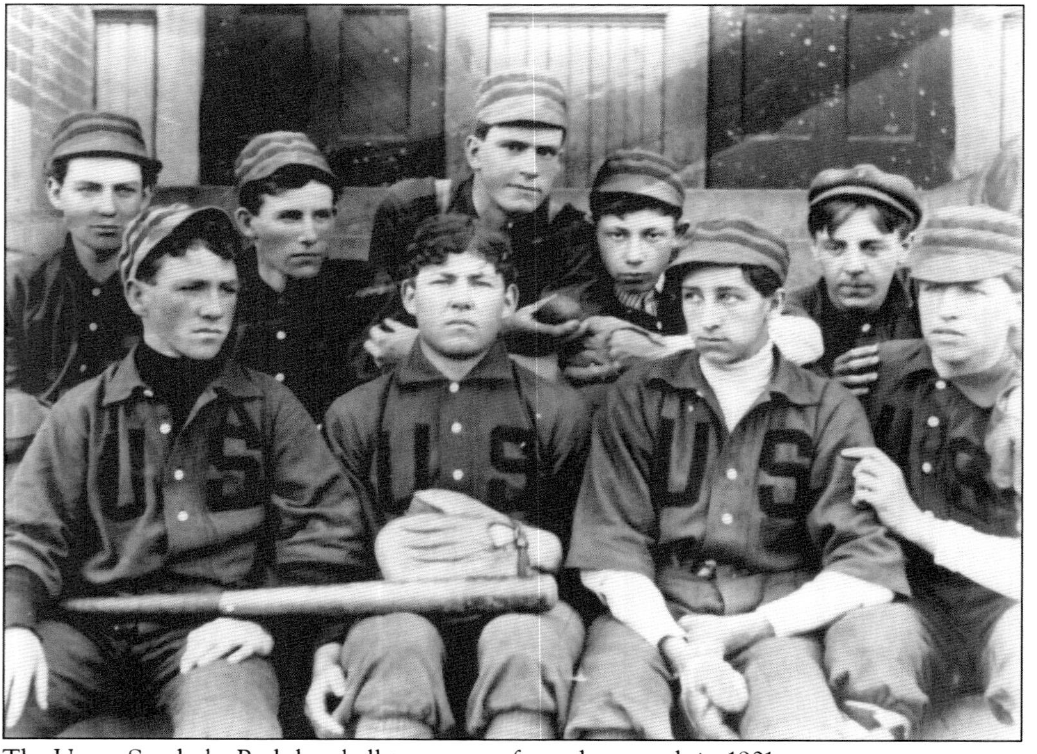

The Upper Sandusky Reds baseball team poses for a photograph in 1901.

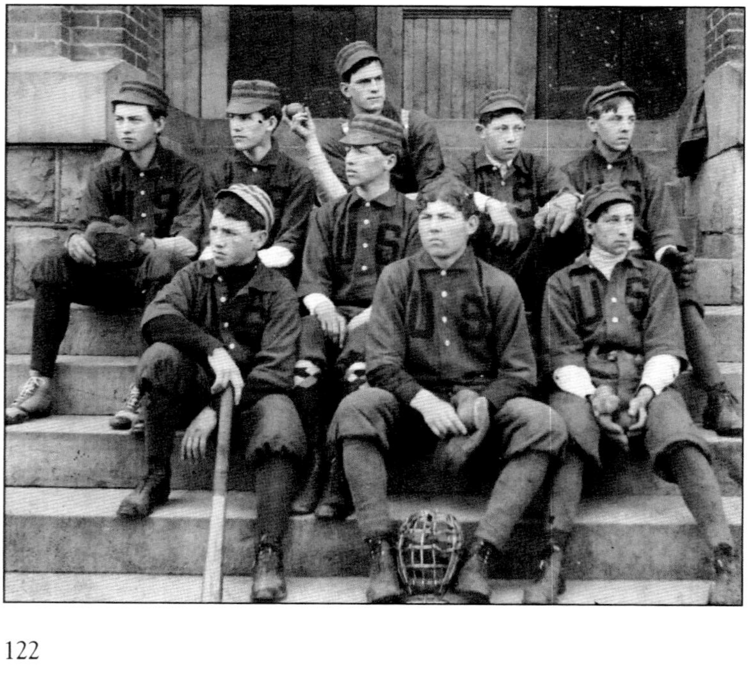

The Upper Sandusky baseball team is seen here in 1901. The team consisted of Bob Hare, second base; V. W. Brinkerhoff, fielder; William Berg, catcher; Charles Hitchcock, shortstop; Ralph Philbrick, first base; Earl Hunt, fielder; Don Golden, pitcher; Bob Henderson, fielder; and Herbert Stephenson, third base.

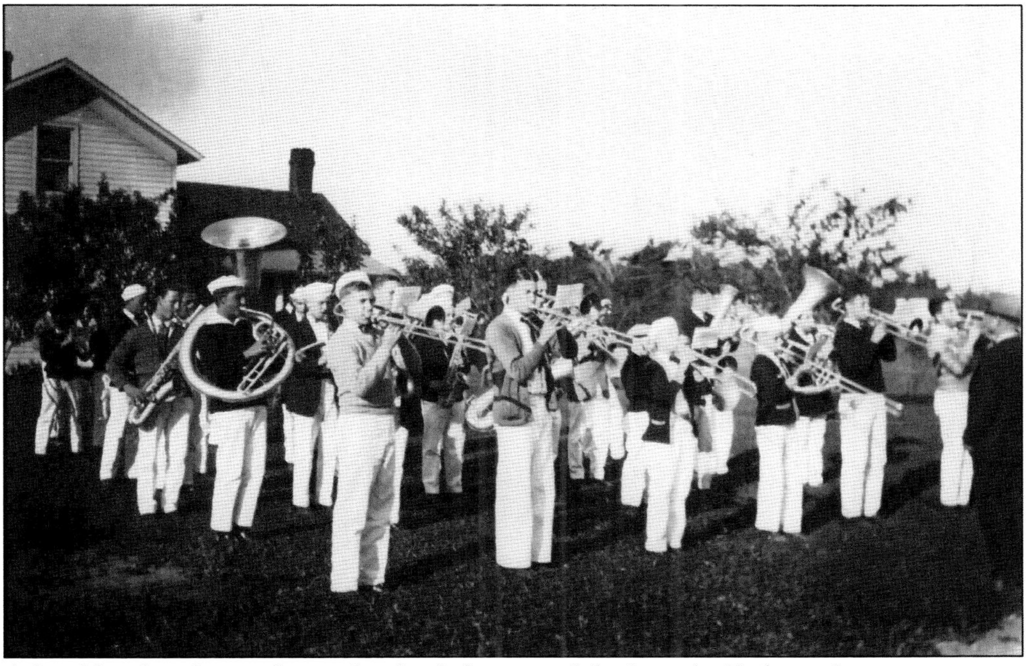

A local band is shown playing for the dedication of the Lincoln Highway. It was a common practice to have local entertainment for these festivities.

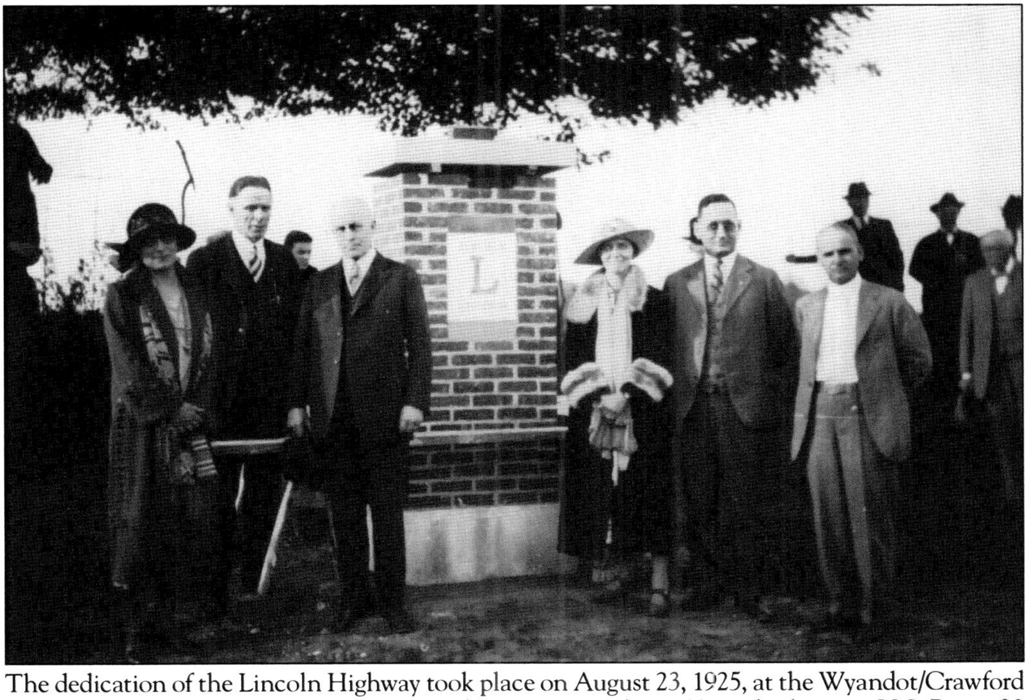

The dedication of the Lincoln Highway took place on August 23, 1925, at the Wyandot/Crawford County line. The route is designated Wyandot County Highway 330 today because U.S. Route 30 was relocated a mile south of old route 30 and is now a four lane highway, opened in late 2004.

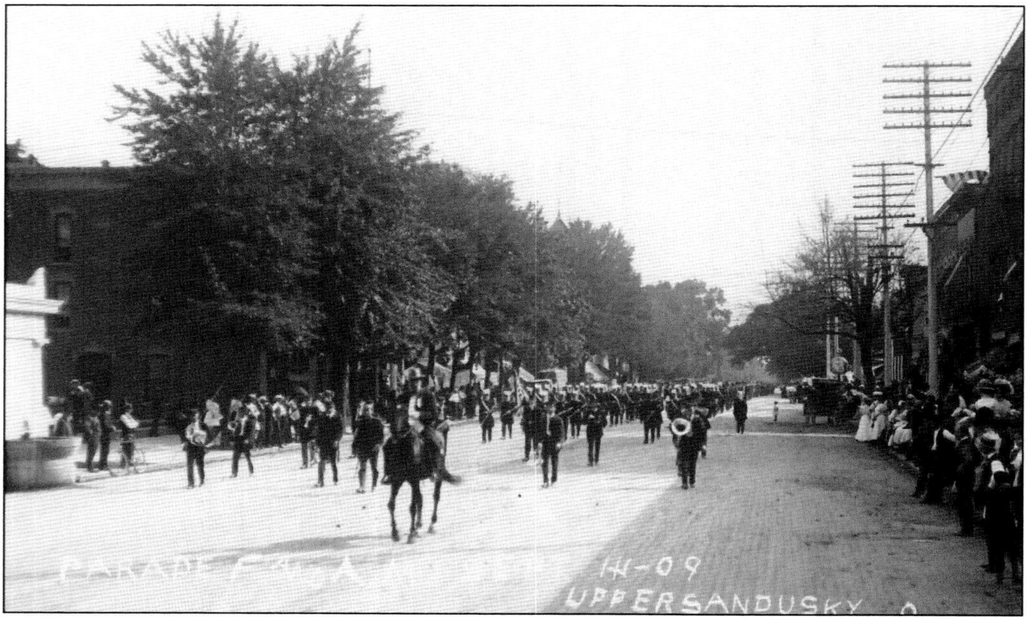

A parade of the Free and Accepted Masons celebrates the laying of the Mason's cornerstone on September 14, 1909. To the left of the lead horse is a partial view of the Stevens Memorial Fountain. The Wyandot County Courthouse is out of sight behind the fountain.

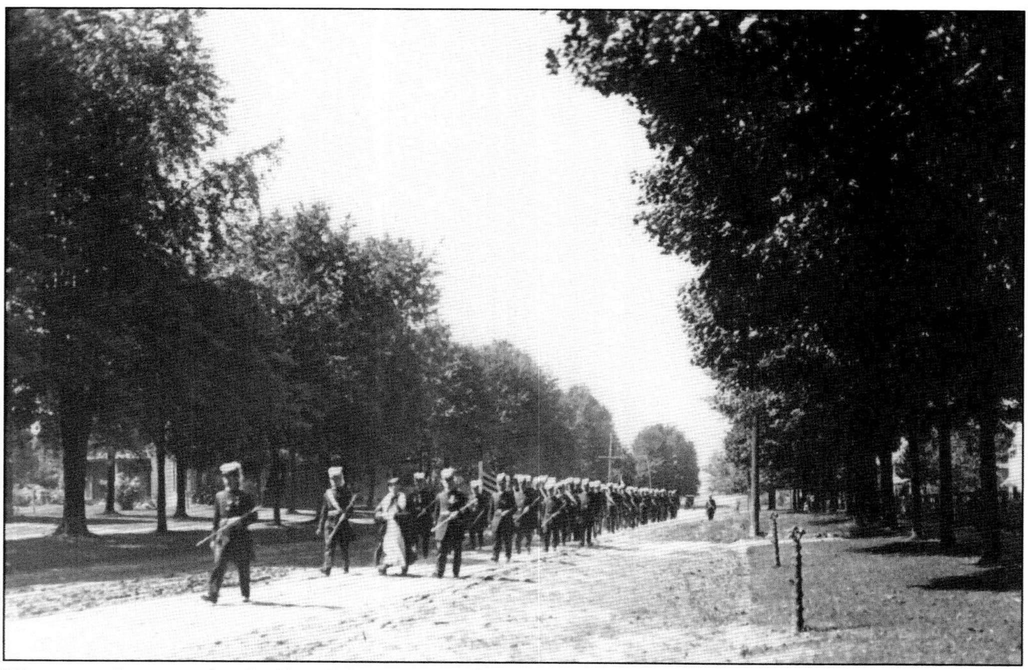

This is a photograph of a Free Mason's parade in September 1909.

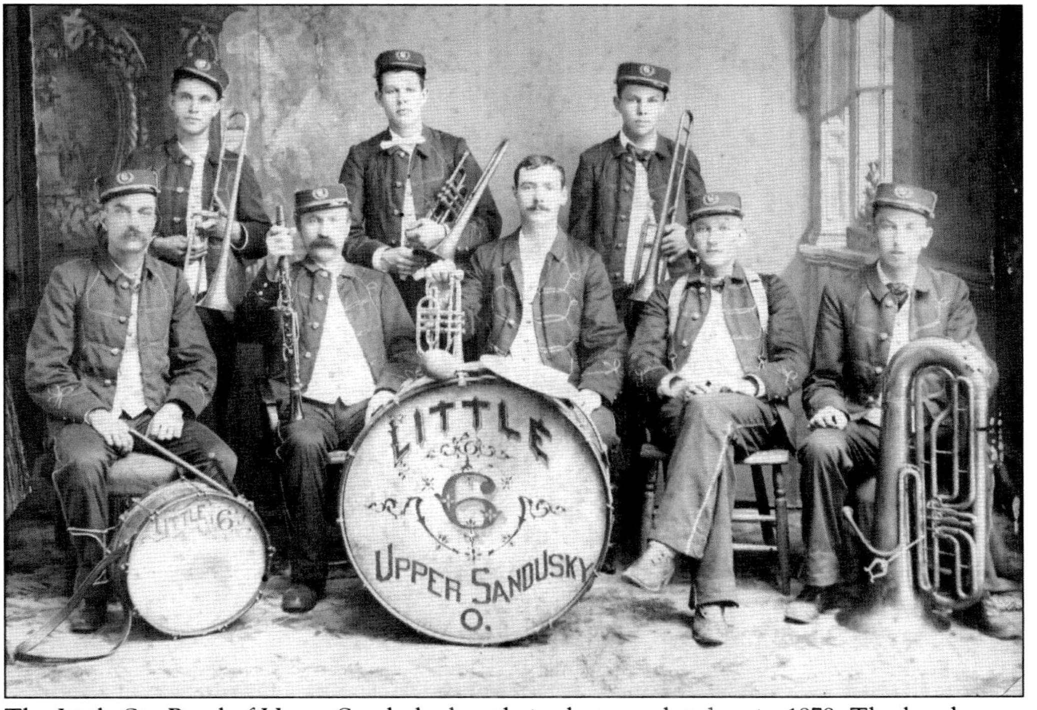

The Little Six Band of Upper Sandusky has their photograph taken in 1878. The band was a popular attraction and was supposed to play for the dedication of the new courthouse on August 24, 1900. When a team of horses pulling their wagon was frightened and went out of control, their instruments were damaged and they were unable to play for the afternoon dedication.

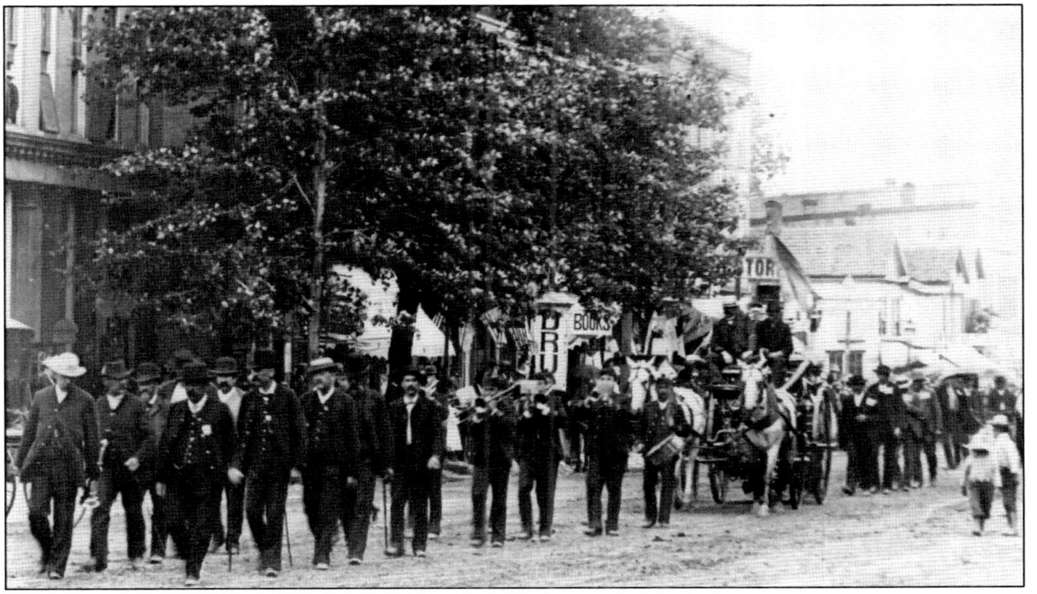

In this parade in the late 1880s, the gentlemen in front appear to be Civil War veterans, which was common at the time. Behind the veterans is a band followed by what looks like a horse drawn fire wagon.

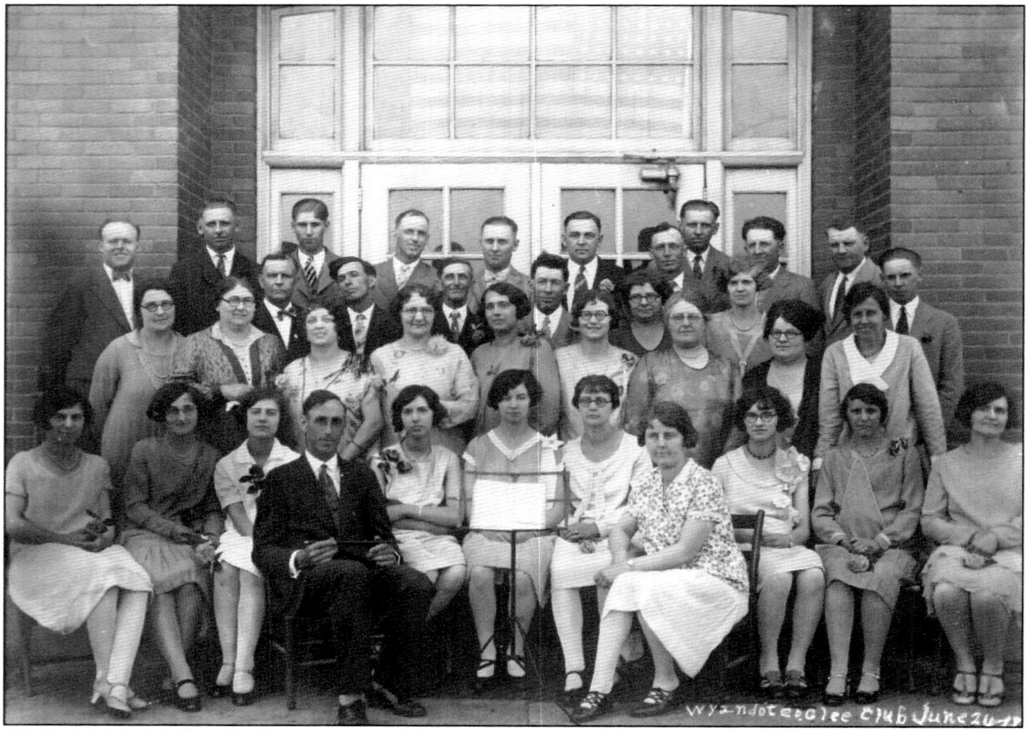

The Wyandot Glee Club is pictured here in a photograph dated June 24, 1928.

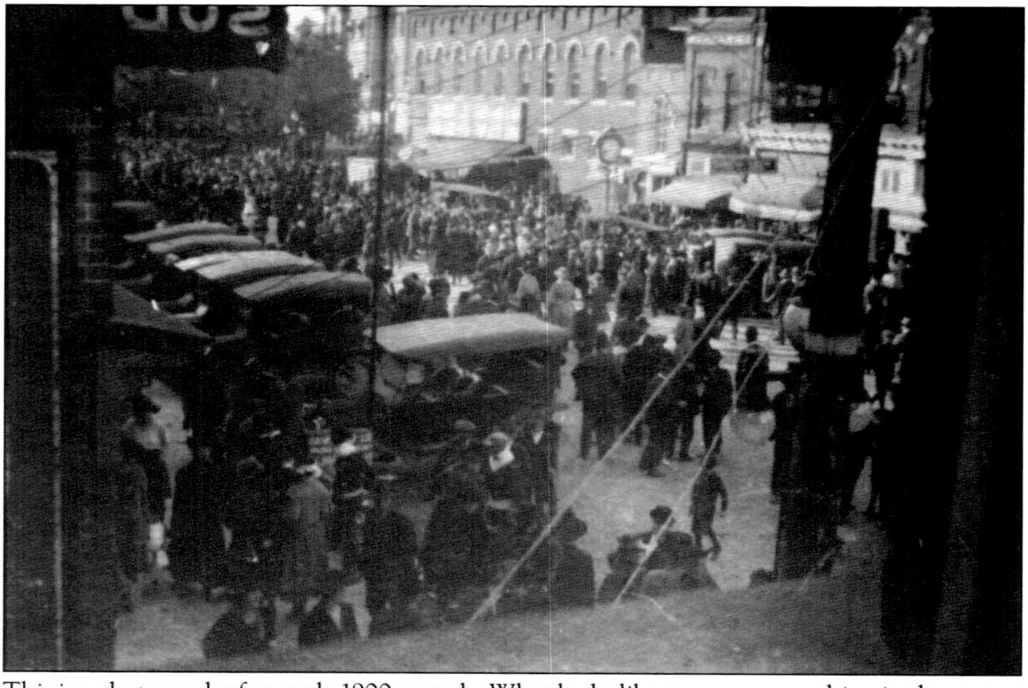

This is a photograph of an early 1900s parade. What looks like troops are marching in the center. (Photograph from the collection of Tom and Marnie Hill.)

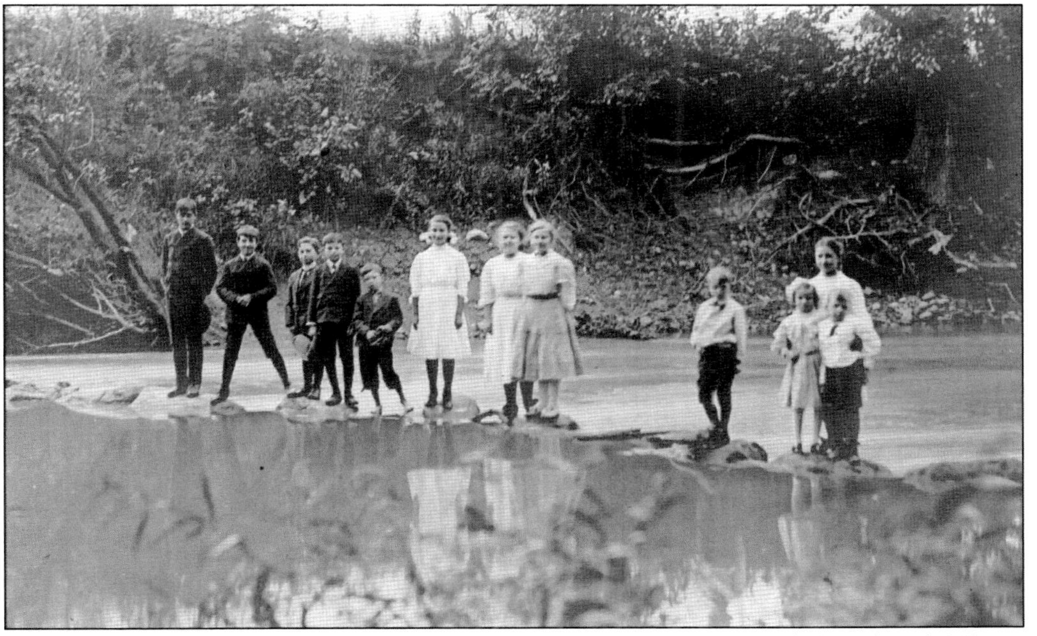

The stepping stones of the Sandusky River, seen here in 1907, were made by Edward O'Brien and friends in 1885, before the U.S. Route 30 bridge between Mononocue and Upper Sandusky was built. The stones could only be used when the river was low enough to safely navigate them. (Photograph from the collection of Tom and Marnie Hill.)

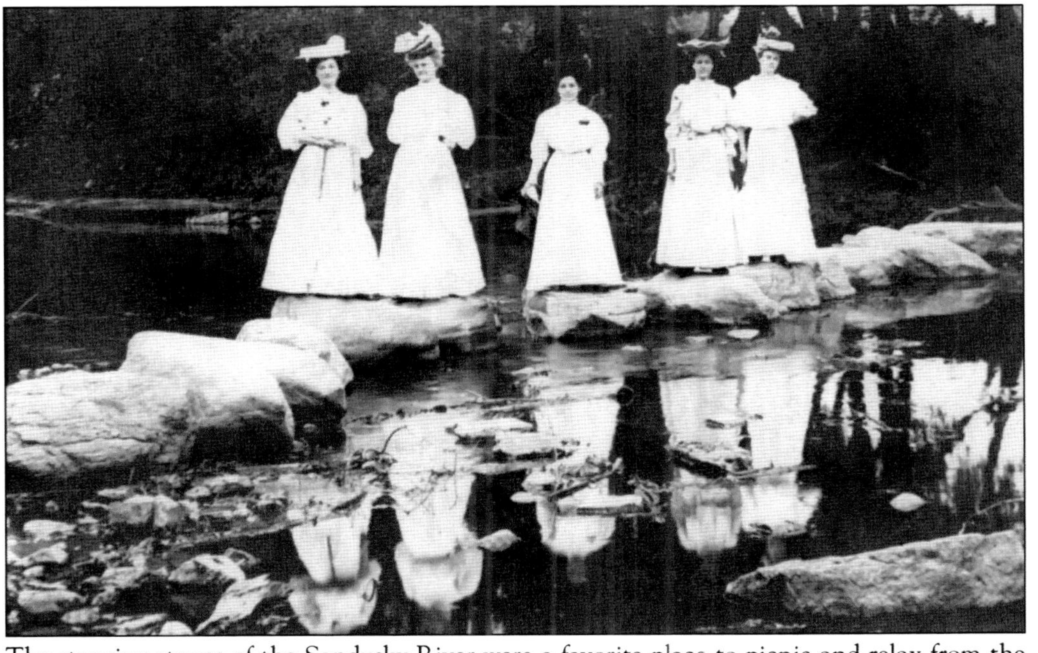

The stepping stones of the Sandusky River were a favorite place to picnic and relax from the rigors of work. The stones are still visible at Stepping Stones Park, which was established in 1997. In 2008, the City of Upper Sandusky erected a pedestrian bridge near the stepping stones. (Photograph from the collection of Tom and Marnie Hill.)

Consistent with our mission to preserve history on a local level, this book was printed in South Carolina on American-made paper and manufactured entirely in the United States. Products carrying the accredited Forest Stewardship Council (FSC) label are printed on 100 percent FSC-certified paper.

MADE IN THE USA